★ BUNNY TALES ★

Behind Closed Doors at the
★ PLAYBOY MANSION ★

★ BUNNY TALES ★

Behind Closed Doors at the
★ PLAYBOY MANSION ★

Izabella St. James

RUNNING PRESS
PHILADELPHIA · LONDON

Cover & Interior design by Joshua McDonnell
Front Cover Photography by James Creighton
Typography: Bodega, Akzidenz Grotesk, and Caslon

Running Press Book Publishers
2300 Chestnut Street
Philadelphia, Pennsylvania 19103-4399

Visit us on the web!
www.runningpress.com

★ Contents

★ To Justin

Prologue

★

"And the wild regrets, and the bloody sweats,
None knew so well as I:
For he who lives more lives than one
More deaths than one must die."

—*Oscar Wilde, The Ballad of Reading Gaol*

There I was, in torn-up jeans and white cotton shirt, with frizzy hair and sun-kissed skin. I had spent all day at the beach watching a shoot for the popular television show *The O.C.* Now I was sitting at a chic restaurant looking forward to some sushi and sake, when I suddenly felt someone's eyes burning into my flesh. I looked over and saw a good-looking man staring at me. He was smiling. I politely smiled back and turned away. Then it hit me. *Oh my God!* I knew him. The whole world knew him. He is one of the few elite actors who are members of the exclusive $20 million-a-movie club. There he was, famous star and still staring and still smiling at me. All of a sudden I became aware of my beach bum look and snuck off to the bathroom right past his table. I reapplied some lip gloss, as if that would make all the difference, and began walking back as nonchalantly as possible. He stopped me. He told me I was astounding—interesting choice of word, but nonetheless flattering. I tried to be witty, but I don't know what I said. It's all a blur.

I went back to my table and asked the waiter to hurry with that sake. It's not like I had a crush on this man, the way we all tend to with certain celebrities; I had never really thought much about him. But there was something about him, the intensity of his eyes. I found him very attractive in person, more so than I ever imagined from his movies. My skin was tingling and I had butterflies in my stomach. He told me he would sit there and stare at me all night, and he certainly kept his promise. He called me the next day. He surprised me with his warmth, his spirituality, and his intelligence. We talked about everything. It was perfect.

And then it happened. He found out I had once lived at the Playboy Mansion. He was livid. I was guilty without having a chance to be proven innocent; he automatically convicted me of all of the indecencies anyone could have possibly committed. He questioned his own intuition because it led him to care about me. I told him that his intuition was just fine; his feelings were based on my character, my heart, my soul, and not based on the circumstances of my life or the adventures I may have experienced. I was still the same good person. He told me he had such hopes for us and had not felt this way about a woman in many years. It amazed me that he was willing to throw it away just because I had lived at the Playboy Mansion. But he was angry and couldn't get past it. He was furious because he liked me, and apparently he felt I ruined our chance to be together. I could not be in his world because I was tainted by Playboy. Once people learned of our association, my past would suddenly become his reality, and he could not deal with that. He didn't *want* to deal with that. I was devastated. For the first time I felt guilty, and I didn't even know why. There was nothing I could say. It was the most suffocating, frustrating, belittling feeling to have to defend myself against accusations that were not valid, that were not only superficial but also inaccurate. My heart was broken.

I had been lucky enough not to be faced with other people's prejudices or stereotypes, and their anger or hatered had never been directed at me. I suppose that gave me a false sense of security; I never anticipated what was to come, and when it came, it struck like lightning. This actor told me I had obviously made some compromises in my past. He told me I had to realize and admit that living at the Mansion was not good for me. Initially I tried to be logical. He simply had it all wrong, and it was up to me to enlighten him. I had only lived at the Playboy Mansion; I didn't commit a crime! Bill Clinton, the leader of the free world, received a blow job from an intern in the Oval Office, and people got over it. Hugh Grant was caught with a prostitute, and people forgot. Winona Ryder got caught shoplifting; we moved on. Paris Hilton had a porno out, and a month later she was hosting a teen awards show. I didn't do any of that! I simply dated and lived with Hugh Hefner. Is that really so bad? If I say that I moved into the Playboy Mansion—the ultimate playground for consenting adults—just for fun, then I may be viewed as an irresponsible, docile blonde. If I say that all the girls there had their own plans and were nobody's fools, then we'll be labeled gold-diggers who used Hef. It seemed like a lose-lose situation. We all make decisions and sometimes they are mistakes. Hopefully we do not make the same mistakes, but we try to learn from the old ones and become better people.

After a few days, my self-doubt and ambivalence about his feelings turned to anger. How dare he? How dare he attack me without knowing anything about the situation? The rage deep within me surfaced. I was not going to allow anyone to talk me into feelings I did not have. After the storm came the calm, long-awaited moment of clarity: my experience of living at the Playboy Mansion was not a compromise. It was me letting go of the steering wheel. It was me allowing myself to be the total opposite of who I really am, to explore life, freedom, and self. All of us at one point or another have imagined what it would be like to live a different life than the one we have. But how many of us actually get the chance to do something completely out of the ordinary in our lives? I did. Yes, I was scared, so very scared to let go of everything I knew, to risk my present and my future. I just opened myself up to the experience, good or bad, right or wrong. It was a conflict between the path I had planned and the path less traveled by, between the right and left side of the brain. I knew I was strong enough not to do anything I did not want to, so I surrendered to the experience.

I believe that to genuinely understand another human being, one must understand where he or she came from. Where I come from has had a tremendous impact on who I became and the decisions I made in my life. My roots are inextricably woven into the fabric of my life, even the most unlikely and unexpected parts. I knew I had to write this book. I could not let this happen again. When I told this movie star I was writing a memoir, he advised me not to do it. In his view, everyone would forever view me as a Playboy Bunny. Did I want that? When I told him it would be cathartic for me to write this, he was still thinking about the way it would impact *him*. I realized he was motivated not by my actions, but by how they would reflect on his own reputation. He said writing a book may jeopardize my chances with other celebrities in the future. I was disappointed; so lost was his own identity, so lost was his loyalty to his real feelings, that it never occurred to him that I would not want to be with someone—celebrity or not—who prejudges me. I knew he was a victim of his fame and a slave to his image, and there was nothing I could do about that. But I could answer the countless questions I was confronted with on a daily basis about life at the Playboy Mansion with Hef. I could finally set the record straight.

Did I really ruin my life? You be the judge.

1: Made in Poland

"Though the Poles were doomed to live in the battlegrounds of Eastern Europe and to fight in many historic conflicts, they were as robust and zestful in the pursuit of pleasure and grandeur as they were valiant in warfare. And no invader has ever conquered the heart of Poland, that spirit which is the inheritance of sons and daughters, the private passion of families and the ancient, unbreakable tie to all those who came before...."

—*James A. Michener*

How did I find myself at the Playboy Mansion? I can still envision that little girl, with pigtails and freckles on her nose, living in Poland and dreaming of America. Back then, I tried to imagine what it would be like to live in this magical place called Hollywood. But never would I have imagined that I would one day be dating the iconic and hedonistic Hugh Hefner and living in his famous Mansion. From living behind the chains of Communism to partying behind the velvet ropes of Hef's exclusive entourage, it has been a long road.

I was born in the beautiful city of Krakow located in southern Poland, an ancient royal city famous for its architectural beauty and cultural heritage. Krakow's historic center houses the largest medieval square in Europe and the impressive Wawel Castle. A city on UNESCO's World Natural and Cultural Heritage list, Krakow is a vibrant, charming, and historically significant center of central and eastern European culture. The entire country of Poland is beautiful—the golden sand of the Baltic Sea's coastal beaches, the lakes of Mazury, the green wilderness of Bieszczady, the Tatra mountains, and the delightful charm of Poland's historic cities. Poland is a uniquely fascinating country, with its scenic landscapes and the romantic tales of medieval knights and battles, kings and splendid castles, contrasted by the dark horrors and destruction of World War II, its determined stand against Communism, and today's modern outlook and booming economy.

Immersed in its turbulent history, the passion and character of Poland is resilient, and the people are spirited, warm, and welcoming. The hospitality of Polish people is legendary; pleasing your guest is a high honor and requirement in Polish homes. The principle of "what's ours is yours" is strictly followed. Poles are very family-oriented, and the family unit includes members of the extended family. As parents age, they often live with their children and grandchildren. Children are raised to honor and respect the elderly. Polish people have many beautiful traditions that are hundreds of years old; they are highly valued and maintained.

Poland is the proud homeland of Pope John Paul II, who was Archbishop of Krakow before he became Pope; Nicolaus Copernicus, the astronomer who developed the sun-centered view of the solar system; and Marie Sklodowska-Curie, who discovered radium, paved the way for nuclear physics and cancer therapy, and was the first woman to receive a Nobel Prize and the first person to receive two Nobel Prizes. The Poles also have a strong musical and artistic sense of identity. Poland inspired its favorite musical son, composer and pianist Frederic Chopin. Few people realize that the land also produced Joseph Conrad; this popular English author of seafaring novels such as *Lord Jim* and *Heart of Darkness* was actually Józef Korzeniowski, born of Polish parents.

Poland is also the birthplace of men who fought for American freedom, such as Casimir Pulaski and Thaddeus Kosciuszko. Kosciuszko, one of Poland's greatest heroes and patriots, fought for freedom with the American Revolutionary Army. Kosciuszko distinguished himself by building and fortifying West Point and became engineer of the Southern Army. In 1783, the U.S. Congress offered him citizenship, land, a pension, and the rank of brigadier general. His indomitable devotion to the cause of freedom made him a symbol of the pursuit of freedom everywhere. Pulaski came to America in 1777 to fight in the war for independence and, as a cavalry general, won distinction in numerous campaigns. Mortally wounded in the Battle of Savannah, he left behind him a cavalry unit that became the nucleus for future squadrons and earned him the title "Father of the American Cavalry." In recognition for his services, numerous towns, schools, highways, and bridges in the United States were named after him.

Poland has a remarkable history of heroism and tragedy. It was the country most devastated by World War II in eastern Europe, losing about a quarter of its population and almost its entire Jewish community. Although blessed in its geographical location, Poland has been unfortunate in its political implications. Situated in the heart of Europe, between Germany and Russia, Poland has always been vulnerable. Poland was the first victim of World War II, which began when Poland was blitzkrieged by the Nazis from the west and later by the Russians who attacked it from the east. Having no natural borders from its aggressive neighbors, Poland had no chance. The aftermath of the war greatly influenced the character of the country. Former Jewish centers in the cities and the stark concentration camps where the Nazis carried out their extermination atrocities, remain as the most stirring reminders of the nation's tragedies. Poland is home to some of the world's most horrific places, including Oswiecim, more commonly known as Auschwitz. Cities destroyed by the war had to be rebuilt from scratch, and the many meticulously restored historic buildings and historic old towns are testimony to the pride and determination of a strong and durable nation.

The war is not just a painful distant memory; it is deeply embedded in my family's history. My dad was born in 1939, the first year of WWII, and his childhood was marred by the terrors and hard times of the war. His family lived on the eastern frontlines of the war in Poland, where the Russian troops were trying to push the Germans back west. Both sides shot anyone or anything that moved, and thousands of Poles were getting killed in the crossfire. My dad's family home was shot at, their only cow was killed, and when the house caught fire, the family horse burnt alive inside as they had no time to free it, barely escaping death themselves. My dad was just a baby, and his father carried him on his back as the family walked for days, over 20 miles in distance to places of safety. He remembers that during the day the people would hide in the forests, and at night they would keep walking to get away from the frontlines. People clustered near streams so they and any animals they were able to bring with them had water to drink. He remembers that many times guns were fired on those gathered, and the waters of the streams turned crimson with blood. When the refugees reached distant towns, strangers took them in and gave them a place on the floor to sleep. They had to beg for food because, when they ran from their homes, there was no time to pack money or food; a minute could be the difference between life and death. My father's desperate situation didn't end with the fight for the frontlines; one of his brothers was killed after trying to clear a local field of landmines. My grandmother, Marianna, died early after the hardships of war took their toll on her, and I never got to meet her.

The war was just as poignant in my mother's life. While my father was born into the hellish time of war, my mother was born a few years after it ended, when the devastated country was struggling to rebuild. My maternal grandfather, Jozef, had been arrested and sent to Auschwitz for protecting and helping Jewish people during the war. He spent more than two years being overworked and tortured at the camp. He managed to survive, but when he returned home he was a ghost of the man he used to be. My grandmother was left to take care of five children and an entire farm on her own. She worked harder than any woman I ever knew. My mom taught me to respect my elders, and I loved my grandma very much. When I was a little girl, I used to make her cards for Women's Day (a European holiday honoring all women), her birthday, and any other occasion. I remember that she always managed to stash away a little bit of money for me so that I could buy myself something I really wanted. I never met my maternal grandfather, though; when my mom was a teenager, he died from the never-ending chronic conditions he developed in Auschwitz. War and its consequences pervaded my identity and life.

It was this shadow of World War II in which I grew up. Not only was the war and its legacy a nightmare carved into the nation's consciousness, but the war had also left our nation at the disposal of our enemy. The Iron Curtain had fallen, and Poles found themselves on the wrong side of it. It was not the side people wanted to be on. We belonged to the Communist bloc, but wanted nothing more than to be on the other side. I remember being keenly aware, even as a child, of the injustice that befell my country. As a way of protesting, I refused to learn Russian, even though it was eventually a required subject in school. I watched the television, looking up to the American president Ronald Reagan, and longed for him to be the president of my country. I admired Margaret Thatcher; she was one of my first role models, an attorney and female leader—she was one of my inspirations to pursue a legal career later on in life. I couldn't help but feel our predicament was unfair; why did *my* country get invaded by Hitler first? Why didn't anyone help, and why did the West allow us to fall under Communist rule? These are not the usual questions a child under the age of ten struggles with, but I did. I think the fact that the realities of the world were the realities of my childhood made me grow up and mature more quickly. But that was not all; I had promised myself that when I grew up, I would not be a victim of circumstance or location. I was going to take control of my life one day; I intended to live in freedom, like others, and experience all that life has to offer. When I met Hugh Hefner, he embodied all of the freedom and fantasies I envisioned as a little girl.

As if having to come to terms with historical past was not complicated enough, having to deal with the reality of Communism was no picnic either. What was Communism? Technically speaking, the government, in the name of the people, owned the factories, farms, mines, and other means of production. People could no longer own their own profit-making businesses and farms, as in the capitalist system. Government economic planners decided what and how much should be produced each year, what the prices should be, and what wages should be paid to the workers. Although the government guaranteed everyone the right to work, the wages were low. Heavy industry such as steel making and coal mining was emphasized. Consumer goods like automobiles, clothing, and TVs became scarce and expensive. Pollution became a major problem, but environmental problems were largely ignored. Housing, built mainly by the government or group cooperatives, was always in short supply. Often, two or three generations of a family lived in a three-room apartment. Newlyweds usually had to wait years for a small apartment of their own. But everyone had a home; homelessness was not a problem. Long lines were a part of daily life, when oranges or bananas appeared at the local grocery store once every few months, the lines went on for blocks. Every day, women would go from shop to shop to get items. Even when in stock, there was little variety of goods. Often there was only one type of laundry soap, one flavor of ice cream, and one kind of coffee.

My father held a high position at the largest steel plant in the country, Huta Katowice, and he earned a good salary. My family had a very good life in comparison to most people. We had our own spacious apartment, a big garden, and we had a car, which was a luxury at that time. My mom had an economics degree from college but was able to stay home and take care of me until I was about seven years old. I am an only child, and my parents spoiled me. Despite the shortages in Poland, I had dozens of dolls, a doll carriage, and a miniature piano; I had a snack bar in my room full of sweets and everything else a child could wish for. I was so loved that I could not imagine sharing the love my parents gave me with anyone else; when my relatives asked if I wanted a cute little brother or sister to play with, I hysterically screamed "No!" Now as an adult, I wish I had a sister or brother to go through life with because nothing is more important to me than family.

As a child, I spent part of my summer vacations visiting my aunt Stasia, my father's sister, who lived in a charming village called Makowiska in southeastern Poland. She, my uncle, and my cousin Adam lived in a great country house with a working farm. They had a barn and every farm animal there is; it was there that I befriended chickens, cows, pigs, horses, and bunnies—of course, bunnies were my favorite. When I lived at the Mansion and saw all the bunnies running around, it definitely took me back in time to my childhood. At five years old, I decided to become vegetarian because I simply could not eat my friends. Every dinner was torture for me as my father would not let me leave the table until I finished my meal, and meat was always the only thing left on my plate. Luckily for me, we had a table that had a middle extension and it provided a perfect place for me to stash my meat and throw it out later. I would also resort to throwing it out the window as soon as my mom was not looking, and when we got my dog Nuka, she would camp at my feet, and I would sneak it all off to her. I also hated eggs, milk, and anything else that came from animals. I have carried that love of all animals with me my entire life. Though I have eased my dietary restrictions, animal welfare and protection has become one of the most important causes for me.

I realize just how very lucky I was and am, having two parents who love me very much and who took care of me my entire life. My parents would do anything for me and have worked hard all their lives so that I could have a better life and a brighter future. My mom is my best friend. She is kind, gentle, and caring. She has always supported me and my decisions, even if it meant she had to make sacrifices for me to realize my dreams.

My father is a hard-working, dedicated man. And though I always knew he loved me, he was the disciplinarian, and he wasn't afraid to take off his belt to teach me a lesson. But I rarely got into trouble; I was a straight-A student. I was responsible and polite. I was also raised as a good Catholic girl. Poland is a predominantly Catholic country, and has a sense of nationhood to which the Catholic Church is fundamental. At a time when people had very little, religion provided faith, strength, and hope. Religion offered meaning in life and beautiful traditions in Polish culture. Valor and patient endurance of the Polish people prevailed through Communism, thanks to a faith that matured in trial and hardship. Back when the country was cut off from the free world, Poland relied on its extraordinary religious faith. The fact that his holiness Pope John Paul II was Polish was extremely significant to me and all Poles. He was the link between us and God. He was this amazing man who spoke so many languages and traveled all over the world feeling at home wherever he went. I idolized him. He was my inspiration. I saw him as a child when he came back to visit Krakow. To me he is the greatest Pole who ever lived.

My parents always taught me about the world and encouraged me to learn. My father would go around the house quoting Adam Mickiewicz, Poland's most famous poet and the leader of Polish romanticism, who wrote many masterpieces, including *Pan Tadeusz*, which have been translated into several languages. As a child I could recite poems by Julian Tuwim and Jan Brzechwa. As I got a little older my father encouraged me to read books by Henryk Sienkiewicz, a Polish novelist and winner of the Nobel Prize for literature whose works have been published in fifty languages. Among Sienkiewicz's most famous novels is the widely translated and filmed *Quo Vadis*, a story set in the times of the Roman emperor Nero, which became the number one worldwide best-selling novel of all time. One of the positive things about Communism was that all education, from elementary school through college, was free. The government in most eastern European countries required all children to attend school until age sixteen. By the 1980s, illiteracy had been eliminated in most eastern European countries.

Having a car allowed us the privilege of travel. My parents have a saying that I was "born on the road" because ever since I was a baby, we were always going on trips. We traveled all around eastern Europe. At an early age I had the advantage of spending summer holidays on the Black Sea coasts of Romania and Bulgaria and exploring Hungary, Russia, and East Germany. Our journeys were restricted to eastern European countries because travel to western Europe was not permitted: most people who got the chance to go "west" would not return. We would arrive home from these trips with unique souvenirs, cute clothes, and school supplies that other children simply did not have.

Although the trips abroad were a blessing, they were often marred with some Soviet encounter. Waiting to pass through the Polish-Soviet border usually took hours. Once at the border they searched the car, intimidated everyone, and made sure it was as unbearable as it could be. Often the return trips were even worse because they questioned what you were bringing back, often subjecting people to body and cavity searches to make sure they weren't bringing in gold. If they found gold on you, they would take apart your entire car, and I mean into pieces. Going through the Soviet border was like going through the gates of hell. I remember being terribly scared as a little child and just trying to sit as still as I could.

Martial law was imposed in Poland by the Communist government on December 13, 1981, to prevent democratic movements such as Solidarity from gaining popularity. Many democratic leaders were imprisoned. The borders were sealed, airports were closed, and access to major cities was restricted. Travel between cities required permission. Curfew was imposed between 10 p.m. and 6 a.m. Telephone lines were disconnected. Mail was subject to censorship. All TV and radio transmissions were suspended (except one government TV channel and one government radio station). Classes in schools and at universities were suspended. Once, after we passed the Soviet border, we were stopped by the police, who berated my parents for going on a holiday; they screamed that my parents should get back to their jobs instead of going on a vacation. My parents were scared, and I just sat curled up in the backseat as quiet as I could, praying that these people would go away.

I suppose the idea of escaping Poland was born out of a desire to change the status quo. Although my parents had good jobs, they were pretty much at the top of where they could go in their careers without having to join the Communist Party. In reality, only the minority of Polish people were members of the Communist Party, though they held almost every important government post and enjoyed many privileges such as better housing and special access to western consumer goods. Most Polish people, however, had no choice but to conform to life under Communism. My mom had other ideas; she had dreams of a better, different life. I don't think she knows just how much I admire and respect her for making that decision, for taking that risk. She was my first hero, and she is still my greatest hero.

Things got worse in the mid-1980s; people were scared that the Soviet Union would send its army to invade Poland and the country would become another Soviet satellite. Life was uncertain from day to day, and my parents were scared. Under the Communist system, the "collective interest" of the people, as determined by the Communist party, overcame any claims to individual rights. The government harshly suppressed freedom of speech, press, and assembly. The government licensed newspapers, other media, and even churches in order to control them. The practice of religion was discouraged. The courts vigorously prosecuted anyone dissenting against Communist-Party rule. At my father's work, when anti-Communist messages were written on the walls, my father was pressured to find out and reveal the names of the perpetrators. My dad was threatened with losing his job and his freedom if he did not collaborate with the Communists. But my father was not only an honorable man, but he also could not betray anyone. He was also a member of the Solidarity movement.

Even though travel to western Europe was restricted, it was possible to get a visa if you knew someone with connections. Luckily, my mom was a resourceful person and had such connections. We were able to get permission to go on a bus trip to Greece. My parents planned that we would go to Greece, and when we got to Athens, we would stay behind and apply for a visa to immigrate to North America. We could tell no one except our closest family. We couldn't sell any of our possessions before the trip because it would raise suspicion. Our extended family was present the day we left, and they were instructed to share the possessions we had to leave behind. Our car, our furniture, our souvenirs, and all our mementos were given away for free. We weren't able to bring very much money with us because if had it been discovered by the border patrol, it would indicate our plan to leave the country.

I was eleven years old, and I do not remember the planning of the trip or packing for it, but I vividly remember leaving my apartment, and in particular, saying good-bye to my beloved dog Nuka. As we were stepping out of our home, she followed me, happily wagging her tail. I turned around and held her in my arms one last time. With tears pouring down my cheeks, I grabbed some of her fur in my hand in a desperate attempt to take a piece of her with me. She was the first dog I ever had. My father took me to a local farmer's market one cold morning, and I spotted a small box with a few puppies in it. They were so little and cold that I needed to do something. I noticed a tiny black fur ball looking at me and trying to get out. I picked her up and never put her back in. I immediately put her inside my winter coat, and she made herself comfortable somewhere in my sleeve. My dad bought her for me and I named her Nuka, after a small black orphaned bear from a popular Japanese cartoon at the time. I waited anxiously all day until my mom came home from work to see if I could keep her. Once my mom saw her, she fell in love, and Nuka quickly became a loved member of our family.

I could not stop crying as we made our way to the bus. My mom told me I could not cry because my sorrowful behavior would imply something more than going on a holiday. But when I looked back at our house, I could see my family on the balcony and I could see my dog's little head between the balcony railings; she was looking in my direction. It broke my heart, and I still cannot get through this memory without crying. She knew we were leaving her, and it killed me inside. My mom told me and I truly believed that we could come back soon and get the dog. The first time we returned to Poland was in 1990, and no one knew where the dog was. She was supposed to stay with my uncle, but he gave her to someone else because she chased his chickens. It was the first time in my life that I felt I failed someone. I could not find her, but I had to believe in my heart that wherever she was, she was loved and taken care of; who could deny such a beautiful, sweet, and loving dog? As for our belongings, they seemed to have disappeared. Some of the souvenirs had been scattered among family members, and I was able to retrieve a few mementos of my childhood. My vast collection of toys, which remained in a perfect state over all the years I had them, was gone without a trace. It does hurt me that my family never thought of putting aside and preserving a couple of dolls or teddy bears, or the countless handmade cards I had made for my parents over the years. It's a very sad feeling to know that the first eleven years of your life did not leave a trace.

The year we spent living in Athens was both fantastic and difficult. The only money we were able to bring with us from Poland quickly ran out and my parents had to find jobs. After living in a hotel for about a month, we moved into a very shabby apartment with a few pieces of furniture. There were many times my father wanted to go back to Poland, because running out of money and working in positions well below his qualifications was very difficult for him. My mom believed it was worth the sacrifice. She was the rock that carried us through. I, on the other hand, was having a blast.

I attended school, where I learned Greek and a few words in English. I met new friends, both Greek and other immigrant children from all over the world. My parents worked, and I had to fend for myself. After school I explored the city with my friends. At eleven years old, I was taking the buses by myself, going to new neighborhoods, and often getting lost but always finding my way home. I would buy myself a souvlaki for lunch and go on adventures every day; Mount Likavitos, the zoo, and I never tired of watching the change of guard at the Parliament building. I learned Greek mythology and went to the Acropolis whenever I could. I was fluent in Greek in no time. I loved the spirit of Greece and really enjoyed living there. I appreciate the people and the culture and fondly remember that time.

I had a paradoxical childhood; I was a happy and loved child who lived in a country suffocated by Communism and longed for a different life. My mother showed me not to be afraid to take life into my own hands.

Throughout the years, when I have found myself unsatisfied with the status quo, I have drawn on my childhood for strength to make changes. My mom also taught me about taking chances in life. My parents sacrificed everything; they gave up their careers, the support and love of their families, and left all of their material possessions. They did that so that I could have opportunities they did not have or those that I would not have had, had we remained in Poland.

I am sure the last thing my parents expected was for me to move into the Playboy Mansion; I did not expect that of myself. But that was what fate brought my way, and I responded to the invitation the same way I had to other new experiences—I was intrigued. I welcomed the experience. I always feel that if I am not receptive to life and all that it has to offer, I am not taking advantage of the gift of freedom my parents gave me.

2: Canada, Eh

★

"I'm not a lumberjack, or a fur trader. I don't live in an igloo or eat blubber, or own a dogsled. And I don't know Jimmy, Sally or Suzy from Canada, although I'm certain they're really, really nice."

—*Molson Canadian Campaign*

After about a year in Greece, our application to immigrate to Canada was approved. We were informed that they were sending us to British Columbia. If it seems surprising to you that we would move to a place someone else chose for us, it seems just as astounding to me as I write this. We didn't have a choice as to where in Canada we were going; I think the Canadian government sends people to areas that need to be populated. My parents had heard that British Columbia was very beautiful, and so we were excited. After a flight that seemed to last for an eternity, we finally arrived in Prince George, in interior British Columbia. We were greeted by some Polish people who lived there, and then we were taken to a hotel. After a few days, they helped us find an apartment. Arriving in Prince George was a major culture shock for us. In Poland we lived in a beautiful historic city, then we lived in ancient Athens bustling with life, and now we had found ourselves in a small lumber town in the middle of the Rocky Mountains. Undeterred, my parents began taking English lessons, and I was sent to school. Mind you I only knew about ten words in English, such as "orange" and "pencil," and I knew the days of the week, but I had learned to say them with a heavy British accent, so people in Prince George had no idea what I was saying. But again, I adapted. I made friends and learned English, my third language, quickly and even won the spelling bee in my school; I may not have know what those words meant, but I sure could spell them!

I enjoyed the novelty of living in a place where grizzly bears and moose frequented people's backyards and where a person didn't go buy a Christmas tree but went to chop it down himself, almost drowning in the snow on his quest for the perfect tree. But the one thing I was disappointed about was that I did not see American Indians with long hair riding horses everywhere. I had read novels about American Indians and fell in love with their culture and way of life. I had a romanticized notion that they still lived in tepees and wore traditional clothes and that I would fall in love with a chief's son—yes, *Dances with Wolves* is one of my favorite movies. My naiveté may seem silly to Americans, but I grew up in a country that was ninety-nine percent homogenous. Until we moved to Athens, I had seen only one African person. He was the only black man in our town, and when he walked by, I would stare at him in awe. He was married to a Polish woman, and they had the most gorgeous children. We called them mulatto, and for me, that word stood for beautiful skin and exotic features. I always wished I had their tan skin. I grew up without any concept or notion of racism. I had no idea that in other parts of the world, people judged each other based on the color of their skin. To me, anyone with a different color of skin was exotic and fascinating, and I longed to meet them and learn about their culture. I never knew what a tremendously different world awaited me.

Just when I was getting settled in my new life in Prince George, my parents announced that we were moving again. I was sad to leave my new friends and my beautiful, wild surroundings. But they saw no future for them in this charming, but sleepy, lumber town; there were few jobs and none of the opportunities they were looking for. They came to Canada to build a new life, to pursue a dream, and they could not stop until they had the opportunity. The plan was to move to Toronto in the province of Ontario, in eastern Canada, because it has a lot of industry, jobs, and growth. So with some money they saved from any odd jobs they could get, my parents bought a van. It was an old white van with only two seats, the driver and passenger. We packed the van with the few belongings we had acquired and embarked on a trip across Canada, the second largest country in the world. Through the natural beauty of British Columbia, the spectacular Rockies of Alberta, the never-ending prairies and plains of Saskatchewan and Manitoba, to the Great Lakes surrounding Ontario, it was an incredible trip—even though I had no seat and was squashed among the furniture in the back. We had never been to Toronto, nor did we have a place to stay there; we just went. This was the spirit that was passed on to me by my parents, this fearlessness, the ability to take a risk and pursue the unknown in hopes of bettering your life. That courageous spirit has been with me all of my life.

We eventually settled in Kitchener-Waterloo, Ontario, about an hour southwest of Toronto. Kitchener is famous for having the largest Oktoberfest celebration outside of Germany. Each year tourists from all over Canada and the United States flock to the town to drink beer, eat sausages with sauerkraut, and sing. Another claim to fame for K-W, as we call it, was that former heavyweight champion Lennox Lewis grew up there (he was born in Jamaica and now lives in the United Kingdom) and attended a high school two minutes from my house. When I met him years later at the Playboy Mansion, the first thing I told him was that we had a Kitchener connection and he got a kick out of that. It was a wonderful place to spend my teenage years. A town made up of family-oriented suburbs and home to two good colleges, it was safe and friendly. My friends like to remind me that I was the new girl in school who showed up at Monsignor Haller Elementary School in the last grade, wearing a short jean skirt and a Garfield sweatshirt, and caught the attention of male classmates. All I remember was being conscious of the way I spoke English and wanting to make new friends—I didn't care about the boys. I was also somewhat anxious about starting grade eight when I had never attended grade five, six or seven—the years I had missed when we were busy moving around the world. Luckily, the Communist-dictated school curriculum in Poland was so comprehensive and at such an advanced level that I was not behind at all despite the years I had missed. In addition, I had begun learning my fourth language, French. I hadn't realized Canada had *two* official languages, but when you already speak three languages, what's another one?

I attended Resurrection Catholic Secondary School, a beautiful new school with wonderful teachers, where I wore the classic uniform of a kilt, white shirt, and black knee-highs. I had a tight-knit group of girlfriends without whom I would not have survived the turmoil of teenage years. Besides playing on the soccer team after school, note-passing and gossiping about boys were our favorite school activities. I was the last one of my friends to lose my virginity. I felt so left out when, during our lunch hour, they would talk about their experiences and compare notes.

I had been waiting for the perfect guy, my first love. And then it happened. His name was Deon. He was a skater boy, with a long mohawk who listened to Metallica and wore Sex Pistols shirts. He dropped out of school, but he was gorgeous and I loved him. My dad was not crazy about him, but we found ways to see each other. I wanted him to be The One. One night when my friend Pamela was sleeping over at my house, we snuck out at around midnight in the dead of winter and walked to his house, which was a few miles away. We brought my mom's butter knives for protection, a fact that still gives us a good laugh. It took us more than an hour in freezing temperatures to get there, but when I got to his house, it was he who wasn't ready, although he was not a virgin. Ironically, he liked me too much to have sex with me. Soon after that he moved to British Columbia, and I had to move on, but I always regretted that he wasn't the one. I decided that I could not wait until someone "special" came around again—that could take years! Out at the all-ages night club my friends and I used to go to, I met a boy who was a great dancer. The way all of the girls liked him and cheered for him made him the hot commodity. His name was Joey and he was another bad boy type; I decided he was going to be the one. Not more than a month after we started dating, I snuck off to his house and we did it. He didn't know it was my first time because frankly, I was too cool to admit it, and he was too immature to notice. I told him Deon had been the first, because in my heart, he was. And that was that. We were driving somewhere when I broke the news to my mom; I had always been honest with her and I could not keep the secret to myself. It was the first time she had been disappointed in me. I hated to hurt or disappoint her, but I learned then that there would be times in my life when I would have to make my own decisions and not always please everyone.

During the rest of my high school years, I dated several guys, but I was highly selective as to whom I became sexually involved with; I was more preoccupied with my grades. Boys were a fun distraction, but school and learning were my passion.

I graduated high school with an academic excellence award for an average above ninety percent, as well as a special award in geography and other achievement awards. My friends were surprised; they didn't know I was such a nerd, but I loved learning and I loved school. Ever since I was a little girl, my family and I had thought that I was going to grow up to become a doctor. My dad never missed an opportunity to give me some early practice by having me bandage his finger or anything else that I was capable of doing. This dream came to a crushing end when, in my high school science class, I was unable to dissect a frog, let alone graduate onto dissecting the baby pig. I wasn't even able to lay it out on the table and consider the idea. I left my class and took a zero on the assignment. That was it for me. I realized I could not be a doctor. That left me with the only other traditionally prestigious and respectable profession: I decided to become a lawyer.

Although there were two universities in town, I didn't even bother applying to them. Kitchener was a great place to spend my adolescence and a great place to raise a family, but at eighteen, I had outgrown it and I was itching to get out of there. I longed for more culture and new, diverse experiences. In the past, it had been my parents who moved around until they found a place where they could build their life; now it was my turn to look for a place of my own. I researched Canadian universities and found out that McGill University in Montreal was rated the number one school that year. With my grades, I could go anywhere. I turned down scholarships at other schools and chose to attend the esteemed McGill in French-speaking Montreal in the province of Quebec. I was not afraid to go to a city I had never seen and where I did not know a soul; after all, I had done it before, albeit not alone. I was sad to leave my mom. She is my best friend, and our bond and our love is so strong that I didn't know if I would survive being away from her. It broke my heart to live so far from my parents, but I had to do it for myself; I had to grow up, have responsibilities, have the freedom to develop my own character. My parents drove me to Montreal and helped me settle in at my all-girl residence. I cried when they left. I missed my mom so much, but we spoke every day on the phone, a custom that continues to this day no matter where we are in the world.

Everyone always says your college year are the best years of your life, and they are right. My time at McGill was the absolute best time of my life. Founded in 1821, McGill is widely regarded as the "Canadian Harvard." William Shatner of Star Trek fame graduated from the school in 1952 with a bachelor of commerce; there is a social activities building named after him. I was attracted not only by the prestige of the university, but also by the beauty and *joie de vivre* of Montreal. People really enjoy life there, not just amazing summer events like the jazz festival, comedy festival, and the Grand Prix, but every single day—even in very cold weather. I loved the school, and I adore the city.

My first year at McGill, I met three of my best friends. Laura and Gena had lived with me at the all-girls residence. My first memory of us going out together was on my birthday; we went to a male strip club. We were 18 years old and without parental supervision for the first time. I don't remember whose idea it was, but Laura and I had a great time giggling with embarrass-ment. Our second year, the three of us moved into a beautiful two-story townhouse on Durocher Street. We would sit at the kitchen window and phi-losophize about life, God, and everything else as we watched the world, especially the boys, go by. We were legends in the "McGill Ghetto," as the school neighborhood was called, three tall (at 5-foot-7, I was the shortest) blondes living together.

My third best friend at McGill was Niki, a tall beautiful brunette, a cross between Cindy Crawford and Geena Davis. She was the first person I met at McGill on my first day. I was lost and looking for orientation. Despite being new there herself, she was calm and collected and showed me where to go. After that I saw her in several of my classes, as we were both Poli Sci majors, and we became friends. She was Greek, and that only made me like her more. Her mom makes the most delicious almond powder cookies, and I was lucky enough to receive a couple of deliveries. I remember Niki and I always grab-bing coffee before our political theory class, discussing how we should go to Los Angeles and become soap opera stars as we waited for the lecture to begin. That was always our Plan B. One day, I convinced her to join the U.N. club and introduced her to my friend Guy, a cadet from West Point, since I was dating another cadet at the time. I had met them at a conference I attended at Yale. I was responsible for a long and complicated romance between the two, causing her a lot of heartbreak and confusion. But she never held it against me. She was the more responsible one; she looked out for me. I was the one who was always getting myself involved in boy intrigues and waiting until the night before to write a thirty-page research paper. I always waited until the last minute, staring at the heap of books that awaited my attention—it was then that I became inspired. I even had the procrastinator's creed poster on my wall "I shall always begin, start, initiate, take the first step, and/or write the first word, when I get around to it." There was a method to my madness however, as I always managed to pull it off and get an A.

My roommates and I had a party at our house once, and all but two of our guests were men. We didn't know how to deal with it, so we got drunk. First year of college was a year of many experiences. We got cheap "Baby Duck" wine at the local *deppaneur* (the "dep" is like a family-owned 7-Eleven or convenience store, and can be found only in the province of Quebec), which was great because we were eighteen years old; the drinking age in Ontario where I lived is nineteen, and you can purchase alcohol only in special government-operated stores, the accurately-called Beer Store and Liquor Store. Not at all like in the States, where in some states you can purchase alcohol at a grocery or drug store. This opened a whole new world of trouble for my friends and I: the first time we got drunk; the first time we threw up in public; and the first time we woke up and didn't know where we were exactly, only to run as fast as we could to our 7 a.m. Spanish class, whose teacher was not amused by our appearance.

It was also a time of experimentation, the first time I smoked pot and laughed hysterically while bingeing simultaneously on Doritos and Tim Horton's doughnuts. Our experience with psychedelic mushrooms was at a party, where we sat paralyzed, staring at everyone, completely convinced that the girl in front of us was a peacock, and our friend's new date looked like an oversized gnome, and in fact we even told him we thought so. College was a time for growth, but also fun. There were ski trips that never saw any skiing and a great trip to Laura's native Bahamas; there was the time I worked as a shooter girl at a nightclub called Angel's, where guys bought me more shots than they bought themselves, and many other fantastic memories.

There was never a shortage of men in our lives. It was during my second year that I met and dated Keith McPhail. He was a gorgeous, fun, loving person. I remember I was shopping for a watch of gold and silver so that I could wear it with both types of jewelry. A few days before my birthday, Keith called me from a party—it was 3 a.m. He said he had something he wanted to give me and was coming over. I protested. I was in Montreal, and he was in London, Ontario. It was a nine-hour drive! He showed up ten hours later to give me the beautiful, expensive watch with a gold and silver bracelet, that he had bought me. He was outgoing and adventurous; he was training to become a pilot. We broke up because of the demands of my studies and his training, but we became best friends. He visited me many times afterward, flying himself and even my friends to Montreal. He always told me he would come back for me one day with a big diamond and ask me to marry him.

After Keith, I dated mostly athletes—football players, to be exact. One in particular affected my life for a long time. Ryan was a quarterback at the University of Waterloo, and I met him when I was home for the summer. We had an instant attraction and spent a fun few weeks together until I had to leave for McGill. I thought we would continue in a long-distance relationship, and we did for a while. Our relationship was so intense that he drove nine hours just to be with me for a couple of hours. With the distance between us, we slowly grew apart, and then I found out he was seeing an older girl at Waterloo; he needed someone who was there to take care of him during football season. I was upset but I had to let it go. I had met someone new as well. Sean was a great guy. I only wanted to be friends with him at first, but he was such a wonderful person that I decided to give the relationship a chance. He was a caring person; he brought me food, took me out, and did amazingly kind and romantic things to make me happy. He was always there for me unconditionally.

But I was too immature to appreciate him. Every time I went home, I saw Ryan. It could not be avoided because he worked as a bouncer and bartender at the bar my friends and I always hung out at when I came home, Loose Change Louis. We just couldn't resist each other. I had never had this illogical, intense desire for anyone and never felt the way I did when I was with him. I did not understand why; I hated myself but I couldn't stop it. I loved Sean, but I was attracted to Ryan and there was no middle ground. Ryan had a girlfriend as well. We had an ongoing affair for more than two years, which ended very badly for everyone involved. Sean found out and called Ryan's girlfriend to tell her what was going on. It was brutal. I was confused; I didn't understand why I allowed it to happen. I learned a painful but valuable lesson about love and lust. I swore off men. I didn't even look at guys for more than a year.

Despite all the fun I was having, it was at McGill that I found my intellectual footing. I started off with a double major in history and political science, but after two years, I found it too restricting. I had taken a couple of literature and philosophy courses and wanted to explore other subjects. I wanted to be a well-rounded person; I didn't want to just know history or just know politics. McGill had the perfect major for me: humanistic studies. This major allowed me to continue my studies of Spanish, philosophy, geography, and classical music. I developed a love for English literature, Baroque art and classical music. I also studied American history and fell in love with the principles and ideals upon which the United States of America was founded. I also longed to take some drama classes, but I put them off. My main extracurricular activity was the model U.N. club. I went on delegations to Harvard, Yale, Georgetown, and the real U.N. in New York City. I was an internationalist and an idealist. Having been raised in Poland, Greece, and Canada, I felt like I was a child of the world. I dreamed of being a diplomat, with the ultimate goal of becoming an ambassador. I decided to become a lawyer specializing in international affairs.

But school was not the only place I learned; life provided the most challenging tests and taught me the hardest lessons. My very last semester at McGill, I went to Kitchener-Waterloo for spring break, and when I arrived back in my apartment, I had several messages on my answering machine. My friend Pamela asked me to call her immediately, and I knew something was wrong. She told me that Keith, my former boyfriend and one of my best friends, was in a plane crash and was dead. I didn't believe it. There must have been a mistake. I felt paralyzed. I have known people who had died but never anyone so young and so vibrant, and so close to me. He was flying a plane with his girlfriend as the passenger, and I guess it was a snowy night in Maine. It was determined that for some reason he thought he was flying at a higher altitude than he really was and he crashed into a mountainside just a few miles from the airport. I spent the night crying, and when morning came, I went right back to Kitchener for the funeral. As much as I was hurting, I knew his family was hurting more. I wrote a poem about Keith, for his family and for myself, and I bought some flowers and spent some time with his family the night before the funeral. I went back to school afterward, but I was not the same person. There is a song titled "Surrounded" by Chantal Kreviazuk, which Pamela turned me onto, that reminds me of Keith: "I was there when you shone as bright as Bethlehem from afar, I was there when you were young and strong and perverted and everything that makes a young man a star, oh you were a star." Whenever I fly, and I frequently do, I think of him. I'm scared of turbulence, so I speak to Keith and ask him to keep me safe. He is my guardian angel in the skies.

Just when I thought things could not get worse, the ice storm of 1998 arrived with a vengeance. Freezing rain, snow, and ice pellets pounded the region for five days. There was no power in the city of Montreal and all over Quebec and Ontario as power lines and trees were falling, brought down by the weight of the ice that covered them. Huge icicles were falling off buildings and would surely kill a person had they hit him on the head; I missed such a fate by a couple of feet. There were at least twenty-five deaths, many from hypothermia and carbon monoxide poisoning because people used whatever they could to stay warm. Because there was no power, many students used candles for light, and when the frat boys next door to my building forgot to blow them out, my apartment almost burned down. I stood in the freezing cold, watching the brave firefighters battle the fire, as I cried and prayed to God to save the few belongings I had, particularly my books and my assignments. The next day, I asked Sean to drive me home to my parents' house in Ontario. I had had enough of winter forever.

A few weeks later, the day before my first exam, I found out that my grandmother had died in Poland. I loved my grandmother very much, but I knew that my grief did not compare to what my mom was going through. My mom was devastated that she was not there with her own mother in her last moments. She felt guilty about leaving Poland and leaving her mother behind. When we left, her plan was to bring my grandma over to Canada. But my grandmother had a life in Poland, and at her age, she did not want to leave behind everything she knew. Plus her high blood pressure and heart condition presented a serious danger for flying overseas. At the time of my grandmother's death, my mom was very sick with a severe back injury. Any type of movement was painful for her, and she was taking strong pain medication. Immediately I wanted to blow off my exams and travel to the funeral with her. When I found out that if I went, I would have to retake some of my courses and that it would delay my graduation, my mom told me I had to stay at school and finish my semester. It was heartbreaking for me not to go to my grandmother's funeral and be there for my mom through her emotional and physical pain. I should have gone; I was unable to study anyway and barely made it through my exams.

The trauma of Keith's death and my grandmother's death made me contemplate my life more closely. I became acutely aware of the unpredictability of life and decided that although I loved studying and burying myself in books, there was more for me to see, experience, and enjoy. My soul needed uplifting, and my body longed for sunshine. My focus changed; I was determined to combine my educational goals with a more relaxed quality of life. I needed a change of scenery, to re-energize my body and my soul. When I was looking at law schools, the lifestyle they provided became just as important as their academic credentials.

Having been in Montreal during the 1995 Quebec Referendum (a public vote to decide whether Quebec would separate from the rest of Canada and pursue a path toward independence and sovereignty; the motion was narrowly defeated by a 50.58-to-49.42 percent margin), I became disillusioned with Canadian politics. Despite the fact that I loved Montreal, the severity of winter had worn me out. The ice storm of 1998 solidified my belief that my future lay south—way south—of the border. I was dreaming of a nice warm place to attend law school. I was California dreamin'. Despite my longtime desire to attend Georgetown University, I applied to two schools in California based solely on their location and the quality of life they provided. Pepperdine University in Malibu was the first to send me a letter of acceptance. Having never been to Los Angeles, I thought it would be a good idea to see the school and check out the city. As I drove by the ocean, down the Pacific Coast Highway, I fell in love before we even reached the "Malibu: 27 miles of scenic beauty" sign. I got this feeling inside, like I was home. The only thing left to do was apply for a school loan. My parents had paid for the majority of my education at McGill, but that was impossible with a private American school; it was just too expensive. There was only one lender in the United States or Canada that was willing to lend money to Canadian students to attend a professional school in the States. And though the interest rate was high and the conditions strict, I signed on the dotted line, with my parents as co-signors, happy to have the chance to fulfill my dream.

The only reservation I had about moving to California was the fact that I would be so far from my parents, particularly my mom. She was very sad that I was leaving her again, but at the same time, she was proud of me and thought I was so brave. It was really hard for me to leave her again and go further than before. But I saw this as an opportunity to change my life and eventually change the lives of my parents. I thought that if I moved to California and established my life there, I would help my parents move there so that they might enjoy the nice weather in their older years. I have always looked forward to the day when I will be able to take care of them and repay them for all that they have done for me. Everyone has something that drives them forward. Gratitude and love for my parents has always been my driving force.

My parents were incredible about the move; a month before school started, they surprised me by buying me a brand-new car. We packed it up and drove across the continent again, but this time it was to the United States: past the Great Lakes states, through the rolling green hills of Iowa, the plains of Nebraska, the splendid mountains of Colorado, the hellish heat of Utah, to the much awaited Pacific Ocean. It was quite a trip, a passage to a new life. When we got to Malibu, my parents continued to amaze me. They bought me the furniture I needed and bought me food and all the necessities. All too soon, they had to fly back home. After I dropped them off at the airport, I stopped at a nearby beach, sat down on the sand, and watched the planes fly up into the sky, wondering if one of the planes was theirs. I couldn't hold back my tears. I was choked up with feelings of gratitude, love, and guilt. I missed them already. I felt alone. But I did not dare allow myself any pity—after all, this was *my* choice. I had to be strong like my mom. I got up, took a deep breath, and entered my new life.

3: Legally Blonde

" Law school is for people who are boring, and ugly, and serious. And you, Button, are none of those things."

—*Elle Woods' father in* Legally Blonde

W hen I started law school, I was full of enthusiasm, energy, and hope. Everyone warned me ahead of time that the first year of law school is tough. It's a time when the school tries to weed out the weak—survival of the fittest. And indeed, a few people did not return for the second year. For me, the first year was a mix of satisfaction and disappointment. I had a couple of professors who inspired me with their passion for the subjects they taught, and those became my favorite subjects and the ones I did the best in. But the majority of the classes were uneventful; I learned what I had to but without any inspiration. And of course there were a few classes I absolutely hated. It wasn't because of the subject; it was because of the professors who taught them. In law school, subjects are taught using the Socratic method, which is a technique of teaching in which the professor asks leading questions to stimulate rational thinking and elicit answers. However, some professors used it as a weapon to break students down and intimidate and humiliate them. Perhaps what they were hoping for was that we would be so afraid of not knowing the answer that we would try harder and be prepared. All it did for me was make me dislike the teacher, not care about the subject, and resent the fact that I was paying thousands of dollars to get verbally "abused." But I loved the law and all that it stood for, and I remained hopeful that things would get better the following year, when I would be able to take some courses in international law.

When I moved to California, I had not had a boyfriend in a long time; it was self-imposed singledom after the Ryan-Sean heartbreak. I was looking forward to meeting some hot Malibu surfers. The movie *Point Break* flashed in my mind, and I imagined tan, muscular boys with long blond hair. I was curious to see what the boys in law school would look like, but I certainly did not have high expectations: lawyers aren't known to be lookers. On our first day of school, the dean asked us to look around, announcing that it was very possible that our future husbands or wives were in this school. I couldn't help but laugh. Pepperdine actually did have more than the average number of good-looking people; maybe it's the oceanfront location of the school and proximity to Hollywood that attracts many beautiful types. Despite the fact that there were a few cute boys around, I was uninterested.

Then one day as I was leaving school, I noticed a leg. The leg had a huge tattoo on its side, almost from the knee to the ankle. I was surprised to see anyone in law school with a tattoo, let alone one so visible. I tried to see the guy, but he was reading the *Wall Street Journal*. I couldn't see his face but I could tell he was tall, well built, and had funky hair (for a law student). I found it amusing. Only in L.A. can you find a hot tattooed guy who is presumably intelligent. A couple of days later, I saw a guy in the atrium looking at me, and I realized it was the tattooed-leg guy. I thought he was cute but didn't think too much of it. There was already a guy in my class who was pursuing me, and I was trying to figure out how to handle that situation. A few days later we had a school bar night at a place called Rix in Santa Monica. As I sat there with my friends, I noticed a tall guy walking into the place; his spiky hair stuck above the crowd. I realized it was "tattoo boy," but I still couldn't tell what he looked like because he was wearing those yellow-lens glasses people wore at the time. After a few minutes, a new friend of mine, the wild red-haired Johnny from New York City, came up to me and wanted to introduce me to his friend. "I'm Justin," said Tattoo Boy. "Hi Justin, I'm Izabella. Do you have some sort of a medical problem that requires you to wear yellow-lens sunglasses indoors?" I couldn't help myself because I already knew he was interested since he clearly asked his friend to introduce us. He didn't say a word, just stood there and stared. Later I gave Johnny my phone number. The next day, the phone rang and it was Justin. I was surprised; he didn't even wait the customary two days. From then on, he called me every day. "So are there a lot of moose in Canada?" he would ask. "Yes, in fact I used to ride moose to school everyday from the igloo where I lived, eh," I replied. This was usually followed by an extended discussion on whether Canadians say "aboot" versus "about"—and for the record, no one says "aboot." He teased me, but I knew it was only because he liked me, the way boys in kindergarten pulled girls' pigtails as a show of affection. And although I did not realize it at the time, he was growing on me. A couple of days later, he called me from outside of my apartment, saying he had some time before his evening class started and he was coming over. His call woke me from a nap, so I answered the door wearing a pair of old oversized floral pajama pants and a tank top. After we hung out watching TV for a bit, he realized he was too late for class and was just going to have to spend the rest of the evening with me. I realized he had planned the whole thing! He never wanted to go to class, class was just an excuse to come over and "kill some time." That night we drank cheap wine and played *Trivial Pursuit* until my roommate and Justin started cheating. I threw a dignified fit and locked myself in my room refusing to come out, but he wouldn't leave. I finally came out of my room, and he apologized and asked for a rematch. I agreed, we kissed, and he left. And that is how we fell in love.

Although I initially didn't think he was my type, mainly because of his tattoos, as I learned more about Justin, I began to see serious potential for a boyfriend. I was happy to find a guy I was attracted to, had great chemistry with, and was also kind, funny, and my intellectual equal. There was also a sensitivity and vulnerability in him that drew me in. Justin learned early on that life is short and we must live each day to the fullest, not worrying about what others say. He almost died when he was 16 years old, when he was struck by a drunk driver while riding a motorcycle with his friend. His friend walked away with minor scratches, but Justin's leg had been shattered. He was airlifted to a hospital, and doctors did not think he would make it. But he did and had multiple surgeries on his knee and hip and spent months in the hospital. He was one of the youngest people in the United States to ever have a hip replacement. The driver who hit him had no insurance; Justin did not get a cent from him. But he never feels sorry for himself, never cries about life being unfair, and never complains about the physical pain that I know he struggles with all the time. Although proudly and fiercely American, Justin is open to other cultures and traditions, even though he has not traveled that extensively, and that was important to me. Although he likes to teasingly say "eh" and "aboot," he loves going to Canada, finds the people warm and friendly, the country beautiful, and Tim Horton's tim-bits delicious. He also eagerly learned many Polish traditions and even a few words in Polish. Most importantly, Justin had tremendous respect for my parents and always treated them with kindness and affection and understood how much they mean to me. I fell in love with his strength, dignity, realism, and kindness.

It wasn't easy having a relationship with him, though. As I found out, he was a hot commodity on the law school meat market. Girls shamelessly pursued him despite knowing we were together. One girl asked a professor to pass Justin an invitation to her party that weekend. Curiously, I wasn't invited nor were many girls at all. He ended up going to the party with some friends. He didn't stay long, and we all met up at a local bar afterward. She came there as well and saw us together. That night when I got home, I noticed the smell of burnt rubber. I circled my car to discover that it had been vandalized. Someone had ripped off my windshield wipers and stuck them in my exhaust pipe. My gut told me it was that girl. She had left the bar a few minutes before I did. She wanted my boyfriend and went to great lengths to invite him to her party. I am sure she wasn't happy when he came to meet me and spent the rest of the night by my side. Years later when I became friends with a girl who had been her best friend at the time, she told me that it was something that this girl was capable of doing.

I was really upset. I had had the car for only five months and my parents had worked so hard to be able to get it for me. How dare she, or anyone for that matter, lay a hand on something that did not belong to her? Furthermore, she was a law student; I could ruin her if I could prove she did it. Instead I let it go. It was the end of the semester, finals were coming up, and I did not want to create a big issue, particularly since I could not prove it. I basically took it out on Justin. I told him I was not going to date him if it meant he was going to allow some bug-eyed girl to mess with me or my property. He finally confronted her one day, about four months later, as she walked out of class. She acted like she didn't know what he was talking about. I didn't care at this point; I was glad he did it, but it was too little too late.

At the end of the semester, I yearned to get away, but I had to plan my summer wisely, because when you graduate law school and look for a job, you must account for how the summers were spent. Since there was not a major international law market in Los Angeles, I became interested in pursuing an internship in entertainment law. Justin had given me a list of Pepperdine alumni who worked in the entertainment industry as possible contacts. The only one that piqued my interest was a guy who worked for Playboy. I imagined it would be fun and exciting to work for a magazine—at the time I didn't know that it wasn't the magazine part of the company. I sent him my resume and we arranged an interview. It went very well, and he said he would give me a call in a few days.

However, in the meantime, I decided that I needed a change of scenery. I wanted to travel, but I had to use my time sensibly. I came up with the perfect solution: study abroad! I wanted to go somewhere I had never been, and Spain was the perfect answer because I could also improve my Spanish skills. I applied for another school loan to go; I didn't need additional loans but I figured if the extra courses helped me graduate a semester early, then it would all even out. I signed up to study in Madrid for two months and decided to follow that up with a two-week vacation in Italy. I asked Justin if he wanted to come. He had never been anywhere outside of the United States besides Brazil, but if I was going to be serious with a man, he had to be cultured. And that meant he had to travel, learn, and explore. We spent the summer living in Madrid. We grew to love our daily *café Americano* and a *Napolitano* for breakfast; for lunch we had *jamón con queso*, and in the evenings we walked around sampling delicious *tapas* such as croquettas and stuffed mushrooms and shrimp sautéed in garlic. We also appreciated the spirit and customs of the Spanish people. We traveled to Barcelona, Sevilla, and Ibiza, and in the process, we fell in love with Spain. We went to Italy afterward, where we met my mom and got to see the Pope in his summer residence in Castel Gandolfo, followed by Florence, Venice, and Rimini. But Justin and I were not used to spending so much time together, especially under the stress and fatigue of constant travel; at the end of the trip, we were ready to kill each other.

Despite my rigorous study schedule at law school, it didn't take long for me to become a bona fide Malibu beach bunny. I went to the beach all the time, lugging my huge law books. I quickly adapted to the local style—the Uggs, the boy-beaters, the short jean skirts. And every weekend, I'd go out to Hollywood and all the hottest clubs. The social atmosphere in law school was not the greatest. Law school is very competitive. There is an enormous amount of intellectual snobbery; everyone thinks he or she is the smartest. And heaven forbid others perceive you as attractive; one cannot be good-looking and smart. People do not like that and will resent you. And there I was, like Elle Woods in *Legally Blonde*, with my blonde hair, pink tank tops, and low-rider jeans. I walked away from law school with only a couple of friends, and that is because they are both confident good-looking women who do not define themselves solely by their intellectual ability, but actually have some personality as well. One of those girls was Vivian; she was a lot like me, and we bonded over our blondeness, our boobs, and our preference for "bad boy" types. It was with her that I first met Hef.

If you had told me then that a year and a half later I would be a member of Hef's "party posse" and live at his Mansion, I would have laughed. But more importantly, I would have been insulted. It was 2000, and I had just started my second year at Pepperdine. To kick off the new semester, my friends and I went to the hot club of the moment—the Sunset Room in Hollywood. I had met one of the owners, Chris Breed, a good-looking Brit who was always welcoming and gracious toward me and my friends. Sunset Room consisted of an elegant restaurant as well as a nightclub, with a large dance floor surrounded by private tables and a bar. In the back, by a beautiful saltwater aquarium, was the passageway to the VIP section. That section included about five cushy booths and another bar, as well as an outdoor section (for the smokers) with another five covered cabanas. I had casually chatted with several celebrities there in the past: Ben Affleck, Matt Damon, and Leonardo DiCaprio. You never knew who you would run into. As we made our way to the VIP room, we noticed Hugh Hefner sitting at a booth with a platinum blonde on either side of him and another older man. Despite the fact that I grew up in Communist Poland and various parts of Canada, I knew who Hugh Hefner was. First, because of his association with Canadian Pamela Anderson—she became famous by being a Playboy Playmate. Secondly, since I moved to L.A., I saw Hef and his troupe of gorgeous blondes frequently featured on TV. My friend Vivian wanted to go say hello, but I was a bit hesitant. I could see all these girls going up to Hef, and I found it more than a little embarrassing. I was intrigued by Hef and attracted to him in a way that I did not understand. What would I say to him? I guess I could tell him I almost interned at Playboy. I didn't realize then that Hef worked from home and never went to the Playboy offices. When Vivian announced she was going to speak with him, I reluctantly went with her.

The older man sitting with Hef made small talk with us and invited us to sit in the booth. This was Doc—Dr. Mark Saginor, otherwise known in Hollywood as "Dr. Feelgood," Hef's personal physician and one of his closest friends. Later, we would learn that Doc also treats the girls in Hef's posse for their assorted medical needs. Hef was very polite and very sweet. He looked at us with a warm smile, making us feel welcome at his table. He was relaxed, drinking his Jack and Coke, with Buffy Tyler and Katie Lohmann sitting at his side, doting on him. He was wearing a black suit and a pink shirt with a white collar and cuffs. I was fascinated with him and the girls. A million questions ran through my mind as I sat there observing them: Were these girls just props? Did they sleep with him? What was their life like? Did he love them? I wanted to talk to the girls, but they seemed in a world of their own. After a couple of drinks, Doc asked us for our phone numbers and invited us to a "Fun in the Sun" party at the Playboy Mansion the following Sunday afternoon. We had no idea what that meant exactly, but we reasoned that if any fun was going to be held in the sun, then it couldn't be too bad.

When I woke up the next day, I remembered the invite to the Mansion and I was nervously excited. The very first time I came to Los Angeles to visit Pepperdine School of Law, my ex-boyfriend Sean and I were driving down Sunset Boulevard when we noticed a Star Maps sign at the corner of the street. We decided to pull over and buy a map for fun. The street corner happened to be Charing Cross Road, and the man selling the map informed us that the Playboy Mansion was just down the street. We had to drive by it. We stopped and took a quick glance at the gates. I wondered what was going on inside, imagining all sort of debauchery. Sean suggested that I walk up to the gate and see if they would let me in to see Hef. "No way, that's embarrassing. Plus I am not sure I want to see what's inside," I said. My only contact with *Playboy* magazine was when Sean and I were driving from college in Montreal to my parent's house in Kitchener, and out of boredom and curiosity I picked up a *Playboy* at the gas station. It was the fortieth anniversary issue and it contained the one hundred stars of the century. I was simply curious about their choices. Sean had always told me I should be a Playmate. Even when I was at McGill, guys used to call me Pam Anderson's little sister, which was silly because we look nothing alike, but the Pam phenomenon was so big in Canada that any girl with blonde hair and boobs was always compared to her.

That Sunday, as Vivian and I drove to the famous 10236 Charing Cross Road address (guaranteed to be on any quality Star Map), we had no idea what to expect. As we approached the gate, a voice coming out of a huge rock asked us who we were and confirmed we were on the list of invitees. As the gates opened and we drove up the winding road, the bright yellow "Caution: Playmates at Play" sign welcoming us, we were guided through the main door of the house into the backyard. There we were greeted by nothing short of paradise: a sprawling green lawn with free-range exotic birds, a pond with ducks, a beautiful pool with a waterfall and nature's truest bounty—sexy girls frolicking in the sun, talking, swimming, playing volleyball. I didn't see anything too crazy; I had imagined I might see naked people prancing around or making out in the deep dark corners of the Mansion, but it was not like that at all. It was surprisingly civilized and tame. At one corner of the pool, Hef sat playing backgammon with two friends, one of whom was Doc. We went over to say hello. As we were walking away, I recognized his Girlfriend and Playmate Buffy Tyler and sat down to speak with her. I thought she was very cool and friendly. I asked her if she lived at the Mansion, and she told me that she and Katie Lohmann shared a room. I asked what it was like, and she told me she was having a lot of fun. I had many more questions, but I didn't want to drill her; I thought she was nice enough to answer any of the questions in the first place.

As Vivian and I stood there taking in the surroundings, we were approached by Jenny—the lady who is in charge of Mansion party invitations—and she took down our information and then took our photos. We got some towels and lay out on the lawn, close to the pool. We just observed these fascinating new surroundings. We also kept visiting the bar, where the bartenders made fresh fruit smoothies and you could order food from the menu du jour. When at the bar, I noticed one of Hef's Girlfriends surrounded by a group of wanna-be Girlfriends. I smiled at her, and she came over to tell me I was pretty. I was flattered by the unexpected comment. At that moment I would have never guessed, in a million years, that this girl and I would be roommates at the Mansion one day and have many adventures together. As evening approached, everyone was slowly leaving to change for dinner. Vivian wanted to stay for the dinner and movie, but I kept worrying about all of the homework that awaited me at home. I also did not want to create additional problems between Justin and I; he was already not too thrilled about my going to the Mansion, and I didn't want to make things worse by staying there until late at night. Vivian and I ended up leaving before dinner. I had a good time that day, but I didn't think I would go back to the Fun in the Sun for a long time; it wasn't worth fighting over with Justin.

This first experience was followed by invitations to all of the Mansion parties. Although I went and was fascinated by the whole Hef party posse scene, I kept my distance from him. Between schoolwork, my relationship with Justin, and going out with my friends, I had no time for anything else. After attending a couple of Mansion parties, I began receiving regular phone calls from Jenny at the Mansion inviting me to come back on Sundays for Fun in the Sun, which was a weekly thing. The problem was that Vivian was not invited to Fun in the Sun, though she was receiving the invites to other parties. I felt really bad about that and, although she constantly told me we should call them and see if we could go over, I never told her I was already invited to them. I was not going to go alone, and I certainly did not want to hurt my friend's feelings, so I just ignored the whole thing. I was perfectly satisfied only attending the parties at the Playboy Mansion.

As for school, I was finally able to take some international law courses and think about my eventual career in law. I began working for one of my professors, Professor Mendoza, assisting him in writing a book about international business transactions. I became efficient at doing research, learned a lot about writing a book, and was able to make some extra money to help pay my bills. He was a great professor, and I am grateful for the experience. However, I was coming to the gradual realization that I was not going to be able to carry out my dreams of becoming an international lawyer as originally planned. It was very likely that I would have to continue my studies with a master's degree and potentially move back to the East Coast, where the international law curriculum was broader. It was probable that I would have to spend some additional years in academia, researching and writing before I actually got to handle the type of cases I was interested in. This was discouraging to me. I really wanted to go out into the world and have a break from studying, at least for a while. I did not know what other area of law I could practice. For the first time in my educational career, the future was not clearly laid out for me.

After my second year, I felt very tired. Justin and I had been arguing a lot, and he would be spending the summer studying and taking the bar exam. I knew he would be more stressed out than ever, and I did not want to be around for that. I wanted to travel again, and it had been several years since I had been to Poland. But I could not waste a summer traveling frivolously, nor did I have any money to do so. I realized that if I could study in Poland, I could graduate a semester early, and I could get school loans to cover my trip. I found the ideal program via Catholic University, which would allow me to take international law courses in Krakow, Poland. It was a perfect opportunity to earn credits and spend time with my family. I had the fortune to study at Jagiellonian University, one of the oldest and most prestigious universities in Europe. It was founded by King Casimir the Great in 1364. Among its most famous alumni are Nicolas Copernicus and the late Pope John Paul II. And its law faculty is regarded as one of the finest in central Europe. It was incredibly inspiring.

After class each day that summer, I went to quaint little cafés to do my homework and explored the city as much as I could. On the weekends the students were able to go on trips. We saw the Royal Salt Mine at Wieliczka, which is like a vast underground city. The historic salt mine is the only site in the world where mining has continued since the thirteenth century. It consists of nine levels going down to a depth of 358 yards and has 186 miles of galleries with works of art, altars, and statues sculpted in the salt, turning a trip down there into a fascinating pilgrimage into the past of a major industrial undertaking. Beneath the mine itself are numerous churches, chapels, and rooms for leisure activities. It is a fascinating underground world where everything is made out of salt; for example, the main cathedral has walls covered with salt sculptures of saints and scenes from the Bible, the altar is made of salt, even the chandeliers are made of salt. Sometimes the room is used for weddings. Wieliczka Salt Mine was entered into UNESCO's first World List of Cultural and Natural Heritage in 1978. I was a little hesitant to go so far under the earth, but it was a fascinating one-of-a-kind experience.

However, the most memorable trip I took that summer was to the Auschwitz-Birkenau concentration camp. Even though I had lived about thirty minutes from it for ten years of my life, I had never been there. It is not a place a child longs to visit. But now in adulthood, I was ready. Not only was it historically and culturally significant to me to visit this place, but it was also personal. It was painful to see the camp, and absolutely heartbreaking to know that my own grandfather had been there. It was such an overwhelming experience that I couldn't find a place within myself to store what I saw and what I felt that day. I had nightmares for several days. I took pictures that day, though I don't know why; I can't bear to look at them. I suppose I needed to prove to myself that what I saw was real. I know I will have to go back one day, to share this experience with others. I think everyone should go there so that the horrors of the past will never be repeated. It's a truly overwhelming look at one of history's blackest eras.

Justin called me several times that summer, and it was nice to hear his voice. Despite the fact that we were on a break and I did not know what the future held, I missed him. He was my best friend, and it was hard not to speak to him and share all of my experiences with him. I knew that no matter what happened when I got back to L.A., he would be a part of my life. I didn't get involved with anyone that summer; I took the time to be by myself, explore Polish culture, reconnect with family, and figure out what I wanted to do next. Being in Poland on my own and having the time to think, I decided I was not ready to jump back into a relationship with him. There were many things that needed to be worked out first, and I wanted some alone time to establish a life that wasn't so reliant on his presence. I came to L.A. to do so many things and I fell in love with him before I had the chance to enjoy the city on my own terms. Now was the time to start fresh. I also thought about Hef and the Mansion from time to time and decided I would go to Fun in the Sun again, now that I did not have the restraints of a relationship. I kept receiving invitations to Mansion parties while I was gone, and I looked forward to going to a party when I got back. That was about the extent of my plans in regard to Hef. I never imagined what the future would bring. I looked forward to being independent, but I drew a certain comfort from the fact that Justin was there for me. I knew that he would be close by, and like I always tell myself, if it is meant to be, it will be.

4: Hanging with Hef

"I couldn't help it. I can resist everything except temptation."

—*Oscar Wilde*

I came back to Los Angeles refreshed and anxious to finish my last semester in law school. In September 2001, right at the beginning of the school year, my friend Niki came to visit me from Toronto. And just as I had done the year before, Niki, Justin and I went out to celebrate her trip and the last semester of my law school career. In a bizarre twist, what happened a year before repeated itself; I ran into Hef again. Not only once but twice that same week: on Wednesday at the Hollywood club Las Palmas (now LAX) and then on Friday at another club called Barfly. Was this fate? After a couple of drinks, I decided to go up and say hi to him. Justin and I became close when I returned that fall, but we did not get back into a relationship. I got my own apartment and he stayed over a lot; we were going to hang out and see where things went. That night, even Justin encouraged me to go say hi to Hef, and so I did. Hef seemed to remember me and was very happy to talk to me; he immediately invited me to come out with him and his girls the following Friday. The next day, I received a call from his assistant, Mary, who invited me to Barfly with Hef and his Girlfriends. After accepting, I was instructed to arrive at the Mansion at 10 p.m., and we would be departing around 10:30.

I was still hesitant; I kept changing my mind until the moment I walked out of my door. What would I wear? Would the other girls be friendly? But in the end, my curiosity won out. And you know what they say about curiosity.

That night, although I didn't know it, I was being recruited. I had a couple of the Girlfriends come up to me and tell me how much fun they were having, how much money they made, and what a great opportunity it was to live at the Mansion. I was told that Hef was interested in me and that I should give it a chance. It sounded almost too good to be true. Then I was told about "the bedroom." After the club, they all go and party in Hef's room. I didn't have to "do" anything at all; it was just a lot of fun. An alarm went off in my brain. I definitely did not want to go to Hef's bedroom, fun or not.

I didn't know him. I don't even *kiss* on the first date, let alone go to someone's bedroom. And was this even a date?

I got out of the limo in front of the Mansion, thanked Hef for the night, got into my car, and went home as fast I could. A few days later, the tragedy of Sept. 11, 2001, occurred. Like the rest of the country, I was devastated, stunned, and scared. To my surprise, I received a personal call from Hef, asking me to go out with them. I told him I couldn't, considering what had just happened, and expressed mild disappointment that he would consider going out at a time like this. He seemed taken aback by my tone and mumbled something about how "life must go on." I agreed that life must go on, but it was much too soon. Later I came to realize that rain, snow, blackout, or any other natural disaster—Hef would still want to go out. Why? So he could have an after-party in his room.

After that, Hef kept on inviting me out and I went out with them several more times, but it was all very casual. Although I found Hef to be very nice and interesting and I always had a good time with him and the girls, I had no plans to get seriously involved with Hef. He invited me to be part of his group, an honor of sorts, at the Mansion's annual Halloween party and even offered to pay for my costume and gave me a makeup and hair allowance. I received a check from one of Hef's assistants. I ended up going shopping with Holly, who was the new girl at the Mansion. It seemed to me that the other girls were not friendly with her and I wanted to befriend Holly. The party was great; it was so much fun being part of Hef's group. I was beginning to imagine myself as part of the party posse, but I disregarded such thoughts for two reasons: I was still in law school, and there was the bedroom issue. I heard from a model that had been hanging out with Hef for a few months that some of the girls had herpes, and it freaked me out. I never had any diseases, and I wanted to stay as far away from them as possible. After the party, I kept receiving calls from Mary; she is the one who calls to ask girls out on Hef's behalf. He rarely calls girls himself. Hef employs an elaborate system of procurement to keep the pipeline filled with willing nubile women. There's a guy named Ron—short, with red hair and a beard—who is always out at clubs cruising for talent and trying to bring new girls into Hef's circle. The ones Hef isn't interested in, Ron tries to date himself. I always see him with his Playboy Mansion notepad in hand to impress the girls and to appear legit, which cracks me up, but I like him; he's a nice person. But Mary has been with Hef forever—she was the house manager at the Chicago Playboy Mansion and has worked for him for decades. It never ceased to amaze me that she would care so much to get Hef the girl that he wanted, that she tried so hard to make him happy and really cared about his sex life and how he was treated. She and Hef have a very special, interesting, peculiar relationship. In my opinion, it is she who runs the Mansion. And so she kept calling and inviting me to go out with Hef, but I always told her that it was my last semester in law school, and exams were around the corner, and I couldn't go out right now, but I would when I was done. I guess I wanted to keep the option open.

By the end of December, I was done with all of my exams, and although my graduation ceremony was not until June, I was officially finished with law school. To start working as an attorney, I needed my license, and to get the license, I had to pass the Bar exam. Without even taking a minute to think about what I should do next, I signed up to take the Bar exam in February and borrowed $3,000 from my parents for a review class. I spent Christmas in Canada with my family, and when I returned, my friend Vivian and I attended the New Year's Eve party at the Mansion. I received a warm welcome from Hef and spent the night partying with him and the girls. I had a great time. I noticed that some of the old Girlfriends were gone and that there were a few new girls "trying out". As I sat there looking at them, I tried to envision being part of the group. Could I do this?

After the party, Hef called and invited me to come out with him and the girls now that I was done with school. Little did he know that this time of preparation for the Bar is much more intense than actually being in school; everyone who was studying for the Bar exam lived, breathed, and dreamed it. It requires your full attention and all of your time. You start with a few hours in class every morning, followed by an entire day of exercises and memorization. But I felt like I needed a break from the mental strain and loneliness (I can only study alone) of preparing for the exam. During the week I attended the review class, and on the weekends, I went out with Hef. I knew I was treading on dangerous ground, but I decided to give it a shot and see what happened. And what happened was that I had a blast! I became good friends with a couple of the girls who were also new to the scene, and that changed the dynamic for me.

Although we had nothing in common, Emma and I hit it off immediately. She is from England, a former Page Three girl (a woman who models topless for photographs published on page three of the U.K. tabloid *The Sun*). She had a pretty tough life; a high school dropout, she had a baby at seventeen and was struggling to make ends meet as an exotic dancer and model. She met a nice man who helped her out; he wanted to come to America, so they got married and he brought her and her son with him. When she first got to Los Angeles, she started doing B movies. When she met Hef, she was having a hard time paying rent. She had tested for *Playboy* magazine before, but despite being very photogenic, in my opinion, did not get approved. She was hoping to become a Girlfriend because of the money and work opportunities with Playboy it could bring her. Although our lives had been completely different, I liked Emma. I realized that, though I was not as bad as other people in law school, I was also a bit of an intellectual snob. I would not date anyone who was not as educated as I was, or befriend women who relied on their looks, or men, to get by in life. The feminist in me regarded that as pathetic. But life at the Mansion forcibly exposed me to a wide variety of characters, and I became more open-minded. Because of my friendship with Emma, I learned how to be less judgmental about people and the things they do in life to survive. I loved her sense of humor and upbeat personality. I like all accents in general but I have a particular liking for the Queen's English. I loved the way she spoke; her swear words were particularly amusing. Before I knew it I was going around saying "bloody hell" and "bollocks" as if I had grown up saying it. No matter how bad my mood was, there were certain words she could always say to make me laugh such as the word guilty, which she pronounced "gui-ee," or when she ordered "tos-ee-os" (Tostitos) and salsa. Emma and I had a lot of fun together; we would drink and dance at the clubs. We were also both in the same initial stages of our relationship with Hef, although she knew she wanted to move in and I still wasn't sure about it. My friendship with her influenced my eventual decisions regarding moving in, living at the Mansion, and even moving out. Now I had a few friends who were entering this foreign world of Playboy with me; we shared our concerns, our fears, and our hopes. The experience was now beyond hanging out with Hef; it became about having fun with my friends. It was exactly that kind of thinking that led me to sabotage myself.

This new lifestyle was not compatible with studying for the Bar exam. I was sacrificing my studies, and I knew it. Hef was planning a trip to New York City at the end of January, and I was told that he wanted to invite me but was not going to because he didn't want to interfere with my studies. I knew that the damage had been done already, and so I asked him if I could come on the trip. He agreed but was concerned about taking me away from my studies. We chartered a private jet and stayed at the Four Seasons Hotel in Manhattan. I shared a room with Roxy, with whom I bonded, but who drove me nuts waking up at 7 every morning. The trip to New York was amazing. We went to see *The Producers*, which was fantastic. We went out to the best nightclubs and hung out with musician Moby one night—he was so sweet and was fascinated by the fact that I had just finished law school. He wrote about me in his online journal, but I have not seen him since then. The best, and most rewarding, was going to a firehouse (Engine 3, Ladder 12, Battalion 7) and spending time with the New York Fire Department—just four months after Sept. 11. They made us lunch, which included a salad made in the biggest salad bowl I had ever seen, and we drank iced tea from mugs so big and heavy that we had to use both hands to lift them. They also showed us how to go down the fire pole; I held on for dear life, screeched all the way down, and plopped ungracefully, but I loved it. Some of the girls were great with the pole—previous work experience, I suppose. We took photos with the firemen and had a truly amazing time.

When I got back to L.A., my priorities had begun to change. Something unexpected happened: I had begun to really like Hef. He was always such a gentleman toward me, always very sweet and gracious. I was flattered that this connoisseur of beautiful women was interested in me. I was hesitant at first because of the fact that he had multiple girlfriends—the Girlfriends; I didn't really know how to deal with that, so I focused on my relationship with him. The age difference, though it is the first thing people bring up to me, did not bother me. I had always dated guys my own age, or two years older at the most, but I liked older men in general. I find them interesting, secure with who they are, and mature—much more mature than any guy my own age. And Hef was all of that and so much more.

He also won me over with being kind and thoughtful. I had mentioned to Mary, who kept a watch on my studies, that I needed a new computer to take my exam on. She was going to check if there was one available at the office that I could borrow. Without waiting for her to find out, I went and bought one on my credit card. When she found out, she called to tell me that

Hef wanted to pay for it. I was overjoyed. Not only was it a tremendous help financially, but it was also a sweet and considerate gesture. Hef continued being very attentive and caring toward me, and I could not help but grow to care about him. I really enjoyed his company.

After the New York trip it was difficult to get back into the rhythm of studying. I would go to my review class and sit among the stressed-out, sleep-deprived, caffeine-fueled students. After class I stopped by the Mansion; it was pure paradise. I lay out by the pool, where the butlers delivered my lunch, I swam and tanned, and I was being seduced by the Playboy lifestyle. I wondered if I should put the Bar exam off for a while; after all, I graduated early thanks to my hard work. I could spend the next few months trying something different and then take the Bar exam in July with the rest of my class. However, because they would not refund my course money or the Bar exam fee, I decided I would just do it for the experience. Hef endeared himself to me even more when he gave me the money I paid for the course review and the Bar exam. I was able to pay my parents back, and it felt amazing.

A week before the Bar exam, Hef told us girls we would be attending the MusiCares dinner gala honoring the chosen artist of the year and the 2002 Grammys, but of course I was excused because both events coincided with the exam. I immediately protested to Hef. I knew the exam was a lost cause, and I did not want to miss out on the Grammys. Hef gave each of us $2,000 for outfits to the two events. We were ecstatic. I got a white dress for the dinner and a white leather outfit—a mini skirt and a matching jacket—for the Grammys. The night before the Bar exam, I attended the MusiCares benefit—my first red carpet event. By the time I got back to the hotel—I was staying at the Radisson, where the exam was taking place—all of the students had long been asleep. The following day I took the exam, and to my surprise, I did fine. The second day of the exam (it's a three-day test), I was distracted. I knew the Grammys red carpet action began at around 3 p.m. and I wouldn't even be finished with the test by then. As soon as I was done, I ran to my room to find out that my limo and security was already waiting downstairs. I did my makeup in fifteen minutes and didn't even have time to do my hair because the show had already begun. I cannot imagine what my fellow examinees must have thought when they saw me strolling out of the hotel in a white leather outfit and getting into a limo. The show was great; we sat right at the front on the side of the stage and had perfect view of all of the performances.

After the show, we went to a couple of after parties, and then the limo brought me back to my hotel. The next day, when it was time for the last day of the exam, I simply couldn't do it. I was tired and could not concentrate. I left the exam room, packed my stuff up, and left without finishing. I later found out that had I made a real effort on that last day, I would have probably passed the exam; my scores until then were good. As things were, I couldn't get a job at a law firm without first passing the bar, and the next bar wasn't until July. My self-sabotage was successful. Now, there was nothing stopping me. But there was someone.

My going out with Hef and the girls was a source of constant fighting between Justin and me. After I graduated from law school in December 2001, he thought my "fling" with Hef and his posse was over, but I was just getting to know them. Justin appealed to my intelligence, independent spirit, and strength to discourage me from being involved with Hef. He told me he was disappointed that I was wasting such a fantastic education to pursue a frivolous life. "What happened to the girl I knew who wanted to become an international lawyer and make the world a better place?" he would challenge me. He was my best friend, and he knew how to get to me. It hurt. I cried myself to sleep almost every night, wrestling with my conscience. When appeals to my ambition didn't work, he turned to insults: "How can you hang out with those dumb bimbos? Don't you have any pride? What happened to your self-respect? You wouldn't be caught dead hanging out with people like that a year ago! Everyone will equate you with them. You will never get a job in a law firm." Although his previous technique made me think about the choices I was making, the insults incensed me and only provoked me further. He hurt me too much, and I had to cut off contact with him for a while. To hell with everyone! I decided. It was not easy to reconcile my bad-girl desires with my good-girl upbringing and defy the predictable expectations of everyone around me. Maybe it was a mistake, but it was my very own mistake. I wanted to live life on my own terms, not as a passive concession to the expectations of others.

I *was* seduced by the Playboy lifestyle. The private jet, the parties, the limos, the Grammys, and the carefree lifestyle were unlike anything I had seen or experienced. It was so different from my disciplined, socially conscious intellectual existence; I could not help but be tempted by it. My true Libra spirit has always been seeking to balance itself. For a long time there had been a struggle between my left brain and right brain.

I wanted a legitimate education so that I never had to go through what my parents went through. Some people think that speaking English with an accent means you are stupid. People don't realize how difficult it is for immigrants to come to a new country with nothing, to learn a new language, and try to make it as an equal. The odds are against you.

And though I dreamed of artistic pursuits, I knew that a solid education would provide security and validation in this world. In law school, I realized that a law degree might not be enough to do what I wanted to do. I started looking into a master's degree in international law, but I wanted to live life a little; I was becoming a perpetual student. I was afraid to think what my student loans would look like if I continued studying. An opportunity for a break came from the most unexpected place.

There was something about the Mansion that just lured you in. It's not Hef himself. It's not the house. It's this enchanting feeling, this aura. There is a spirit to that place that makes your skin tingle, your mind relax. It makes you lose your inhibitions. Hef and his lifestyle seduced me with the promise of a privileged and peaceful lifestyle. Not to have to worry about rent, bills, and all the other mundane details of life that preoccupy most of our time—that meant freedom to me. Freedom to explore a different side of life. It is Maslow's hierarchy of needs: When our basic needs are satisfied, we can look to satisfy our higher desires and allow our sexual animal off the leash. It's an addictive lifestyle. After I spent time at the Mansion, the Bar review class simply did not have a chance. The rigor of class illuminated the freedom of the Mansion—it was exhilarating. I did want a break from studying, though the Mansion presented the extreme of anything I could have possibly had in mind. But I believe in destiny. There was a reason this opportunity had presented itself to me. This was a fork in the road, and I had to choose. It wasn't a fair choice. Of course I would choose the road less traveled; the way of the Bunny.

Even though we were Hef's Girlfriends, there were certain benefits that Emma and I were not getting and could not get because we did not live at the Mansion. The most important was the weekly allowance—only the girls that lived at the Mansion could get a weekly allowance in exchange for living under Hef's set of laws. This is very surprising to most people; they have no idea that we are given an allowance as Hef's Girlfriends. Initially, the financial issue was one of necessity; we were going out with Hef all of the time, yet we did not have the money to buy new outfits, and when you go out several nights a week, you quickly run out of things to wear. Secondly, the late-night partying is not conducive to maintaining a nine-to-five job, so we needed an allowance to pay our bills. However, the benefits of living at the Mansion, like most things in life, came with many strings attached. To live at the Mansion, you had to follow the rules, and there were many rules. But the one that we really got stuck on was the curfew: Everyone had to be on the Mansion grounds by nine o'clock every night—unless we were out with Hef at a club or a function. People honestly did not believe us when we told them we had a curfew at the wild and crazy Playboy Mansion. Nine o'clock? But nothing fun happens before 9 p.m.! And that was exactly the point. From this one rule derived many consequences: I couldn't go out to dinner with my friends; I couldn't go out to clubs with my friends; I couldn't have a night off and go sleep over at a friend's place; I could not take acting classes because most of those took place in the evenings; and on and on. Though we later learned how to bend this rule occasionally, this was a major hang-up at the time. Secondly and generally speaking, our freedom was limited; our lives were no longer really our own, we were now a part of the group. Interestingly, it wasn't always like that. The girls that came before us were allowed to do much more than we were, but they screwed up and Hef learned from their mistakes. Emma and I would constantly debate whether we could handle it if we did move in, and it became an "I will if you will" type of situation.

I really didn't know if I could live at the Mansion; I didn't know if I could play the role that was expected of me. And make no mistake, most of the time we were all playing a role: playing Hef's Girlfriend, playing like we were friends, being chatty and polite with all of the random folks always coming over. It was exhausting. It is a show. I really should add all of that experience to my acting resume: dumb blonde eye-candy. It's like when you long to get a certain job, or long to meet someone famous, and then you have the chance and you ask yourself: Can I really do this? It is much safer being a "normal" person and admiring from afar, but it takes a certain resolution and courage to actually step up and live in a world so unfamiliar and that is not as safe as the one you live in.

I literally made a list of pros and cons to help me make up my mind. The cons included my relationship with Justin, the sex issue at the Mansion, and falling off my career path. The pros included having a unique experience, taking a chance, and living life to the fullest. After I sabotaged the Bar exam, there was nothing for me to do besides wait for the results, though I already knew the outcome. Once I had decided that I would hang out with Hef and the girls and become part of the "party posse," moving into the Mansion was inevitable. After all, why devote all this time to the whole scene and not receive the same benefits as the girls who lived at the Mansion? It was my time to play, or my time to waste. As long as I was paying my bills and not taking my parents' money, I was doing okay, or so I decided. In the end, my stubbornness and determination to be independent and experience life on my terms won out. I am an only child; I never had to compromise, share, or give in to anyone. An opportunity to move into the Playboy Mansion, regardless of the consequences and implications, does not come every day. Besides, I could always move out; we didn't have to be there for a specific period of time, and we never signed any contracts or confidentiality agreements as to our relationship with Hef or our life at the Mansion. I was always in charge of my life.

Starting January 2002, I was hanging out with Hef and the girls on a regular basis; I slept over at the house in one of the available bedrooms a couple of times a week and I became an official Girlfriend of Hugh Hefner, an occasion commemorated by a unique Playboy necklace (the same one that is given to Playmates, the pendant on the necklace is actually a pin) that you cannot buy. Emma and I made an effort to come out on "movie nights" and watch the old movies with Hef, and hang out with him on Saturdays, knowing how much he enjoyed our company and how important it was to him that we be there. Basically, we made extra effort to be there during the times we were not "required" to be there. Hef noticed and officially asked us both to move into the Playboy Mansion in April 2002, and we accepted. We were excited! It is so strange after so many months of deliberating whether we could, should, or would move in that as soon as he invited us to do so, we jumped at the opportunity. After all, it was just Holly, Tammy, and the two of us that were invited to move in. It was a privilege for him to invite us to move in—we knew how many girls wanted our position and how many thousands of dollars he had to pay for our rooms at the Mansion. For me it was all about having the unusual experience of living at the infamous Playboy Mansion. Moving in also meant receiving a steady allowance. Although he had been generous with Emma and me, those were random acts of generosity, and we needed something more regular to count on. So we began the process of moving our things in.

The most complicated task was to tell my parents that I was going to move into the Playboy Mansion. I told my parents that I worked for Hef. I told them I had to live at the Mansion for convenience, which was true. They never knew about the different aspects of my relationship with Hef. My parents were not wholly comfortable with my living there; my father constantly asked me when I would fulfill what he thought was my destiny and be an attorney. My mom was supportive of my decision as long as I was happy. My father's idea of a good person was someone who worked hard and was a productive member of society. His code was honor, work, and education. My mom knew how independent and spirited I am, and she gave me what I needed: love and support. However, if she knew the full extent of my relationship with Hef, she would never had allowed me to move into the Mansion. Ever.

5 : The Crib

"Mid pleasures and palaces though we may roam,
Be it ever so humble, there's no place like home."
—John Howard Payne

When you think of the most famous residences in the world, which come to mind? The White House, Graceland, Taj Mahal, Buckingham Palace, 10 Downing St., maybe the Neverland Ranch, and surely the Playboy Mansion. And now, one of those places was my new home! Except the Mansion is like its own little country, with a hedonistic ruler and its own special laws. It took a while to get used to the idea that I lived at the legendary Playboy Mansion. Every time I pulled up to that famous gate with the talking rock and it opened automatically for me, I would take a mental step back and think, *How did I end up living here?* At the beginning, everything was so new and exciting; we were having the time of our lives. The Playboy Mansion is a peculiar place. First and foremost, it is Hef's house. It is also Hef's office, an office that employs approximately ten other people at any given time. There is also house management, the video department, the people that work on Hef's scrapbooks, the butlers, the maids, the gardeners, the animal department, and security. Then of course it became our house as well. All in all, it's a lot of people. The main problem I had with that was the lack of privacy; the only privacy I ever had was in my room.

The Gothic Tudor house was built in 1926 for a British businessman, Mr. Arthur Letts. According to the house legend, Mrs. Letts haunts the Mansion. I never saw anything ghostly or experienced anything peculiar, but the house does have a creepy feel at night. One of the other Girlfriends, Bridget, with her love for murders and other unpleasantries, believed in the spirit of Mrs. Letts roaming around the Mansion—that's why she had the ghost-talker come do a séance on one of the episodes of *The Girls Next Door*. It was Hef's great love, Barbi Benton, who found the house. Hef fell in love with it and purchased it in 1971 for a million dollars, a great investment considering it is now worth an estimated $45 million. It was originally intended to be the West coast counterpart to the now nonoperational Chicago East Coast Mansion. The Playboy Mansion had a "sister" house built next door, which was there before Hef bought it. Though smaller and slightly different, its layout is a mirror image of the Mansion. Hef purchased the neighboring house in 1996. His wife, Kimberly, and their two teenage sons live there.

The Mansion wasn't like people think—with James Caan ordering drinks at the cabana bar, and bikini-clad women running around. Instead, it was strangely quiet throughout most of the day. The only people you ever saw were the small army of gardeners and groundskeepers it took to maintain paradise, and Hef himself, barreling along one of the shaded walkways in his silk pajamas and slippers, clutching a sheaf of papers on some mysterious errand. Although the house is large, approximately 21,000 square feet, it doesn't feel that big; there is no danger of getting lost in it. The layout is actually quite simple: The basement contains mainly storage and other functional spaces. On the ground floor are all the common areas, the second floor houses all the bedrooms, and the third floor, or the attic, houses the scrapbooks and video department.

When you enter through the huge golden oak main door, you find yourself in what is know as the great hall. If you keep going straight through this area you'll get to the backyard. The great hall has an ornate desk with Hef's picture hanging above it and a guest book below for guests to sign and leave

Hef messages. There is also a bench and a throne chair. A painting of Hef's second wife, Kimberly Conrad Hefner, also decorates the great hall. During the parties, there is a dance floor put in here, and on the weekends it is an area for guests to mingle. For us girls, it was the place to meet before we went out to clubs or events. We always posed in the great hall for the first of many photographs taken during a night out.

To the right of the great hall is the walnut-paneled formal dining room, with a long oval table and cushy blue seats all around. On the weekends, other chairs are added to accommodate as many guests as possible for the buffet dinner. Hef's seat is at the head of the table with the chairs immediately next to him reserved for the Girlfriends, his brother Keith, and his closest friends. There is also another small round table by the window, to accommodate extra guests, and the food tables are along the other walls. There is a Jackson Pollock painting in the dining room that I admired though Hef told me it was a replica; the real one was sold some years ago. Right next to the dining room is the Mediterranean room, a small garden-like breakfast/lunch room that is only a door away from the butler's pantry and then the extensive kitchen.

The kitchen is open twenty-four hours a day; my favorite thing about living at the Mansion was being able to order food anytime. All I had to do was press "0" on my telephone, or from anywhere in the house, and order anything I wanted. If I could not decide, I would order two meals and eat a portion of each. The way it worked is the butlers would write down our order and when it was ready, they brought it to our rooms on a tray. Now they have a computer to type the order into and keep track of the food. We could order anything anytime! Whatever the craving was, it would be fulfilled. My friends loved visiting and ordering French toast with fresh berries for breakfast; I used to get it all the time too. For lunch they made an awesome Cobb salad or a club sandwich. My favorite dinners were chicken fajitas, salmon, penne pasta in Alfredo sauce, or cheeseburger and fries—they make the best "skinny" fries at the Mansion! And I can't forget the fresh chips and guacamole. We were really spoiled. But things weren't always perfect; some butlers were less efficient than others and only realized they forgot about your order when you called an hour later wondering why the club sandwich was taking so long. That was the downside; we were not allowed to go and make our own food, even if we were hungry and didn't want to wait. In fact, we were not even allowed in the butler's pantry. After so many of Hef's previous girls hooked up with the butlers, there was a strict rule about no socializing with the staff.

People were not the only ones benefiting from the kitchen and butler service; our dogs were pretty spoiled too. My dogs would eat chopped up chicken twice a day (and dog food once a day), which was ordered along with my breakfast and lunch. The butlers would bring it on little white dishes. This was very helpful when I began interning at the Playboy Entertainment Group Inc. a couple of days a week, and I could call them and ask them to feed the dogs; leaving food for them was not an alternative because pugs are piglets and would eat it all. I became so used to pressing "0" and reaching the butlers that when I started working at Playboy, I would press "0" on my phone and say, "Hi, this is Izabella, can you please take two chicken dishes to my room for the pugs and make sure they have water." It never ceased to elicit a colorful response from the confused company operator: "Who is this? Chicken for pugs? What the hell are you talking about?" I always laughed at myself: This reliance on pressing "0" was out of control. I was actually really embarrassed at how spoiled I was, and I was embarrassed on behalf of the dogs; they were spoiled as well. Sometimes as a special treat I (and I was not the only one) would order a lamb chop for them, but I always made sure to ask for one with as little meat as pos-sible—I just wanted the bone for the dogs to chew on. Then, one day when I tried to order two chops the butlers told me that the chef was very angry that several of us girls were ordering lamb chops for their dogs when they were bought especially for Hef (lamb chops were one of his very favorite meals). I certainly did not mean to offend anyone, particularly the chef—I just wanted the bones. The butlers thought it was funny that Emma and I got in trouble for eating Hef's chops, and I never ordered them again.

Back to the house tour. On the opposite side of the great hall, if you make a left from the main entrance, you will see a beautiful wood twin balustrade staircase, and as you pass under it, you will find the living/family room, although it more commonly functions as the movie room. During the week the room is like a family room with brown leather couches, a piano, and a couple of tables. This is where the Christmas tree stands during the holidays. On movie nights the couches are arranged and rows of chairs are added to accommodate the guests in front of the giant movie screen. Behind the movie screen, which is left down most of the time, stands an old but beautiful tiger print sofa, which I was told is where one of Hef's Girlfriends, who is also a Playmate, used to have sex with one of the butlers. Past the movie room is the library, with not too many books in it at all. It has a desk where Hef writes his notes for the movies (on Friday nights Hef introduces the movie of the night by reading his notes about the movie, things like background, meaning, etc.), as well as a worn-in couch and a table where Hef plays backgammon on Sundays when the weather is not suitable for outdoor activities, and a cozy fireplace. Hef is always seen interviewed in this room, surrounded by pictures of his family and Girlfriends and an interesting sculpture of Barbi.

Between the movie room and the library is a secret door disguised by the carved wood paneling on the wall. There is a hidden button that when pressed opens up the door and reveals a staircase that leads to a wine cellar. It's all very James Bond. Emma and I snuck down there one night to retrieve a bottle of my favorite wine, Cabernet Sauvignon. I had ordered a glass from the kitchen, but they had an overstock of Shiraz and that was the only wine they were going to serve until it was finished. *What?* Hef always announces on television that we have a five-star kitchen, but what kind of a five-star restaurant has only one type of wine? So I took the matter into my own hands and searched for the legendary wine cellar; one of the brave butlers showed us which secret button to press on the wall to get the door to open. The next day, one of the butlers reported that a bottle of wine had been removed from the cellar and Hef came charging to my room, upset, as if I committed a crime. Hef's previous Girlfriends had gone down there and taken a few bottles of

Dom Pérignon, which cost him a lot of money, and from then on girls were not allowed to go to the cellar. Hef came to have a "talk" with us about it as if it was a major transgression. It really surprised me that he was so mad; it was just a regular bottle of wine. I was also mad for being treated like a child: "I am sick and tired of drinking that vinegary Shiraz all the time just because they have an overstock of it," I tried to explain. "How many more months do I have to drink it for, Hef? I would go to the store and buy it myself but I already got yelled at by a butler for having a bottle in my room!" That was another rule: No *bottles* of alcohol in our rooms. Again, it was because girls in the past had drinking problems and so now Hef did not allow bottles in rooms. All I wanted was one glass of Cabernet to relax and I got a huge headache instead. But that was the nature of life at the Mansion. In the end, Hef promised to have the kitchen cabinet stocked with a better selection of wine, and told the kitchen staff that the guests could drink the Shiraz, but the girls were to have any wine they wanted. Another battle won.

And that is all there is to the downstairs—not as many rooms as one would imagine. Unlike the glamorous celebrity homes you usually see on *MTV Cribs*, the Mansion does not have a formal living room or any fancy rooms at all, nor does it contain any remarkable pieces of furniture or decoration. I guess it would be futile to have very expensive and luxurious things when the house is used to entertain so many people on a regular basis.

To get to the second floor, you walk up the twin staircase, at the top of which you will find a brass sculpture lovingly referred to as "brass ass," in the crack of which, messages are left for Hef. The upstairs is organized in a very straightforward way. You have one long hallway (in the shape of an L) and all the bedrooms are located along it. The first doorway you encounter upstairs is Hef's bedroom. After Hef's room are bedrooms numbered from two to six, along with a few closets along the way. At the end of the hall, after bedroom six, you take four steps down and that is where the offices are located. It used to be the maids' quarters, but the four small rooms have been converted to home offices. When Emma and I were moving in, Holly lived in Hef's bedroom and Tammy had the next room, bedroom two. Bedroom three had three beds and was used by visiting girls, so whoever took that room had to share (later, before I moved out, Bridget had the other beds removed and it became her bedroom, as it remains at the time of my writing). Then there were bedrooms four and five, which had a connecting bathroom. At the end of the hall was bedroom six, and though it was the second smallest room, it had its own bathroom, so that was the room I chose. I did not want to have to share a bathroom; I really wanted my privacy and wanted to be able to enjoy a relaxing bath without feeling like I was inconveniencing someone else. I also didn't want Hef popping by all the time and checking up on me. I didn't realize that during the day, I would have the least privacy because the offices were next to my room. Every time I walked in and out of the door, everyone looked down the hall and saw me. Tammy once told me that every girl who occupied that room did not stay long at the Mansion; the room's distance from Hef's room was symbolic of the distance the girl wanted to keep from the group. Ironically, this applied to me in some respects, but I did end up living at the Mansion for a much longer time than I expected.

In the hallway connecting the bedrooms is a gallery of photos taken throughout the years. The walls are literally filled with pictures; every celebrity imaginable is there: Brad Pitt and Jennifer Aniston, Robert DeNiro, Jack Nicholson, Bruce Willis, Jim Carrey, and hundreds more. There are also pictures of Hef's friends and Girlfriends over the years. Sometimes at night when everyone was sleeping, I just walked up and down the hall and looked at all the pictures; it could take hours. The Mansion also has an attic, a third floor with slanted ceilings, where Hef's scrapbooks are stored. Hef has 1,500 scrapbooks documenting his entire life. When he was young, he started documenting his life by drawing cartoons of people and events in his life. When he got too busy to draw, he began using photographs, articles, and other mementos. Hef kept love letters he got from girls, photos, and other special tokens. This is the reason he took hundreds of photos every week, everywhere we went. No moment could be lost. The scrapbooks are an egomaniacal obsession.

The attic is also where all of the movies are kept, as well as the video department. Hef is a huge fan of classic movies and documentaries and is a dedicated film collector. He currently has more than 4,000 movies in his library on three-quarter tape or DVD. There's a full-time staff of people in a control room, who TiVo and tape better versions of old movies, documentaries, history programs, etc. There's also a staff whose primary job is to transfer film from three-quarter tape to DVD. The video department also videotaped shows for all of us when we we're gone, so that we could watch them later; they also kept an eye out for any news regarding, or mention of, Hef and Playboy.

There is also a basement area used for the laundry, and storage, with a creepy underground walkthrough to the gym, which itself is located underground. Besides the main house, the property also has a guesthouse, a four-bedroom cottage with shabby décor that houses Playmate hopefuls and Playmates who visit. The guesthouse is really outdated and needs a makeover; I heard that Holly was undertaking a remodel, and I certainly hope she was successful. Located beside the guesthouse is an aviary, which is home to many exotic birds—as well as fish—which I am sure served to wake the guests bright and early. On the other side of the guesthouse is the beautifully maintained tennis court, with benches and a bar area and tables. That is were the haunted house is built for the annual Halloween party. I used to take my pugs to the court every day and play soccer with them using one of the tennis balls.

If you follow the path running through the front yard from the guesthouse, you will find the game house, with the infamous padded-floor room (the carpeted floor has a very thick pad underneath to make it bed-like), which is surrounded by mirrors and TVs. The floor in that room is soft, but it is by no means a mattress. Maybe it was at one time, back in the swinging '70s, but it has been worn in and worn out long ago. Besides pinball machines, a pool table, and several video games, the game room also has two other connected bedrooms; the red room and blue room—named after the color of the sheets and accessories. All you will find in these rooms are a bed, a ceiling mirror, and a phone. These rooms are very popular during parties, when they provide mischievous guests privacy for sexual liaisons or other interesting activities. Beside the game house, among the trees and shrubs, is the pet cemetery, where metal plaques commemorate the lives of beloved pets such as Mama Dog and Dior, Kimberly Hefner's beloved Doberman.

On the other side of the main house is the backyard. The grounds of the Mansion are definitely the most beautiful things about the entire property. When you walk out of the great hall into the backyard, you find yourself in paradise. Hef always told us that this is not what the grounds looked like when he bought the house, and it took a while for him to transform it into his own Shangri-la. First there is a large green lawn where the exotic birds roam. In the summer, a volleyball net is set up in the middle of the lawn, and there is also a large trampoline out there all year round. To the right is a tropical lagoon pool with a waterfall. Hef said he chose a naturalistic pool with rocks to blend in with the beautiful property because he just could not imagine putting a square cement pool back there. The pool is a variation of a kidney shape, and it wraps itself around a small hill; if you go all the way back around the pool you will find a path that leads to the top of the hill from where waterfalls plunge into the pool. Back in the '70s and '80s, girls used to suntan there naked and couples snuck out there to make love in the sun or under the stars. Maybe that is why helicopters still fly over the Mansion grounds almost every day, often circling repeatedly over the pool area. Also, on the top of this hideaway, embedded into the ground, is a large piece of stained glass, which, if you peek through, shows you the grotto underneath.

The pool is connected to the infamous Grotto by two passages: one is a few feet under the water through a rock—I never swam through it because it gave me a claustrophobic feeling. And the other entrance is under a waterfall. The grotto is amazing. It feels like a romantic cave. It is warm, cozy, quiet, and seductive. The grotto is a combination of the pool with its cold waters and five hot-water whirlpools—you can walk right from the cold water into the hot water of the whirlpools. The whirlpools are all different; there is one that is like a bed—the water is only a foot or so deep so that people can lay in it. Another is very small but deep, a full body space—you just stand in it, and the pressure massages your entire body. Yet another is a cozy little sit-down, and the main, largest whirlpool is about waist-deep with the sitting area all along the side of it. Big white candles are scattered around the grotto. There are also green mattress pads (like you would find on a futon) conveniently placed in the remote dark nooks of the grotto.

The pool and grotto are connected to a series of bathrooms, changing rooms, and showers that feel like they are outdoors—one wall of the shower is glass that faces the outside but is blocked from public view by luscious tropical plants. This area leads to a narrow winding staircase, down into the basement area connected to the house, where you find a well-equipped gym, as well as a steam room and a room with two professional tanning beds. On the other side of the pool is a Koi pond, also the favorite hangout of many ducks. One of my favorites was Zeus the goose (he was a Canadian goose, so I felt a particular bond with him), who passed away when I lived at the Mansion. We all loved him; he used to cruise around when the girls were tanning and hang out with them. I think he had a thing for Bunnies. He kept quacking at you as if he was telling you something. Hef wanted to get another goose, but we were afraid we could not find another like Zeus. There were several other birds that became favorites such as the trumpeter who loved being around people; the trumpeters are a small family of birds restricted to the forests of the Amazon basin in South America. They are named for the trumpeting call of the males. They are dumpy birds with long necks and legs and chicken-like bills. There was also the nutty African crane that would stalk us. I was always afraid he was going to nip at me. There are also pink flamingos and beautiful peacocks walking the grounds, as well as many other rare and exotic birds in the aviary. My favorite was Corolla, a Moluccan cockatoo usually found in the Philippines and the Moluccan and Indonesian islands. Moluccans are light pink to salmon colored with a beautiful large orange crest. Corolla is darling; she would say hello and always put on a show, which consisted of wing flapping and exaggerated head movements, when you came to visit her. She stuck out her foot to indicate that she wanted you to take her with you, but once you did she refused to go back to the other birds; she was happy to stay with you. I always told Hef that I would steal her some day.

Next to Corolla's day hangout (the birds spent the night in the aviary but were brought out during the day into the backyard, where they had tree posts with umbrellas to hang out on) was the zoo. Hef is one of the very few individuals in the country who is lucky enough to have a private zoo license. Most of the occupants are monkeys, such as the squirrel monkeys that you can hand feed. Grapes and bananas are placed in a little container by the cages, and you can walk in and they will gently take the grape out of your hand with their tiny little hands, peel off the skin, and eat the juicy inside. There were also two bigger monkeys, Coco and Pepe, who tried to scare you off when you walked by, hurling themselves at the bars of the cage. We also had bunnies and an owl that had been injured and was living out her last days in the safety of the Mansion grounds. We had a kinkajou—a nocturnal animal which lives in trees and looks like a cross between a monkey and a raccoon—which we used to sneak down and take a peek at nightly. (Though they are usually found in rainforests, a kinkajou named Baby Luv has recently been spotted on the red carpet with Paris Hilton!) Whenever things got stressful and chaotic in the main house, it was so relaxing and wonderful to walk around the grounds and spend time with the animals.

Last but not least, on the roof of the house are two huge gargoyles. I think they are awesome, but they stay covered the entire year; they only get uncovered for Halloween. At the Halloween party, they flap their wings and breathe smoke. I asked why they stay covered most of the time, and I was told that they are unsightly and would scare people. More unsightly than two blobs on the roof covered and wrapped in cloth? Yeah, *that* doesn't look ugly. I know they look ferocious, but they are there to ward off evil spirits and are nothing to be afraid of. Plus, with all the characters always coming to the house, Hef needs all the help he can get keeping the bad ones out.

As for the furniture in the house, it is an eclectic collection. There are some nice pieces such as the desk in the great hall and the hand-carved throne chairs, and the furniture in Hef's formal office is quite nice; however, the rest of it is just worn out and shabby looking. It has been around since the '70s and maybe even longer. I imagine some pieces came with the house. Certain things have been replaced as need arose, and so the house is furnished with a random collection of things that do not necessarily belong together. It is not what I imagined it would be like. If they ever liquidate the estate and auction off the furnishings, I would advise the Smithsonian to put a bid in early on some of these ancient treasures. I have been to houses of celebrities and wealthy businessmen, houses that are beautiful and spectacular as expected. The Playboy Mansion, however, is just shabby inside, much to my surprise. The most beautiful parts of the Mansion are the architectural built-ins, such as the wood carvings in Hef's room or the staircase. In my opinion, the greatest accessory of the house is a small Salvador Dalí painting hanging in the alcove between the dining room and the great hall. I am a big Dalí fan, and I was fortunate enough to see his works, my favorite piece among them, when I studied in Spain. I always thought if the Mansion was on fire, I would grab my two pugs and the Dalí. I just could not understand why Hef did not care as much about the general appearance of the interior of the Mansion as he did about the outside. I suppose he was more focused on the beautiful women surrounding him than he was on his actual surroundings. Maybe it's because the Playboy Corporation wants to maintain it in its "original" décor, to keep it the way it was during Playboy's heyday so that after Hef passes, it can become a museum. Hef has said repeatedly in interviews that he would like the Mansion to be purchased by the Playboy Foundation and used as a Graceland-type attraction. He wants to perpetuate the legend and mythology related to Playboy.

Or maybe it's because Hef does not own the house and the company keeps a tight budget on furnishings? Many people do not realize that Hef does not own the house; Playboy Enterprises and its shareholders own the house. I was shocked to learn that. Before we moved in, the other girls and I learned that the reason Hef was so particular about who moved into the Mansion was that he had to pay rent on each of the rooms. And the rent is ridiculously high: at one time he mentioned he had to pay something like $8,000 to $10,000 a month for my tiny room, and even more for the two bigger ones! If I remember correctly, he pays $25,000 a month for his own bedroom. You could rent a gorgeous beach house with that amount of money, even here in the over-the-top housing market of L.A.

The bedrooms were in an even more inferior state than the common areas downstairs. Each bedroom had unmatched pieces of furniture; the bed frame, dresser, table, and desk were all different colors, types of wood, and even period styles. It was like someone went to the Goodwill and bought what she could in order to provide the basics for each room. I give credit to each Girlfriend for her decorating skills and being able to give each room some personality. Besides our mismatched furniture, our bed mattresses were old. I don't know how old they were, but they were worn out and stained; it was disgusting. You would think Hef could buy new ones so that we did not have to sleep on soiled mattresses. It simply wasn't in the budget, I guess. The sheets were also used. When Emma and I moved in, we asked Hef if we could have some money to furnish our rooms, to get mattress pads and new bed sheets that would be used only by us, and get a few things to decorate the rooms. Thankfully he agreed to give us a few hundred dollars; we had to turn in all of the receipts for things we bought and were reimbursed. Because I had to give up my own apartment when I moved into the Mansion, even though I was still paying rent on it, I brought over some of my personal belongings to fill the room. In the end we managed to turn our Mansion rooms into livable and cozy spaces.

Hef also permitted us to have the rooms painted and recarpeted. For some reason he strongly preferred creamy white-colored carpet for the Girlfriends. We asked for darker carpets, but we were refused. He liked our rooms to look like little girl rooms, white carpet and pink walls. The white carpet looked great at first, but with two dogs and butlers delivering food in dirty shoes and occasionally spilling things, the carpet was gray and stained in a matter of three months. And even though we lived there for more than two years, we were not allowed to replace the carpet again. We had to live with that dirty stained carpet until we left. But I am not surprised Hef did not care about our carpets: the one in his bedroom had not been changed for years. It was literally the color of diarrhea. It became significantly worse when Holly moved in with her first dog and then got another. The dogs were not house-broken and relieved themselves on the carpet. Many a late night or early morning we stepped in her dog's pee, or worse, poop. When we used to go to see Hef on Friday morning to get our allowances, we always had to wait a few minutes as he walked around to pick up the poops. Holly finally talked him into having the carpet replaced when we went away on a trip. Unfortunately, the carpet chosen for him by the staff was dark blue with different colored patterns, which made poop-spotting much more difficult. Poor Hef used to strain his eyes looking around in the mornings, and our accidental step-ins increased. I saw on their reality show that she got two more dogs—that's four dogs! I imagine it's just one poop landmine after another in Hef's room.

The carpet in the upstairs hallway also had not been changed in who knows how long. Everything was just old and stale. Archie the house dog would regularly relieve himself on the hallway curtains, adding the scent of urine to the general scent of decay. At the beginning, I ignored all of these things because I was having too much fun to notice. But as time went on, the glamour and excitement of living at this famous address was replaced with disdain for all of the dirty, smelly things. I am glad to see that having a television show has encouraged Hef to replace the hallway carpets and update some things in the house; it is looking much better than it used to. Nevertheless, the Mansion is still not the highly glamorous place many people imagine it to be. In a sense, I wish Hef had kept the cameras out of the Mansion, and maintained that aura of mystique and fantasy that the Mansion had before.

6 : The Blonde Boob Brigade

"I'm not offended by all the dumb blonde jokes because I know I'm not dumb... and I also know that I'm not blonde."

— *Dolly Parton*

In 1998, after ten years of marriage, Hef and "Playmate for a Lifetime" Kimberly Conrad separated, but Mr. Playboy was not lonely for long. With the help of his friends, Hef re-entered the L.A. nightclub scene. Like Austin Powers, Hef was hermetically unsealed and came out ready to swing once again. As he repeatedly mentions in interviews, "I discovered a whole new generation that was waiting for me to come out and play!" It certainly helped that he had his own troupe of Playmates to take out, and a magazine that many young women longed to pose for. Hef has learned that going out with beautiful women attracts even more beautiful women. It is not a coincidence that Hef always goes out with large groups of blondes and at one time had seven Girlfriends; the publicity is priceless.

The original party posse was composed of the "Foursome": Brande, Sandy, Mandy, and Jessica. Hef met Brande Roderick at a nightclub in 1998, and then met Sandy and Mandy Bentley, the twins, a couple of months later at Garden of Eden, another Hollywood nightclub. The twins wanted their friend Jessica to move into the Mansion with them. Although not attracted to Jessica specifically, Hef agreed because she was part of the package. Hef and the girls were seen out on town, and Hef was getting back in the limelight. He realized that four Girlfriends were better than one and that all of this attention was good for business. Things changed in the middle of 2000, when his beloved Brande, after becoming a Playmate and Playmate of the Year, moved to Hawaii to join the cast of *Baywatch Hawaii.* Her departure changed the group dynamic. I'd heard that by August, the twins and Jessica were asked to leave the Mansion. The Mansion regulars cite many outrageous reasons for why the twins were finally ousted. Whatever the cause, Hef had enough, and it did not end pretty. Although I have been around them many times, I do not know them personally. All I know is what I have heard from the butlers when I lived there, that they were high maintenance, that they used to sleep with some of the staff, and that they had many other things going on outside of the Mansion. They knew how to play Hef, and it worked for a long time. I believe it was these girls that ruined it for the rest of us; Hef spoiled them and then ended up being disappointed and hurt. He would never be that generous and trusting later on.

After the "Foursome" fell apart, Hef needed new girls. Enter Tina Jordan. He also met her at a nightclub, and Tina became his main Girlfriend and helped him recruit a new group of girls. This is when the concept of the party posse was born. The original seven Girlfriends were seen on the videotaped Playboy special *Inside the Playboy Mansion* and composed of Tina Jordan, Regina Lauren, Cathi O'Malley, Buffy Tyler, Katie Lohman, Stephanie Heinrich, and Tammy. This was the era of Girlfriends becoming Playmates. One after another almost identical blonde appeared in the pages of *Playboy.* Becoming Hef's Girlfriend was synonymous with becoming a Playmate. Hef must have been happy to realize that the monthly need for new centerfolds also meant that he would have a steady supply of Girlfriends. But the scheme fell apart on both the personal and business levels. First, the readers supposedly became tired of seeing Hef's Girlfriends in the magazine, not necessarily because they were Girlfriends, but because they all looked the same: platinum blondes with fake-looking breasts. Secondly, making the Girlfriends Playmates seemed to backfire because as soon as they got their title and a new car, they left. Some of them wanted a quick fix: they got the $25,000 that the Playmate title paid directly, and the upper tier of modeling or acting jobs it could lead to, or the prestige one could trade on. For Hef, it was another tough lesson learned, one that again affected our lives when we moved into the Mansion. The ghosts of ex-Girlfriends came back to haunt us.

That group fell apart too, quicker it seemed than the previous one. These were young girls who just wanted to have fun. From what I heard, after getting a new Escalade, Buffy drove it to see her boyfriend in Texas; Hef found out, and she was kicked out. Regina apparently was asked to leave for trying to sell Hef's smoking jacket, among other things. Cathi and Katie left for reasons unknown to me. When Katie, Buffy, and Cathi left, Dalene Curtis, Kim Stanfield, and Michelle joined the group. When Regina left, Christi Shake joined. And a new girl, Holly Madison, had just moved in; I remember how excited she was to finally be living at the Mansion. I first met Holly weeks before she moved in. She was one of those girls who came to the parties and Fun in the Sun. It looked to me like she was always trying very hard to get Hef to notice her by hanging around his Girlfriends. I guess Holly's efforts paid off. Tammy asked Hef to allow her to move in, and he agreed. From what I heard about Holly, she had moved to Los Angeles from Oregon and worked at Hooters as a waitress. She couldn't afford a place to live; she was sleeping on someone's couch, and begged Tammy to help her. Holly was invited to stay in bedroom three which had three beds in it and was used by girls who were visiting. As soon as Holly moved in, she began an intense sexual relationship with Hef. She was the only one who had sex with him regularly and replaced his main Girlfriend, Tina, in all of the bedroom duties. My guess is that she knew what she had to do to stand out and she did it. I remember a couple of weeks after I started going out with Hef, some of them said they didn't mind the fact that Holly was becoming intimate with Hef and spending so much time with him because it freed them up. She didn't seem to have any friends, and I always made a point of being nice to her and sitting beside her since no one else did, until a girl named Bridget came along.

Within the three months it took for me to finish my last semester in law school, the group had dwindled to Tina, Tammy, Holly, and Michelle. Dalene left after Hef made her a Playmate and helped her get a new car. I don't know why Kim Stanfield left, but I heard that Christi Shake got caught with a boyfriend in Maryland and had to leave as well. Holly was ecstatic because she didn't like sharing a room with Christi, and now that the other girls were gone, she had her own room. Besides the fact the group was now reduced to only four, the girls knew that Tina Jordan was planning her exit as soon as everything with her centerfold was settled. When Tina left, Michelle planned to leave as well. She already had a place in a beachside town, and would get up early and drive there to get her apartment prepared for move in. Tina's lay-out was initially rejected and she had to reshoot it. There was talk about how she was too old and didn't have the fresh girl-next-door look and the editors were tired of making compromises to get Hef's Girlfriends into the magazine. But Tina had devoted a lot of her time to Hef and did not want to leave without making her dream of becoming a Playmate come true, and she was certain that it was bound to happen very soon. On our trip back from New York, she confided in me that on a trip to Las Vegas with Hef, she and the girls snuck downstairs to gamble and she had met a man who became her boyfriend. In fact, he was from New York and she snuck out to see him when we were there. We heard rumors that she was caught seeing him by Hef's security, but Hef never let on that he knew anything.

Because Tina was preparing to leave, she tolerated Holly's aggressively possessive behavior toward Hef; it made her feel better knowing that a potential replacement was waiting in the wings. I didn't think Holly would ever become the main Girlfriend: it seemed to me that she didn't have that certain *je ne sais quoi* that previous main Girlfriends had. She was reserved and aloof and didn't have the charisma that Brande and Tina possessed. When Tina finally left in February 2002, Holly moved in immediately. I truly believe Hef was not ready for anyone to move in so quickly, but I think he knew there were no other options and Holly was the only one asking for the job. From then on, Holly devoted herself to becoming Hef's first lady. This effort, which appeared premeditated to me, involved her physical transformation, mannerisms, adapting his interests and habits, and carefully examining what traits and characteristics he liked in other women and trying to adopt those as her own.

When Tina left, the group had to be restructured; Hef was left with only two girls, Tammy and Holly. At the beginning of 2002, when I became his steady Girlfriend, there were so many girls wanting to become Girlfriends that it was normal for Hef to go out with as many as fifteen girls. We didn't mind the extra girls because they entertained Hef and we wouldn't have to. But there was a group of favorites that included Emma and Lea, a fellow Canadian rocker girl. Roxy, a single mom, established a secure place in Hef's troupe through her friendship with Tina. There was another girl that was always around named Stacy Burke; she seemed much older than everyone else and was a fetish model. I didn't know how she got into the group. For two months, Holly and Tammy were the only girls living at the Mansion with Hef, and they wanted to keep it that way for as long as they could because they were getting more money and more of everything, but then Hef asked Emma and me to move in.

Of course a couple of the other girls became unhappy about that and decided to take matters into their own hands. Roxy moved her stuff into one of the rooms in the guesthouse. I believe she wanted to plant some roots to feel more secure about her place in the group now that her friend Tina was gone. Roxy also had a daughter, and it seemed to me that she used that fact to remain in the group as long as she did; she always told us that Hef would not kick her daughter out on the street, and she was right. Initially her daughter stayed at the Mansion only on the weekends, but soon began spending most of her time there, staying in her mom's room. I felt for the 12-year-old girl; she was a very sweet, polite young girl, and I did not want her to become a victim of all of the Mansion drama. Hef told us several times that he was not fond of Roxy and that he felt there was no attraction there, but he did not know how to end the relationship. We thought it was silly that this powerful businessman did not know how to break up with a girl, but I was glad to see his soft side.

In the meantime, Lea moved in. She is a model who didn't want to give up her friends and her independence, but the lure of the allowance and her need for a new car, coupled with our efforts to get her to move in, finally swayed her to do it. But she was focused and determined and left within months. She saved every penny and got a nose job and a new car, then she split. I admired her for her discipline. I didn't want her to leave because I really liked her and had fun with her; plus, I knew that someone less likeable was bound to take her place.

Stacy also made herself comfortable in a guestroom; she even moved her cats in. Hef actually liked Stacy's personality—she watched movies with him and didn't cause any trouble; plus, she was a willing bedroom participant, so Hef was glad to let her stick around. One day Emma called me to come over to Lea's room. They wanted to show me something on the computer—still shots of Stacy in a very graphic adult film. We also called Tammy to show her what they found. We couldn't believe it; we knew she had done fetish stuff but not a full-on porno. None of the Girlfriends really wanted Stacy in the group. I thought she was an embarrassment. At the Grammys, she wore some latex get-up; at the Midsummer Night's Dream party, she dressed up as a horse with a gag in her mouth and Hef had to have a talk with her about it. She was a nice, unthreatening girl, so she stuck around, but the porno was just too much; we didn't want that kind of association. Tammy said we should show Hef; we all agreed, and I was the one sent to get him. "Honey, Lea and Emma found something on the Internet, and we want you to see it," I said. Holly, who was also in the room with Hef, followed him. The girls showed him what they found, and we unanimously told him it was not cool with us to have Stacy in the group. It was the one and only time that we as a group had "voted" someone off. Hef knew what had to be done and did it. Although

Stacy was allowed to come to the Mansion for movie nights and was welcome to attend the parties, she would no longer be part of the group or go out with us. Some months later, I heard that she thought it was me who got her kicked out, but that was not the case. Lea and Emma were the ones who had found the dirt on her. Stacy continued to faithfully come to the Mansion every weekend (although she lived in Long Beach), and had confided in others that she was waiting for us—me and Emma—to leave because once we were gone, no one would object to her rejoining the group. Poor girl, I never told her that I always thought she was a nice person and that it was the whole group who voted to get rid of her. That is why almost two years after Emma and I moved out, she is still not back in the group and never will be if Holly has anything to say about it.

When Stacy was ousted, her space was quickly taken by Emma's friend Susan. She worked at Neiman Marcus, was sleeping on a friend's couch, and was looking for a break. Emma introduced her to Hef at Barfly, and she immediately asked him if he had any vacancies at the Mansion. A few days later she moved in. Susan was Canadian like me (I am a Canadian citizen, consider myself Polish-Canadian, and hope to be American as well), and I thought she was sweet. She had lost her mom to cancer, did not have a father, and longed for a sense of family. She was recently divorced, and from what she told us, she was a trophy wife who had been emotionally abused by her husband. It appeared to me that she had some work done, though she never wanted to admit it to us. I once asked her who did her veneers, and she screamed that her teeth were perfect and real. When a couple of months later one of her veneers cracked, and Hef announced in the limo that her insurance didn't cover the replacement veneers, I thought she was going to die of embarrassment. She seemed to me to be a helpless girl, with no skills in life other than modeling—Susan wanted Hef to buy her a computer, but didn't know how to turn one on. I think she relied on her looks and on men to take care of her. We became friends mostly because Emma was our mutual friend, and because I felt sorry for her; I felt like she needed us. Susan reminded Hef of his wife Kimberly's blue-eyed cool blonde look, and he liked that. He was always very gentlemanly and romantic with her; it drove Holly crazy.

There was another girl, Bridget, who began hanging out with us. We were all introduced to Bridget in 2002 when she came to the Playboy Mansion one night to meet Ray Manzella. Ray used to be Pamela Anderson's manager, and was Jenny McCarthy's boyfriend and tireless manager, who finally got her the gig on MTV's *Singled Out*. He had also been married to one of Hef's ex-Girlfriends, Sondra Theodore. Many women hooked up with Ray, thinking that he would see something special in them and they would become the next starlet. Bridget and Ray were going out on a date and met up at the Mansion. Bridget got to wait with us in the dining room as we waited to go out on one of our club nights. I recall Holly needed a jacket to wear that night and Bridget offered her own jacket. She seemed like a nice girl, but I thought she was very average looking and I didn't give her much notice. Ray was a playboy, and we were used to seeing him bring a new date to the Mansion every week. And so what happened to the other girls happened with Bridget; after a couple dates with Ray, the "relationship" ended. On one Sunday movie night, I saw Bridget crying in the corner of the great hall, and I asked her if she was okay. Then I approached Ray and asked what happened. He had gone out with her a couple of times, and I guess she read more into it than there was.

After her break-up with Ray, out of pity or habit, the girl was invited to come over to the Mansion for Fun in the Sun. Because Ray was not interested, Bridget moved onto the next obvious man—Hef. She liked costumes, so she would dress up whenever the occasion allowed; for Cinco de Mayo, she dressed up as Carmen Miranda; for Fourth of July, she was the Statue of Liberty. Although I thought the costumes were tacky, Hef found these tactics charming. Again, out of habit or desire to get laid, Hef invited Bridget to go out with us one night. We happened to see Ray that night at Barfly, and it was obvious to everyone but Hef that Bridget was trying to make him jealous. She was dancing with Hef and giving him kisses, all the while watching to see how Ray reacted. But Ray had found himself another young wannabe starlet and did not pay attention; he seemed relieved to have Bridget off his back. She then concentrated wholeheartedly on Hef; she regularly watched old movies with him on Fridays and Saturdays, and was a very willing bedroom participant. It wasn't like Hef met her, was immediately attracted to her, and had to have her move in; it was a slow, gradual process. I think she realized that if she put in the time and made herself the perfect companion, she would get into the group. She was always there, cheery, unthreatening, and before we knew it, she was one of the Girlfriends.

In October 2002, a Halloween party scandal got Tammy kicked out of the Mansion. Tammy had been there the longest of anyone and wanted to stay until she accomplished her goal of becoming a Playmate. If Tina could do it, then she could as well. But it was not to be. It all started when I finally agreed to hang out with Tammy outside of the Mansion. She asked me to come with her to a party in Malibu that a friend of hers was having. I was not busy, and of course my love for Malibu meant I didn't need an excuse to spend time there, particularly in a house that belongs to Sting in the Malibu Colony. That is when I met Jason Davis; Jason is the grandchild of billionaire Marvin Davis, and brother of Brandon Davis (Mischa Barton's former boyfriend). Tammy said Jason was nice but heavy-set. Tammy had this brilliant plan that she would get his butt in shape, marry him, and live happily ever after. I liked Jason, he had a unique sense of humor and a sweetness about him. We became friends instantly. The party was fun; Paris Hilton was there with Jason Shaw, her boyfriend at the time, and hottie Mark McGrath, of Sugar Ray, was there, but he was with his girlfriend. We ended up staying too late and got in trouble when we got in past our curfew. We ran up to Hef's bedroom and started making excuses for why we were late, but Hef knew I wasn't to blame. He knew it was Tammy and that I was just along for the ride.

A couple of days after that incident, Tammy came to me with a favor. She wanted me to put Jason Davis on my Halloween party guest list. Hef allowed all of the Girlfriends to invite a few (about five or so) friends or family members to each party. It was made clear to us that we should invite girls, so inviting guys was a bit tricky—it was best to pair them up with a girl unless they themselves were celebrities or had some sort of "value" to Hef. Since the day I met Jason, he called me every day and we had become friends, so I was happy to put Jason on my guest list. However, Tammy then asked if I could also put one of Jason's friends on the list. I told her I couldn't do it because I wanted to invite some of my friends; plus, it would be hard to have another guy on my list. That is when she told me about the money. She said that those guys were paying her $1,000 each to put them on the list and that she would give me half if I agreed to put them on my guest list—she would keep the other half as a finder's fee. The thing was, Jason was my friend and I would not take money from him to invite him to the party. But he really wanted his friend to come, and since the payment for that was already arranged with Tammy, I thought I might as well try to get his friend in, and if I was to get anything in return for that, it was just a bonus. One day after Jason and I had lunch together, we went shopping and I saw a Gucci watch I considered buying. Jason offered to buy it for me in appreciation for putting his friend on the list, and I accepted it. I later realized Tammy did not have space to put Jason on her list because she had bigger fish to fry. Apparently she was going to try to get Brandon Davis in for a lot more money, and if I would put Jason and his friend on my list, she didn't have to do a thing but was still making money. I had been told that Brandon was not welcome at the Mansion because it was the place where he got a bit out of control at the last party he attended.

If that had been it, maybe she could have gotten away with it. But when Emma and Lea found out about this scam, they did the same thing except they charged people even more money, something like $2,000 a person to get them on the list. From what I know, Roxy got wind of it and because she had nothing to gain, she told Holly about it. Holly promptly reported it to Mary and Hef. And then came the official summons from Hef. We were each called in to have a private discussion with Hef in his office. We were scared because we knew someone was going to go down for this. When I went to speak with him, he asked me what happened. I told him the truth as far as it concerned me, and I never blamed anyone; I never pointed to Tammy as the ringleader. I told him that the people on my list were actually my friends, and I admitted that though I knew Jason's friend, I only invited him because of Jason. I told him that Tammy arranged to receive $2,000 for getting Jason and his friend into the party, and I was to get half of it. I told him I did not know the details of Tammy's other arrangements. I told him about the watch, and Mary told me to give it to her, but I told her I would just pay Jason back for it because I was going to buy it anyway. And I did pay him after the whole thing fell apart. I don't know what the other girls told Hef, but I imagine they did what they had to in order to save themselves. Needless to say, the Halloween guest list was scrapped and we weren't allowed to invite anyone. In the end, I was disappointed with myself for getting sucked into that whole thing. Jason and I continued to be good friends, and I tried to clear his name with Mary and Hef, but my efforts were futile.

We knew something bad would go down. Tammy, Emma, and I went out for some margaritas to talk things over and de-stress, but instead we got drunk and came up with a crazy idea: we were going to get tattoos. We drove over to Shamrock Tattoo on Sunset Boulevard and got little pink Playboy bunny tattoos by Chris Garver of the new reality show *Miami Ink*. Emma and I each got one on our "lower abdomen," and Tammy on her ankle. We went home and showed Hef our battle scars, wanting to show our devotion and our apology. He seemed amused, but I knew it wasn't enough. The Halloween party went on as usual, we had a lot of fun, and for a moment I wondered if all was forgiven. But it was not: immediately afterward, Tammy was asked to leave.

When we broke any of the rules, Hef would act very disappointed and make us feel bad. It seemed like he loved making us feel guilty. But the thing was, if anyone started crying, he would back off and be sweeter than ever. I remember I had a fight with him once about something minor; Hef confronted me and we got into an argument. Being an emotional person, I started crying. He walked out of my room, but came back twenty minutes later to give me a hug and to tell me he loved me very much and he wanted us all to be happy. I could tell that this was not going to be one of those situations. I felt like this was Holly's silent victory. I heard her tell Hef what a trouble-maker Tammy is, and Hef finally let Tammy go. I could tell Hef was sad to see her leave; I knew he cared about her. He was also sorry to see her pets go; after all, he had bought her Pinky, the capuchin monkey, just a few months earlier. But he didn't want one bad apple to spoil the rest of the group.

In my opinion, Tammy was not fond of Bridget, and Bridget was intim-idated by her and kept out of her way. Tammy's leaving gave Bridget courage to push for official Girlfriend status. At about the same time, Lea left; with her goals accomplished, she didn't want to stick around. So when Bridget finally moved in, our steady group was formed: Holly, Emma, Susan, Roxy, Bridget, and me. This was the group that was together the longest and is most prominently featured in my story. We only had one more change later when, in 2003, Hef let Roxy go right before Playboy's fiftieth anniversary celebra-tion. For the next six months, it was just five of us until a girl named Candy moved in for a year. Candy tried to stay neutral and remain under the radar. Even after she left, she continued to hang out with Hef and the girls. After she left, it was just the five of us: Holly and Bridget on one side, and Emma, Susan, and me on the other. That was when tensions reached their peak. A few months later, immediately before we all left in May 2004, Hef met an 18-year-old named Kendra and she was the last to move in. Since then it has just been the three of them, Holly, Bridget, and Kendra, the girls featured on the current reality show *The Girls Next Door* on the E! network.

7: The Fabulous Life

The first few months at the Mansion, we partied like rockstars. We went out to clubs three or four nights a week, we attended events, and we hosted parties at the Mansion. We drank too much, stayed up until morning, and then slept until the afternoon. Then we would get up to go to the beauty salon where an army of people attended to us, to prepare for another night out. One person would be blow-drying the hair, another would begin curling the dry pieces, another was painting our nails, while yet another was giving us pedicures; somewhere in between we would get our makeup done as well. All this while trying to eat something—thank God they served food! This easily took four hours. However, if hair color touch-up was needed as well, then you would have to be there for at least six hours. We seriously overdid it with the salon at the beginning because we knew Hef expected us to look good and we wanted to please him. We were spoiled, but we knew how lucky we were, and we were grateful to Hef. We were young; we had money, cars, and all the nice things money can buy. We also had time.

We learned pretty quickly that everything at the Mansion revolved around a routine. Hef spends every day of the week in the office—not his office, but Mary's. She sits at the desk, while he is usually sitting on the floor with his back against an office couch. However, every single evening has a specific designation and is rarely altered. Mondays are "Manly Nights," which means Hef's "manly" (his term) friends come over for dinner and a movie. They have a special menu to choose from, and afterward they eat and chat. This is the only night when Hef lets his friends choose the movie by a vote, and it's usually a classic. Tuesdays are "Family Night," when Hef's sons Marston and Cooper come over with their mom, Kimberly, and, with Hef, they have dinner and watch *The Simpsons*. To my surprise, this did not last very long; they would leave early and Hef usually spent the rest of the night playing Monopoly with Holly and Bridget. It was strange to me that he didn't play a game with the kids or spend more time with them instead of the Girlfriends. Wednesdays, Hef plays cards with a few of his guy friends, and then he and us girls would go out at 10 p.m. Thursdays were usually unplanned; this was the night Hef used to take us out for dinner, and we got to pick the restaurant. I loved going out for dinner with Hef; it was a night out, but it was intimate, and we were all able to talk and bond. And because Hef let us pick the restaurant, we got to go to some of our favorite places, such as Asia de Cuba, Koi, Katana, Boa, Mastros, or Morton's. Friday is "Casablanca Club," when several of Hef's friends and guests come over for cocktails, buffet dinner, and a movie from the '30s or '40s. After the movie we would gather downstairs and go out to a nightclub. On Saturdays, Hef usually works on his scrapbooks; in the evening, like on Friday, there is a buffet dinner and a classic movie. Sundays, he plays backgammon at "Fun in the Sun," followed by buffet dinner starting at 5:30 and a movie at 7. Sunday night is the only night Hef watches a current movie; it is usually a new release that is in theatres.

Our official obligations were limited to going out on Wednesday night and Friday night. Occasionally there was dinner on Thursday, which I always enjoyed. And very rarely something came up on Saturday nights. Hef also expected us to be around for "Fun in the Sun" on Sundays, but I usually got out of that by making a quick ten-minute appearance. It was very relaxing and fun and I used to love it when I first moved in, but I just couldn't sit in the sun all day long. It was also a day Justin had off, so I usually spent some time with him on that day. Hef would constantly come up with ways for us to spend more time together, which Emma and I automatically axed unless it was something we really wanted to do. We already spent three or four nights together, and that was enough, not because of how we felt about Hef, but because of the drama that was bound to arise among the girls. There were many times I literally did not see Hef for two or three days.

In aggregate, we were *required* to spend only two nights and one day with Hef. That leaves a lot of time for personal pursuits. Each day, from the moment we woke up until 9 p.m., we could do whatever we wanted. The curfew on the nights that we did not go out was the hardest rule to follow. There were days when we had Playboy obligations, such as photo shoots with Hef or other special events that came up, but most of the time the days belonged to us. We would always leave a message on our door so that Hef knew where we were, though mostly it was just a general "Running errands" with an added "Love you, Hef" to reassure him as he walked past our doors.

As we went out on our daily adventures, we considered the possibility that we were followed or were being spied on, but as time passed, we realized that if this was the case, we would have gotten kicked out by now. So we continued to feel free to do whatever we wanted. And we realized early on that we could do just about whatever we wanted. When I began hanging out with Hef, one of the Girlfriends got up every morning at 7 to go to her apartment in Huntington Beach and came back every evening. She got her place ready for when she left the Mansion and hung out with her friends, but when it was time to be at the Mansion, she was there. I always remembered that. I knew all of the previous Girlfriends had their own lives, separate from the Mansion, and I tried to maintain one as well. It was the ex-Girlfriends who taught us about breaking the rules and getting away with it.

For the first time in my life, I had no real obligations and it felt strange but wonderfully liberating. Old habits die hard though, and I started looking for ways to make myself useful. I knew I would be returning to the real world one day, and I wanted to maintain contact with it. I was the only one out of the Girlfriends who had a *real* job. I began interning at Playboy Entertainment Group Inc., at the suggestion of Hef's assistant, Mary. She said she did not want my legal education to go to waste and asked me to submit my resume. I don't think they really had a choice though, as Mary called the legal department and basically had them give me a position. I felt uncomfortable about this kind gesture. I was definitely qualified to work there but because of my irregular schedule and obligations to Hef and the Mansion, I am sure they would not have offered me a job without Mary's intervention. Hef did not allow any Girlfriends to work. I think he did not want us to be independent. He did not want me to have a job, but Mary convinced him it was a good idea. He acquiesced, but I know he did not like it. Also, I had my school loan to pay every month and since he wasn't helping me in that regard, I think it made him feel like allowing me to work was really him helping me to pay it. I was excited to work and get some experience, particularly at a company my famous boyfriend had founded. I was a little embarrassed about the way I acquired the job, and I wondered how the people would view me, and if they were bothered that they had to hire one of Hef's blonde clones. Never mind that I was an educated and deserving person. To compensate for my Playboy bunny look, I dressed like a total nerd the first few times in the office, but everyone dressed so casually at Playboy that I quickly abandoned the long skirts and loose sweaters. My hesitation was unwarranted; everyone I worked with turned out to be very nice.

Around the corner from my office space sat a nice guy who was about my age. His name was Henry, and we quickly became friends. We would innocently flirt with each other and go out for coffee often, but we were just friends. It was a few months later, when we were out at a club with Hef, that Roxy accused me of having a boyfriend at work who I go out with for coffee all the time. I believe she did it because there were rumors about her having a boyfriend and she was trying to divert the attention. We started arguing and she made me so angry that I pushed her. Hef grabbed both of us and told us to stop it. I had never seen him so mad. He was trembling, and I was afraid he might have a heart attack. We stopped, but the damage was done. The idea of me dating this guy was firmly planted in the infertile soil that comprised many of the minds of my fellow bunnies. Sometime later, when Henry was no longer working at Playboy, I wore a shirt with his band logo on it to be supportive and advertise his band. Little did I know that when I wore it, I confirmed for some of these girls that he was indeed my boyfriend.

On my birthday, not too long after that nightclub incident, I had received a gift from Stacy Burke, which I thought was odd because we were not really friends, but I figured she was doing it for Hef, not me. The gift was a "Hef's Hunny" mug that she had made, a silly hat, and two Oh Henry chocolate bars. We all laughed at the strangeness of the gifts, to the point of tears. I laughed, thinking that she was a stranger bird than I originally thought. I don't even like Oh Henry bars! Sure enough, Hef said he liked them, and he opened one up right there and had a bite. I told him he could have the other one as well. Later as we sat in Emma's room and I pondered the peculiarity of Stacy's gifts, the girls suggested that the reason she gave them to me was because of my friend Henry from work. *Ahhh,* a light bulb moment! Stacy thought that she was being clever by giving me Oh Henry bars because I supposedly had a boyfriend named Henry. She thought she was outing my secret. She wanted to make me nervous and uncomfortable in front of Hef. Uh, my dear Stacy, the joke is on *you.* Henry was never my boyfriend. I am sure Stacy did not come up with that prank on her own; I think she had co-conspirators. In any case, thanks for the laugh, girls! It was a hoot!

After Playboy moved its offices from the heart of Beverly Hills to Glendale, my work became more irregular and sporadic. I was not even a part-time employee. What used to be a ten-minute drive to work turned into an hour-and-a-half drive to work. It was much more difficult to leave work and be at the Mansion for photo shoots or appearances that came up at the last minute; and during the year we celebrated the fiftieth anniversary of Playboy, events were popping up every day. When I first had to commute to the new office, Hef would ask me every day how long it took me to get there and back. Hef does not like long drives. I remember when Tammy wanted to go to a concert in Irvine and he said, "Where is *that*," as if it was in another state, while it was an hour away in Orange County. But then again, he gets to shuffle down the hall to work in his pajamas, so I guess any work commute would seem far to him. I told Hef that many employees were disappointed about the move, but he told me Playboy was saving about a million dollars a year in rent with the move: soon after Playboy moved to Glendale, *The Los Angeles Times* ran an unfavorable article about it, and it seemed like a sensitive subject. I constantly told Hef that it would be nice if he could visit the office and that it would boost employee morale, but he would just smile and say nothing. In a way, I represented him when I was at work, so I wanted to do something nice for the people that worked for my boyfriend. Since I could not bring him by, I brought them the famously delicious Mansion cookies whenever I worked. I also invited my boss from the office for dinner and a movie on a Sunday night. She had worked for Playboy for a long time, and was always very kind and understanding toward me, and I wanted to give her a unique experience.

One of the best things about being one of Hef's girls was the fact that we got to experience a lot of great events. Whether it was going to the Grammys or having a "backstage" tour of Sea World, there were many cool experiences. Going to Sea World in San Diego was actually one of my favorites. We got to travel on our own train, the Scottish Thistle, which was fully catered. And at Sea World we got a private tour and got to go behind the scenes to interact with the animals. I fell in love with a walrus who gave me a kiss and a sweet Beluga whale that looked like a pure white big marshmallow.

We also went to several Los Angeles Lakers basketball games. Hef is friends with Dr. Jerry Buss, the owner of the Lakers, so we were often invited to come watch the games in Buss's suite. Usually we would go during the NBA playoffs, which also coincided with Hef's birthday. Buss always had a gift and a birthday cake for Hef. For his seventy-sixth birthday, he got him an awesome Lakers jersey with "Hefner" and the number 76 on it. The thing about Buss is that he also has a little group of girls hanging out with him, but he prefers young Latinas instead of blondes. The last time we went to watch the Lakers, Buss had also invited Ron Rice, owner of Hawaiian Tropic, who showed up with his own personal entourage of Hawaiian Tropic girls. As we all posed for a picture, I couldn't help but laugh—was this some sort of a club? Older established men who surrounded themselves with girls. Buss is a very generous, kind man, and I always enjoyed being his guest.

The downside of being a Girlfriend was the fact that I—and I am sure I was not the only one—wished that these experiences were being shared with people I loved. When we used to go watch the Lakers play in Jerry Buss' box, I could not help but think about Justin. He loves the Lakers; he knows so much about the team, its history, and its highs and lows. I wished that he could have had that experience instead of me, because even though I appreciated it, he would have appreciated it more. I got to meet Jeanie Buss, Dr. Buss' daughter, who was very sweet and sincere and gave me her business card; the whole time I could not stop thinking that it should have been Justin who was talking to her. I was grateful to experience many of the things I did, I just wished I could share them with other people I cared about.

One of my favorite things was attending the engagement party, and then the wedding, of Carmen Electra and Dave Navarro. At the engagement party, we hung out with former Guns 'n' Roses guitarist Slash and his wife, which was way cool for me since I am a G'n'R and Velvet Revolver fan. The funniest thing happened at the party, which I remind Carmen of whenever I see her: Emma and I went to the girls' bathroom and were waiting for a stall to open up when we heard some noise in the last stall but didn't give it much thought. All of a sudden, Dave and Carmen emerged; he was buttoning up his pants and she was fixing her clothes. We all broke into applause. Having a quickie in the girls' bathroom at your own engagement party was classic! They seemed to make a great couple. We were lucky to be invited to their wedding, though of course we missed the actual ceremony because Hef did not dare miss watching his classic movie on a Saturday night, even though he has seen them all at least ten times. We got to the Saint Regis hotel in Century City just when the reception started. It was a Moroccan-style reception. Carmen looked absolutely beautiful with her hair up and, a classic gown, and the groom performed shirtless onstage with his friend Donovan Leitch. It was a lot of fun, and some of the guests included the Osbourne family and Flea from the Red Hot Chili Peppers. Then came the moment for Carmen to throw her bouquet; I certainly did not want to catch it, so I moved to the back to let the other ladies fight it out. Carmen must have a good arm because I saw the bouquet coming right at me, and I extended my hand and grabbed it. All of a sudden, Traci Bingham launched herself at the bouquet, I fell, she fell on top of me, and she ended up with the bouquet. I sat there on the floor with petals in my hand, hoping that the MTV cameraman didn't catch that because I was wearing a short dress. *I just got tackled*, I thought. Traci must have really wanted that bouquet. But Traci is funny like that; whenever I see her at parties, she is always having a good time.

Of the formal Hollywood events and awards we attended, my favorite was the Grammys. The Grammy week celebration started off with the MusiCares benefit dinner, which is always a lot of fun because you get to watch various artists perform renditions of songs by the artist that is honored that year. In 2002, it was Billy Joel, and when we went again in 2004, it was Sting. I remember Bridget whining and complaining in the car that she did not like Sting and did not want to go. Genuinely surprised, I asked her how she could not like such classics as "Roxanne" or "Every Breath You Take" and said even if she didn't, she should be appreciative of the experience. If looks could kill, I would have been dead, but as soon as she faced Hef, she was all smiles. The Grammy Awards were a lot of fun. The Staples Center was always packed and filled with excitement. In 2002, some of the performances included memorable showings from U2, Alicia Keys, Bob Dylan, OutKast, Mary J. Blige and the Dave Matthews Band. Also, Pink, Christina Aguilera,

Mya, and Li'l Kim took the stage and sang the heck out of their ubiquitous Patti LaBelle remake from the *Moulin Rouge* soundtrack. The 2004 awards included performances by Sting and Sean Paul, Martina McBride, The Black-Eyed Peas and The White Stripes, as well as a first-time ever funk collaboration by OutKast, George Clinton & Parliament Funkadelic, Earth, Wind & Fire, and Robert Randolph & The Family Band. In a special segment, Luther Vandross was honored by Celine Dion, Alicia Keys, and Richard Marx, who performed two of his greatest hits. It was amazing, like a concert featuring the year's best songs. Afterward we went to the Grammy parties, but we never stayed very long. It was enough for Hef that he was photographed with all of his Girlfriends on the red carpet, hopefully he would get enough publicity out of that; we didn't actually need to go and have a good time, did we?

Every year we also attended the Golden Globes parties, all of which take place at the Beverly Hilton, just down the street from the Mansion. We would watch the awards on television at the Mansion and then make our way to the after-parties. It was always great to go and see the actors whose work I admire, but it was never *fun*. Every party we went into, Hef did not want to stay very long, usually because the accommodation was not to his liking, meaning we were seated among other people—without a velvet rope and security lined up all around us. The first year we attended the Globes after parties, Hef felt uncomfortable and claustrophobic and kept wanting to go to the next party. In an hour, we had walked through all of the parties and were headed home. Then he sat there in the limo and talked about what a great night it had been. Emma and I looked at each other in disbelief. Was he for real? We thought he was just saying that to brainwash us. Was he used to really stupid women who accepted his version of each event or experience? It began to dawn on me that it did not matter what the girls wanted to do, but what Hef wanted, and what it seemed Hef wanted was the publicity. After that, he was ready to go home.

The following year I thought the Golden Globes might be different. It started off okay as we spoke with the ladies from *Sex in the City*. Then we had a friendly chat with Tom Hanks, who seemed like a very nice person. We also met Susan Sarandon, who asked us to take a photo with her son Jack, which later appeared in *US Weekly*. But for all of the A-list celebs who were cool and friendly, there were other ladies, dates of men we did not even recognize, who gave us unfriendly looks. We were used to it. Their husbands' or dates' heads spun 360 degrees just to look at us and the women did not appreciate it. I understood where these women were coming from, but it made me feel bad and I felt it was unwarranted. Soon after we got to the party, just like the year before, Hef got all hot and bothered about the crowds and lack of private space and wanted to leave. At that moment, Adrian Brody was trying to speak with him, but Hef was in such a hurry he didn't notice the award winner, and physically shoved and pushed us to leave. We were upset that he treated us like that, and we were embarrassed that he brushed off Adrian like that, even though it was done unintentionally. As soon as we go to the elevator, Shauna Sand, Playmate and former wife of actor Lorenzo Lamas, and I pointed out to Hef that Adrian Brody was trying to say hello to him. I was particularly interested in meeting the young and talented actor because of his role in *The Pianist*. Being Polish, I am familiar with the story depicted in that movie. I also wanted to ask him what it was like to work with Polish director Roman Polanski, a man it is my dream to work with. Hef, who was also a fan of the film, felt embarrassed about what happened, and we returned to apologize and speak briefly with Adrian.

Another film-related event we attended annually was the American Film Institute (AFI) Awards. One year it was in honor of Tom Hanks, and we were seated with Heidi Fleiss and Tom Sizemore, who had starred in *Saving Private Ryan* with Tom Hanks. I thought the AFI was having some fun with us by making the interesting seating arrangement: let's sit the Hollywood madam and the Hollywood sex king together. I was a little embarrassed by the whole thing, but what could I do? Heidi and Tom Sizemore told us how they met and how in love they were, though later when I read about their rocky relationship in the paper, I wasn't really surprised. The awards show was interesting to watch, and the food was tasty, but what I remember most about this event is that it was so cold in that room that all the girls kept pulling on the table cloth to cover themselves up with it.

The next year, the AFI honored Robert DeNiro. I was thrilled because DeNiro is one of the actors I admire most. That event was also a lot of fun, partly because Emma would always get drunk at these formal dinner galas we went to, and she would start acting silly. It was up to me to make sure she behaved, but she would crack me up. Holly, as per usual, appeared annoyed when we were having fun. Emma and I stared in admiration at Leonardo DiCaprio and Jude Law as we watched clips from DeNiro's films and listened to his colleagues recount making these films with him. The nice thing about the AFIs was that they always gave each attendee a collection of films of the actor they were honoring.

One other memorable experience was being invited to participate in the finale of the very first season of *The Surreal Life*. Corey Feldman, a Mansion regular, would be marrying his fiancée, Susie. Another participant on the show was Brande Roderick, one of Hef's former Girlfriends. The wedding was lovely, and the reception was a fun, casual buffet-style dinner around the pool. We hung out with Vince Neil of Mötley Crüe and his sweet fiancée, Leah. We wanted to stay and have a good time, but of course, as with any other event, we left before the real fun actually started.

The best birthday party we went to was for Vicki Iovine, who is married to Jimmy Iovine, the head of Interscope Records. Vicki is a former Playmate as well as an attorney and an author; I really wanted to meet her because we seemed to have so many things in common. The nice part was that they were our neighbors, so we could just walk across the street to the party. Vicki's guests included Dr. Dre—whom I thought very handsome in person—Bono, Sheryl Crow and Lance Armstrong, Mark McGrath, and Maria Shriver and her brother. It was a lovely party, and even though it was Vicki's birthday, the guests were given goodie bags of Philosophy skin products as they were leaving.

We also had a blast stopping by Gene Simmons and Shannon Tweed's house when *MTV Cribs* was filming an episode at their new house. They had a beautiful house, spacious and bright. The best thing was Gene's office, it was a Kiss fan's fantasy; it was huge and covered in unique Kiss memorabilia. Shannon Tweed is Hef's ex-Girlfriend, and she actually met Gene Simmons at a Playboy Mansion party. She was very nice. We met her sister Tracy once at a cocktail party, and she told me she used to stay at the Mansion when her sister Shannon was dating Hef. She asked me which room was mine, and when I told her it was six, she informed me that my bedroom was once a swingers room. I thought it was hilarious, and when I was back in my room that night, I laid in bed wondering what other memories the walls of this room held and how strange it was that I found myself in it.

When I look back on life at the Mansion, I am grateful for all of those unique and one-of-a-kind experiences. I feel like I acquired a lifetime's worth of fantastic memories.

8 : The Booty

"If women didn't exist, all the money in the world would have no meaning."
— *Aristotle Onassis*

The amount it costs to take seven Girlfriends to the movies and treat them to popcorn and snacks? $100. The monthly cost of hair color for seven blondes at a Beverly Hills Salon? $10,000. The yearly amount spent on silicone implants at a Beverly Hills plastic surgeon's office? $70,000. The publicity you and your company get by having seven young blonde busty Girlfriends? Priceless. Having seven young blonde Girlfriends didn't come cheap, but most men in Hef's position spend that on one girlfriend, or an ex-wife, so he was getting a pretty good deal.

There is never-ending speculation regarding whether we were paid money to live at the Playboy Mansion and how much. The truth is we got an allowance of $1,000 a week. Every Friday morning we would go to Hef's room and ask for our allowance: a thousand dollars counted out in crisp hundred-dollar bills from a safe in one of his bookcases. We disliked this process for two reasons: one, we had to go there during a small window of time to catch him after he wakes up but before he goes to his office, otherwise it would take days to get it. And life was so unstable at the Mansion that we always felt that we had to get it right then, because we did not know if we'd be there tomorrow. Additionally, not only was it uncomfortable and slightly embarrassing to always have to *ask* for the money, but also, to make things worse, Hef used the occasion as an excuse to bring up whatever he wasn't happy with in the relationship. He put us on the spot, making us feel uncomfortable. He would tell us what needed to be changed and speak to the other girls about it. Most of the complaints were regarding lack of harmony in the group, or lack of sexual participation, or that we didn't watch movies with him, or that we didn't want to spend as much time with him as Holly and Bridget.

Although he always told us that we were his family and he gave it to us out of love, we often felt like the allowance was not given out of concern or generosity. He used it as a weapon to make sure we would never leave; whenever we were out of town and missed the Wednesday and Friday going-out nights, he did not want to give us the allowance. Every time I went to see my family, he was quick to remind me that if I went, I would not get my allowance. As if I would not visit my parents for a thousand dollars? One time I had to go back to Canada to renew my visa—as a Canadian, I was in the United States under the NAFTA visa reserved for professionals such as attorneys, doctors, etc. I had to go back to renew the visa at the border because the company I worked for—Playboy—did not want to pay for the process. I did not want to travel in the dead of winter, and I did not have money for the extra expense of the flight, but I had to go. Before I went, Hef told me I would not get my allowance when I got back. I was upset, and when I returned, I told him that it was unfair of him to not give me the money when the trip was out of necessity, and I had to spend money I did not have on the flight and the visa. He gave in and gave me my allowance, but I resented him for being so cold about it. We needed that allowance; it was not a luxury. Two of the girls had children and had to pay for their school expenses and extracurricular classes. When Hef asked us to move into the Mansion, some of us still had our apartments because the leases did not end for many months, so we had to pay the rent and other bills. But Hef didn't concern himself with that reality. My greatest burden was and still is my school loan. After eight years of post-high-school education, the loans accumulate, and I was enslaved to the financial institutions. How far does $4,000 a month get you when you are paying $1,500 for an apartment you don't live in and $1,300 for school loans? Sure, girls who didn't finish college or had prior obligations and shopped downtown in the discount district could save lots of money, but most of us didn't have that luxury.

Before I moved into the Mansion, I heard that Hef had paid off some of the school loans the girls had. Having finished undergraduate studies and law school, I certainly had more than enough school debt. Although it had nothing to do with my decision to move into the Mansion, I was hopeful that maybe Hef would help me out with the loans. Any amount of money would have made a tremendous difference in my monthly payment and my future outlook. I knew that my loans were incomparable to the other girls he helped, since they usually got a real estate license or went to a community college for a year. He did know how burdened I felt because he questioned me about where I was spending my money, and I told him that $1,300 every month went to my loans. But he never offered, and I was too intimidated to ask him. What hurt my feelings was the fact that any time a camera crew was around, the first thing out of his mouth was, "Izabella is an attorney." He liked to brag about it to people, as if it validated the quality of women he dated. It hurt me that he used it as a promo tool but never extended any help toward me. Anyone who has postgraduate education knows how it feels to enter the world weighed down with so much debt—it's truly hopeless. And there I was dating a man who could have changed my life without ever being deprived of any luxuries. What was strange to me is that Hef would gladly pay for any plastic surgery, necessary or not, but he would not help me with school loans. I couldn't understand his priorities.

Besides the allowance, there were occasions when we got extra money. For every major event we would attend, such as the AFIs or Golden Globes, we got a $1,000 clothing allowance for a dress and shoes. Special occasions such as the Grammys or the Oscar parties might merit $2,000. We would be given checks from Hef's secretary, with the name of the event on them indicating how it was to be spent. Of course we were not obligated to show receipts and prove we spent all the money on the clothes and accessories, so some of the girls bought cheaper outfits and kept the rest of the money. I always spent it all as required, because we were expected to look good, and we needed the clothes because we were constantly attending events and parties.

Besides cash, there were many other benefits associated with living at the Mansion. Hef covered all of our medical and dental expenses; although in the past he paid for teeth whitening, he stopped doing that in 2002. He did pay for porcelain veneers for many girls, but it was one of those major things you could ask for only once in a while or as a birthday gift. There were also other incidentals such as computers and accessories for our cars, and he even helped me pay off a credit card that I had run up before and during my life at the Mansion. We also had an account at the renowned Jose Eber salon on Rodeo Drive (easily $500 a week for hair styling and coloring, plus $2,500 every three months for hair extensions). And we had an allowance for massages, facials, manicures, and pedicures and even laser hair removal at other salons. Initially, we had unlimited facials and massages, but when girls started abusing this privilege, we were permitted each treatment only once a month and would get only $100 toward it regardless of how much it cost us. We lost the privilege because some of Hef's previous Girlfriends got Botox injections, but had the salon (not Jose Eber) write them up as massages and facials. One of the Girlfriends went to the salon to inquire about this arrangement and Hef's secretary got wind of it and brought it to a stop. Roxy, one of the girls who was suspected of doing this, tried to blame one of my friends for it and it brought about my first fight at the Mansion (there were three). I confronted Roxy and told her that I was not going to stand by and let her blame my friends for this. I did not want to fight with her, but I wanted to stand up for others. That is how I got my nickname of being the "mouth" of the group; when there was a problem, they looked to me to express it.

Another great perk of being Hef's Girlfriend was getting a new car or simply a better car if you already had one. Most people assume that Hef bought the cars for us outright, but that was not the case. He bought the Bentley twins and his prior Girlfriends $100,000 cars and bought them anything they wanted. But when a former Girlfriend took off with her new Porsche or Mercedes, Hef learned to hold back. Things were quite different when we came along. We were allowed to choose a car and then he would give us a $10,000 check for the down payment on the car and would make the monthly payments and pay the insurance for as long as we lived at the Mansion. That way the car would be paid off if one lived at the Mansion for the entirety of the payment plan, which is usually three to four years. However, because most of the girls left before that, they would be responsible for making the balance of the payments. Many Girlfriends who moved out of the Mansion after a year or so were not able to maintain the monthly payments and lost their cars. But we were the more practical generation. We knew to upgrade to better cars, but we would never get the kind of cars the previous Girlfriends got because we would not be able to make payments on them after we left. Again, a lesson in moderation learned from other's mistakes.

When Emma and I moved into the Mansion, Tammy, who had been there for two years, had a Porsche Boxster, and Holly had a hand-me-down Escalade that was left behind when Buffy Tyler was asked to leave the Mansion. When Holly moved in, Hef offered it to her because he was already paying for it. She accepted it, but it wasn't her car of choice. Holly had a hard time driving the huge truck, regularly getting into problems for which Hef was paying. I was the first in the newly formed group to ask for a new car. Since Emma and I were the only ones officially living at the Mansion, besides Tammy and Holly, and Emma had just received breast implant surgery from Hef, I had to be the first to ask for something new, although it was always easier to follow in another's footsteps when it came to asking Hef for things. It was kind of intimidating, but Tina told us that Hef likes to be asked; he enjoys feeling needed. I mustered up some courage, presented my case for why I needed a new car, and held my breath. He said yes, and I was ecstatic!

What I really wanted was a black Escalade, but apparently Holly complained bitterly over the fact that I was going to get the same car she had. Tammy called me while I was car shopping to tell me that I should not do it or it would create problems. I didn't understand it since Holly always seemed to talk about how she didn't want that truck and was going to trade it in as soon as she had the opportunity. Furthermore, she had a white one that was raised up on huge monster wheels; I wanted a black one with chrome rims— a totally different look, especially since Cadillac had come out with a new, altered model of the car. My understanding is that Holly went and complained to Mary as well, and when I called to say I found the car I wanted, negotiated the price, and filled out the papers, I was told by one of Hef's assistants that I had to find another car. I was hurt, sad, and thought it was unfair. I went to look at other cars the next day, and I found one similar to the Escalade, the Chevy Tahoe. When I called Hef's assistant, who usually took care of the money, to give her the details, she told me that it was too expensive and I should look for something cheaper. I was confused; it was already pre-approved by Hef. It wasn't just what she said, but the way she said it: she was condescending and acted like the money was hers and not Hef's. I broke down crying right then and there in the dealership. This was such a joyous occasion for me, and it was agreed to by Hef, and now I was being denied, again? It was embarrassing enough to go to the dealership as Hugh Hefner's Girlfriend and to tell the salesman that I did not have the permission to get the car, but to have Hef's assistant yell at me on the phone was over the top. Eventually I spoke to Mary, who realized the silliness of the situation, and I got the green light for the Tahoe. I was really happy. I had it totally custom made with the chrome grill, sunroof, 22-inch rims, DVD player, TV, back-up camera, and navigation system. In the end it cost as much as the Escalade, although I paid for the upgrades with my own savings. And the biggest irony of it all lies in the fact that less than six months later when Tammy left, Holly ditched the Escalade and got herself a white version of Tammy's black Porsche Boxster.

After my unpleasant experience, it was much easier for the rest of the girls, but no one ever really got their fantasy car, the way previous Girlfriends had been able to. Emma was next, and she got a Land Rover (she is British, after all), but she had to get one that was used and had frequent problems with it. If a girl got the new car she wanted, she could not get any of the accessories, or she got the car she wanted, but it was used. No one believed us if we told them that Hugh Hefner would not pay for our cars, and that some of the girls had to get used cars. As for Hef's assistant, I never got over the way she treated me, and we had recurring problems throughout my life at the Mansion. I could not help but feel that some of the employees resented us; I felt that they saw us as frivolous young women who didn't know how good we had it. Although my feelings or pride were sometimes hurt by the condescending manner in which I was being spoken to, I was always friendly and respectful because that is how my parents raised me. I was not some girl Hef took in off the street; I had a professional career ahead of me and if I was working in my profession, I would be doing all right without Hef.

An additional benefit of being Hef's girl was plastic surgery: Hef kept a running account with a Beverly Hills plastic surgeon. In star-studded beautiful Hollywood, you can never be too perfect. The level of preoccupation with perfection was even higher at the Playboy Mansion. When I first met Hef and his Girlfriends, I heard that he paid for their plastic surgeries; mostly it was breast implants (around $10,000) and nose jobs ($8,000). One girl who had a baby had a tummy tuck, and a couple of girls had liposuction. I was surprised to find out that a couple of the girls who were trying to join the group were doing so solely to get some plastic surgery out of the deal. It was a strange concept to me at the time, that one would get involved with someone only for a nose or a pair of implants. But they were models and thought that a smaller nose would get them more jobs. I didn't have a plastic agenda in mind when I met Hef, but since "everyone was doing it," I succumbed to peer pressure. Although it might not be a priority, many girls at some point wonder, "If I could change one thing about myself, what would it be?" This innocent self-inquiry is no longer philosophical when someone is willing to pick up the tab and arrange everything for you. Hef wasn't just willing to pay for the girls' plastic surgery, he told me more than once that he had the skin under his chin (and his neck) tightened. I am not sure if that was the only thing he had done, but he looks great for his age.

Major things, or things that cost a lot, were something we usually requested for our birthdays. All of the girls always knew what they really wanted from Hef, such as a boob job or porcelain veneers, a nose job, or whatever it was, and they always planned ahead of time when they would ask him for it. We had to wait a couple of months until after we moved in, and a birthday was usually a good occasion to ask for the most expensive things. For our birthdays, Hef always gave us the same thing: a small frame with a photo of you with him, and a card with $2,000 cash in it. In addition, you would get your surgery or whatever it was. The previous Girlfriends taught us to always ask for what was most important to you first, just in case you left the Mansion before you had a chance to ask for anything else. If you stayed long enough, then you could get everything you wanted; for example, Emma got her breasts and her nose done, her veneers, and Hef paid for her green card, which costs thousands, and all of that adds up to a lot of money. She was really good at getting things from Hef by being extra affectionate and using baby talk. I just couldn't do that; when I needed or wanted something, I simply explained myself in a logical manner. Needless to say, it didn't work as well as the baby talk and kisses.

What does a millionaire playboy boyfriend get you for Christmas? We each got $2,000 from Hef as well as various gifts. We would see these huge bags with our names on them under the mantle and we were so excited to open them! That was until we actually looked at what we got. The first Christmas I spent at the Mansion we got the most random collection of gifts. There was one terrific item, such as the diamond Playboy bunny necklace with a sapphire eye, which you can buy on playboy.com for $1,500, but the rest of the stuff left a little to be desired. There were several items that came from the Smithsonian catalog, like small glass ducks, sea life nesting dolls, a pillbox in the shape of a turtle, and cloisonné boxes. Those are nice items for someone who collects those things, like grandmothers who put them in their display cabinets, but not for girls in their twenties living at the Playboy Mansion. We went to our rooms and laughed—what the heck are we going to do with all this stuff? We couldn't even give those things away; no one we knew wanted them. Out of curiosity, one of us tried listing them on eBay but got no bids. We thought Mary, Hef's assistant, must have ordered these things, but then we were told it was Holly who chose them. Because the gifts used to be great, some girls only remained at the Mansion until Christmas to get the gifts. Now the message was: *don't bother waiting*. The rest of the things we got were Playboy items, like T-shirts and earrings and small knick-knacks. But even those things were the ones that Playboy could not sell and were on clearance—for example, the shirts we got were orange and purple. We loved the necklace but we were disappointed overall; we went to our rooms and laughed at the duckies, turtles, and other animals we had in our possession. No one in the outside world would believe us if we told them what we got for Christmas from Hugh Hefner. The thing was, Hef didn't even know what we were getting. It was all ordered by his staff, with the assistance of Holly.

The second year was a bit better; we got all Playboy things (company discount must be high). But again, they were things like Playboy neon lights, Playboy blankets and pillows . . . Playboy overload. I kept a few of the items, but the pink Playboy décor did not suit the wine-colored velvet couch and mahogany furniture I had in my apartment. We didn't get any special items like the diamond necklace we each received the year before. A major issue arose with the necklaces we wore because we wanted one that Holly had. We were all given Bunny necklaces when we became Girlfriends. These were the exclusive, official Playboy necklaces that were given to the Playmates. At Christmas time the first year, Hef gave us each a white gold Playboy bunny necklace. We loved our necklaces, but sometimes when we went to events, we wore outfits accented with gold, so we told Hef that we really wanted the same version but in yellow gold. However, Holly already had one because he had given a gold necklace like that a year before all of us were Girlfriends, and she did not want us to get them. We were told that Holly asked Hef not to get the gold necklaces for us so that she could distinguish herself by being the only one with a yellow gold bunny necklace with diamonds. We did end up getting gold necklaces, but they were $50 ones, not like the nice one Holly had. Again, we gave most of the stuff away.

The best presents we got were the ones we bought for each other. Each year Hef gave us a certain amount of money to buy gifts for each girl. There were seven Girlfriends, and he gave us $500 to spend per girl, so we got $3,000 each. The first year we decided to only spend a $100 on each other and spend the other $2,500 on gifts for our families and Hef. The second year, Hef was not going to give us any money to buy each other gifts at all. We were all so upset and disappointed; I had a feeling it was Holly who told him it wasn't necessary. Emma and I went to talk to him and basically told him that if he didn't give us money to buy each other gifts, then we wouldn't be able to get each other anything. We already had to buy presents for our families, for him, and for so many people who work at the Mansion and it all added up. Finally, he agreed to give us the money, but Holly said that if we didn't spend all of the money he gave us on each other's gifts, she would tell him what we were doing and we would get in trouble. We outsmarted her; we did spend the full $500 on Holly and Bridget, but all of the other girls had a side agreement to only spend $100 on each other's gifts and use the rest of the money on Hef, the staff, and our loved ones. As for Valentine's Day, the most romantic holiday, Hef didn't really get us anything. Each year we got a heart-shaped box filled with a couple of pairs of Playboy underwear, a Playboy tank top, and maybe a pair or two of Playboy earrings or something. No flowers, no chocolates. That was all we got from Mr. Romance himself.

What did we get Hef, you may wonder? What do you get a man who has everything and doesn't like new things? We gave him photos. That was the standard, a nice large photograph of ourselves. We also got him stuffed animals. That was pretty much all you could give Hef. During his birthday and the holidays, Hef got so many gifts from various people. Most of the things were taken by Holly since she shares his room, but sometimes he split things among all of the girls.

When I think of all of the things Hef paid for on my behalf, nothing means more to me than my dogs. I am and will remain eternally grateful to him for buying me my first and second pug. I had not had a dog since the day I left my first dog, Nuka, in Poland, and that in itself was a very significant and emotional thing for me. Many years later, when I was old enough to think of purchasing my own dog, I went to the library to learn about dog breeds and to choose one that was right for me. My research led me to believe that a pug was perfect for me, though I had never even seen a pug. Two years went by until I saw my first pug puppy in a California pet store; it looked like a little alien dog. I was in love. Pugs have a relatively large head for their body size and big bulging eyes set far apart with tiny little buttons for a nose. I had never seen anything cuter, but my love was obstructed in two ways: the places I lived did not permit dogs, and pugs cost more than a thousand dollars. For a student's budget, that meant a large part of a semester's fund. During the two and a half years in law school, I visited many pet shops and played with many pug puppies, but I always walked away sad. More than once I thought that stealing one wouldn't be such a bad idea.

You can understand then that one of the things I loved most about living at the Mansion was that it was so animal friendly. Almost all of the girls who lived at the Mansion had a dog, and I thought it was terrific. That was a big draw for me. About two months after I moved into the Mansion, I went into a Malibu pet store and saw the cutest pug girl I had ever seen. I took her into the play pen area and she did two things to win my heart: she gave me a kiss and then she went and attacked one of the toys. She showed me affection and personality within seconds, and I was hooked. I called Justin to tell him I found the love of my life and needed to know what to do. Justin knew I had wanted a pug for so long, and he encouraged me to get her. I called Hef and explained to him that I found the cutest pug ever and asked if I could please have her, and he said *yes*. I could not believe that this little puglet was mine! I picked out a few puppy necessities, which totaled more than $2,000, and we were off. I could barely drive home to the Mansion, looking over at the little pup in the passenger seat trying to chew her way out of her new kennel. I was devastated when we had to go out that night and I had to leave her behind—it was one of those nights when obligations and feelings conflicted. I was obliged to Hef for getting her, but I resented the fact that I had to go to the same boring bar where my presence was not necessary, while I had a brand-new little puppy who really needed me on her first night here. Luckily one of the girls just had a nose job and was staying in, so she looked after my baby. I went out that night and made an effort to be close to Hef and have a good time with him; I was grateful and I wanted him to know that.

I could not decide on a name for her. It was hard to come up with something that was cute enough and yet reflected her strong pug personality. It was my mom who suggested the perfect name: Balbina. In Poland there is a story about a little goose named Balbina who is an adventurous, independent little girl. It was perfect.

I hated to leave her alone. Whenever I went out for an extended period of time, particularly when I went to work for the day, she would sit by the door and howl. Yes, she would howl like a little smooshed-faced wolf. I decided that I had to get her a sibling. I recalled seeing a man walking his two pugs at Third Street Promenade in Santa Monica: one was fawn and the other black. They were named Salt and Pepper, and I thought that was adorable. It was the first time I ever saw a black pug; the second time was when I was in Malibu and saw a man with a black pug—it turned out to be Dick Clark. He and his wife could not believe their pug was younger than Balbina because it was twice as big. I decided that what Balbina needed was a black baby brother. I contacted several breeders. (When one of them found out I lived at the Mansion, she was so excited to tell me that she and her husband were swingers too! I thought that it was so funny that people think the Mansion is still swinging like it was in the '70s. We didn't actually swing. If I am not mistaken, swinging implies a change of partners; there was no change of partners at the Mansion, it was just one man and his seven Girlfriends. I finally found a breeder in Missouri who had three baby boy pugs. She e-mailed me the photos and I chose the one for me, and Hef gladly paid for little Bogart.

When Bogart arrived, I took Balbina to LAX with me to introduce them on neutral territory. When we got to my room at the Mansion and Balbina realized Bogart was staying with us, she hid under the bed and could not be lured out. I expected instantaneous love between them. I called Justin crying, "She hates him. Did I make a mistake?" He told me to relax and give them a couple of days to get to know each other. When Bogart playfully grabbed Balbina's tail the next day, she realized that he was more than just a pest who played with *her* toys and shared the attention of *her* mommy. She realized that she had a play partner. From then on it was, and still is, puppy love for those two. Of all of the things I got out of the Mansion, the things that changed my life the most are my dogs. The unconditional love they bestow upon me each day, the way they make me laugh every day, is priceless. And I will be eternally grateful to Hef for having brought them into my life.

The most famous pet Hef ever bought anyone must be Pinky, the capuchin monkey (like Ross had on *Friends*) he bought Tammy, which was featured in the *MTV Cribs* episode. Tammy had found a website about capuchins and showed it to him. After careful planning, Hef bought her the monkey for about $7,000; he was able to purchase the monkey because he has a zoo license. When the monkey arrived, it seemed to be much younger than it was supposed to be and we felt bad for the little baby. Tammy had to feed it formula and change its diapers—after putting a hole in the back of the newborn-size diapers for the tail to come through. Tammy, who loved pink, named her Pinky. Problems arose when she got older and we suspected that she might be a he (we could not tell for sure.) Pinky was sweet, she made cute little noises and gave kisses, but she also got into everything and was known to pee or poop on you on occasion. Still, I was lucky enough to monkey-sit a few times, and I will always remember those moments fondly. After the *MTV Cribs* episode aired, Pinky became more famous than us girls and people constantly asked about her. Many times after Tammy left the Mansion, people would still come up to me and ask, "Are you the monkey girl?" It made me smile.

In sum, we were living the good life. We had a boyfriend who took care of us and even gave us spending money. Not bad for lying by the most beautiful pool all day drinking daiquiris, shopping on Rodeo Drive, and partying all night at the most exclusive places in Hollywood.

9: Hef

A Portrait of the Playboy as an Old Man

"Here's to the crazy ones. The misfits. The rebels. The trouble-makers. The round heads in the square holes. The ones who see things differently. They're not fond of rules, and they have no respect for the status-quo. You can quote them, disagree with them, glorify, or vilify them. But the only thing you can't do is ignore them. Because they change things. They push the human race forward. And while some may see them as the crazy ones, we see genius. Because the people who are crazy enough to think they can change the world, are the ones who do."

— *Jack Kerouac*

In his twenties Hugh Hefner worked for *Esquire* magazine as promotion copywriter for $60 a week. When *Esquire* moved its offices to New York City, Hef asked for a $5-a-week raise, and he was denied. He quit. In 1952, with $600 in his pocket and $8,000 borrowed from family and friends, Hugh Marston Hefner started his own magazine. Hef could not afford to pay women for centerfold photos and did not know women who would willingly take off their clothes for him at that point. Instead, he bought pictures from a local calendar company, and his choice made all the difference. The first issue of *Playboy* featured nude photographs of soon-to-be-very-famous Marilyn Monroe. She had posed for the pictures a few years earlier when she needed money. The first issue of the magazine sold 50,000 copies, and the rest is history. Some years later *Esquire* came and offered him the job back and the raise, but he was busy ruling an empire. An oversized $5 bill with Hef's face on it hangs in the game room as an eternal reminder of the humble dream that became a fantastic reality. An empire built on dreams.

It is obvious that the magazine is Hef's true love and passion. Day in and day out, I heard him shuffle down the hall to the offices next to my bedroom to do his work. At his age, he could easily stop working and enjoy his life. But I don't think he considers what he does work; the magazine is his life. The magazine allowed him to blossom not only intellectually but also sexually. He grew up in a strict, Puritan Chicago family. His father was an accountant, his mother a Methodist disciplinarian. He has said there was never any show of affection in his house. Hef was an average-looking guy, who was rejected by his first love, and eventually married the girl next door, to whom he lost his virginity. According to his own admission, Hef created a new persona for himself. This new guy was Hef, the Playboy, the suave magazine founder whom girls loved and was a sexually free being. His entire identity is related to the magazine. It had brought him not only his riches but also an active personal life. Back in Chicago, and more recently in Los Angles, most of the women who were being photographed for the centerfold also stayed at the Mansion. Hef has said that during some years he was involved with as many as eleven out of twelve Playmates being featured any given year. Hef was used to dating more than one woman at a time, and that explains why there were six or seven of us when I lived at the Mansion. It was something he was accustomed to.

Hef would constantly relate everything to *Playboy*. As in the movie *My Big Fat Greek Wedding* where the father believed that every word originates from the Greek language; Hef believes that everything is somehow connected to *Playboy*. And yes many times, the stories made me proud. Sometimes he was just over the top, but it was amusing and I understood his pride. Without *Playboy* he would still be the awkward-looking guy with dreams of romance. When you look closely, Hef is something of an anomaly in his glamorous surroundings.

At the most basic level, Hef is a creature of habit. He is the most regimented person I have ever met. His life revolves around a strict schedule, one that has not changed for decades. He wakes up every day between 10 and 11 a.m. He eats an English muffin with butter and strawberry jam, reads the newspaper, puts on his black silk pajamas, and makes his way down the hall to the office where he works until about 5 p.m., when he eats his daily (instant) Lipton's chicken noodle soup and crackers. He is still the editor-in-chief of *Playboy* magazine, while his daughter from his first marriage, Christie, is the CEO of Playboy Enterprises, of which the magazine is a small part. To create the magazine, Hef literally pastes up articles by hand, goes through photos with a magnifying glass, picks the Playmates himself—he even selects the jokes. And most afternoons, you'll find him in the den off the main foyer, where some starry-eyed journalist practically wetting himself to be inside the Mansion listens as Hef holds forth on the First Amendment, the events of the day, and his place in history. As discussed earlier, the evenings are equally structured; each night has its designation.

Hef is a true original, one of a kind. I loved the fact that he walks to the beat of his own drum. He sleeps in until he wakes up naturally; there are no alarm clocks, so the day starts when he is ready. His office is down the hall, where it is convenient for him. He wears pajamas all the time; black silk pajamas for work, and various colors during the evening. His favorite are the purple ones because they match his smoking jacket. He sleeps in baby-blue flannel pajamas; there are also identical ones in pink for us girls to sleep in. When he goes out, he wears the black Armani suit and custom-made shirts in all different colors with white collars and cuffs. He also has his one casual outfit; a pair of jeans, a red casual shirt, and a grey tweed-ish jacket. That was the one outfit he always wore on our casual outings, if we went to dinner at a casual place or when he went to the dentist. I wanted to buy him a new pair of jeans, a new "casual" shirt, and a more stylish jacket, but anytime we tried to give him something new and improved, he just thanked us and continued with his old ways.

Hef eats all of his meals in bed; breakfast, his later afternoon soup, and then dinner, which he eats late at night, usually as he prepares to watch a movie in bed. On buffet dinner nights, he sits at the table and drinks his classic Jack and Pepsi, while everyone eats. He never seemed interested in what was being served at the buffet—he has a list of a few things he likes and sticks to those tried and true favorites. The kitchen has specific instructions on how to make his food, and there is another set of instructions on how to serve it to him—each food item has a specific place on the tray. The butlers have a book downstairs so that they can always follow the specific directions, because Hef does not like things to be different. His favorites are lamb chops, fried chicken, and the occasional cheeseburgers and fries. His dinner always comes with applesauce and a glass of cold milk, and sometimes with potato chips. Hef also enjoys a Häagen-Dazs strawberry ice cream cone for dessert, which he got me hooked on as well. What was really peculiar about Hef is that when we went out for dinner, he would not eat the restaurant food. Our kitchen prepared his regular lamb chop dinner, along with the applesauce and peas, and would have it delivered to the restaurant before we arrived for our dinner. And when the restaurant kitchen was taking a long time with his dinner he would always get anxious and annoyed—after all, it was already prepared. So even though he took us out for sushi and all sorts of other things, he never tried any of it; occasionally he nibbled on something he recognized, but he always ate his own food made just the way he liked it. The one thing we got him to try was *edamame* (soy beans); at first he was skeptical, but then he liked them so much he began to order them, and still does, all the time.

Christmas and Thanksgiving were the only two occasions each year when Hef ate dinner at the dining room table with everyone else. He sits at the head as always, and the Girlfriends follow on each side. Also seated at the table is his younger brother Keith with a date, and his daughter Christie and son David with their significant others. The other usual suspects are seated elsewhere. Christmas at the Mansion was fun and festive. It was not a religiously significant experience; it was a secular Christmas. On Christmas Eve we had a buffet dinner and a movie. On Christmas Day we also had a buffet dinner followed by a movie. The buffet dinner includes turkey and ham, always amazingly prepared. Because we watched a movie after dinner, it was basically like any other Sunday but fancier. After Christmas dinner everyone gathered in the living room/theater for a group photo, which we usually had to do twice because the group was so large. We opened our presents on Christmas Eve after the movie. We'd all run to Hef's room and start off with the stockings. Then we moved onto the huge bags under the mantle with our names on them; one bag for every girl. Thanksgiving was fairly similar, a formal buffet dinner and a movie. I would have dinner with Justin and his family during the day, and then return to have dinner at the Mansion.

As for alcohol, Hef is loyal to his pal Jack Daniels and Pepsi. Occasionally he had a Mai Tai, umbrella and all. Once in a while we got him to do a shot with us, usually something sweet like a Red-Headed Slut. He always drinks in moderation throughout the week, but there were times that Hef got drunk on the nights we went out. Emma would turn to me and say, "Dude, your boyfriend is wasted, you better keep him in line," and then we would look at him lovingly and laugh. We could always tell when he had a buzz because his shirt would be open down to the middle of his chest, and he would be busting a move on the dance floor. He was always so giddy and chatty with us; it was cute and I liked it when he got drunk and silly. Hef definitely had his endearing moments; he was charming and witty. I loved it when I recognized him in one of those good moods. He would make these adorable dolphin sounds. I have a few pictures of when he is at his most silly and human, and when I look at them I remember those moments fondly.

Another thing I really love and respect about Hef is his soft spot for animals. He has rescued many animals, which now call the Mansion their home. He allows the girls to keep many pets. I cannot imagine many iconic men like Hef, who picks up the poop of his Girlfriends' dogs and doesnt mind it. I always found it charming. He genuinely likes and cares for all animals. If I know anything about human nature, I know that a person who cares about animals is a good person.

One of the things I admire about Hef is the fact that he is a gracious and generous host. He holds dinners and parties for his circle of friends all week long and throws fantastic, elaborate, and expensive parties for many lucky invitees and the various charitable causes he participates in.

He is also giving on a personal level. The things I remember dearly include the fact that when my parents came for my law school graduation, he invited them to come to Magic Castle—a restaurant that also offers various magic shows—with us, and they had a great time. When my mom visited on her own, he invited her to come to dinner with us on more than one occasion; she had a great time and felt honored to share the experience with all of us. When my friends came to visit, he always welcomed them and invited them to come out to dinner with us or whatever it was that we were doing at the time. When my friend Niki came to Los Angeles for her bachelorette weekend, Hef permitted all of the girls at the party to stay at his $4 million "Playmate house," which was used for the filming of *Playboy: Who Wants to be a Playboy Centerfold*, down the street from the Mansion. He also invited them to come to the Mansion for their meals and to come out with all of us to clubs. Not to mention that he allowed me to throw Niki's bachelorette party poolside and in the grotto. As far I know, she is the only woman who had her bachelorette party there. I am grateful for his generous hospitality because my family and friends got to share with me the experience of living at the Mansion. My parents were so excited to be at the Mansion New Year's Eve party; they had never seen a party like that before or even had the chance to enjoy something like the grotto—they got to live out many people's dreams. I am appreciative because Hef, whether directly or indirectly, brought happiness to the people I love and care about. I know some people who watch *The Girls Next Door* cannot believe how Kendra's grandma or Bridget's family like Hef so much. They do not understand how warm, kind, and polite Hef is. And they forget that the parents or family don't necessarily know the full extent of the relationship between the girls and Hef; from what they see, their girls are being treated wonderfully by this kind older gentleman.

Hef is used to entertaining; he has a big group of friends he considers his "extended family," whom he wines and dines all week long. The open-door policy toward his friends stems from childhood, and many of his friends are in a time warp with him. We got to know Hef's friends at the weekend buffet dinners. The most important one in the group is Keith Hefner, Hef's younger brother, a very gracious man who I like very much. There is also big band leader Ray Anthony, who had once been married to American actress and sex symbol Mamie Van Doren, and is the sweetest man. There were many more that I never got to know despite living in the Mansion for more than two years. I heard that when Hef was married to Kimberly, she trimmed the guest list and the frequency of the gatherings. His friends called it the Dead Ball Era, when parties became black tie instead of lingerie. I can certainly understand Kimberly's motives; she was married and had two small children; she didn't want a bunch of people always hanging around the house.

Although I know that some people genuinely care about Hef, some seemed to me to be taking advantage of his generosity. They were there several nights a week set aside for dinner and the movie. When we watched the movies, Hef and us girls were on the leather couch. The second couch was reserved for Keith and his date, and other alternating guests. The rest of the guests sat in chairs behind and beside the couches. There were also some pillows in front our sofa on the floor, where about four or five people lay. Sometimes the movie would be of interest to the kids and Hef's sons would come over. I remember a few of the people complaining about the kids taking their spots. I could not believe their nerve. These were Hef's children—the man who owns the house and kindly invites them to dinner and to watch movies with him several times a week. How rude.

Sometimes the guests were "banned" if they crossed the line with a Girlfriend. Apparently, one Fun in the Sun Sunday Roxy was having a water fight with someone and accidentally splashed a male guest. The man grabbed her by the arm and scolded her. She complained to Hef, and he was banned. The man gave it some time and apologized to Roxy and Hef. Eventually all was forgiven—Hef has a good heart, and the guest was allowed back into the exclusive Mansion circle of friends.

Meanwhile, Hef's relationship with his real family seemed very casual if not strained at times. His daughter Christie, who runs Playboy Enterprises, ignored the fact that we were his Girlfriends for the most part. Since the day I met Hef, I have wanted to meet Christie Hefner, the young female CEO of the most famous men's magazine. I imagined her to be articulate and intelligent. And so it happened that a couple of months after I met Hef, Christie and her husband were staying at the Mansion for a couple of days while in town for a benefit. Christie was in great physical shape, very confident and charming when she wanted to be, but she did have an intimidating quality about her. Christina Santiago, in her Playmate of the Year acceptance speech, said, "Christie, you scare me." Hef introduced all of us girls to his daughter, and when he came to me, he informed Christie that I had just graduated from law school. "You know, before I took over the magazine, I was planning on attending law school as well," she told me in a very friendly tone. I was pleased to have her respect and told her that if I had had the opportunity she had, I would have passed on law school as well.

Holly, who didn't seem to care much for Christie, informed me that Christie does not like "the girls." I could understand if she did not like the Girlfriends mainly because we were an unnecessary expenditure. Hef was paying rent for the rooms we lived in, giving us spending money and paying for our cars, plastic surgeries, and other things. Clearly that money could be spent on other things, or could just be preserved as part of her and the other kids' inheritance. I totally understood. But at the same time, we *were* her father's Girlfriends. Maybe now that a reality show centered around the Girlfriends is on television, bringing Playboy a lot of attention and publicity, she is more accepting of the remaining three Girlfriends. When I started dating Hef, I learned from his friends that Hef and Christie clashed on several issues, such as the cost of his lifestyle—not only the Girlfriends, but also the parties and other entertaining expenses at the Mansion. I remember Hef's birthday party in 2002 had to be downsized as a result of cutbacks. He didn't seem happy about it, but he went along with it. It is also my opinion that Playboy owner-ship of adult channels and acquisition of The Hot Network, The Hot Zone, and Vivid TV from Vivid were largely driven by Christie. I think Hef would have been happy just to have the magazine, but financial reality dictated otherwise. I don't think he is proud of the more graphic aspects of the business, but that's the cash engine that drives the company.

Besides Christie, Hef's most famous child, there are also three sons. Everyone knows about Marston and Cooper, his two young sons with former Playmate Kimberly Conrad. Marston and Cooper seem like great kids. Besides being mischievous—boys will be boys—they were very creative and artistic. Even as little boys they were making films, starting their own play magazines, writing stories, and creating Web sites. I believe they have a wonderful future ahead of them. I can only imagine how strange it must be to grow up in the environment they are in. I was told by one of the butlers that now, as they enter their teenage years, they are starting to realize who they are; they understand their wealth and power. He also told me that they are becoming more rebel-lious, and that Cooper has been sent to boarding school and Marston may join him soon. In my opinion, they are good kids. I remember on Christmas they went to a novelty store with their mom and came back with little gift for all of us, which they left by our bedroom doors. I got a Hello Kitty wallet and stick-ers. I was touched by the gesture. All of us girls put some money together and got the kids presents in return. I think the boys will make terrific successors to the Playboy empire. They are good-looking and very social and have good manners. I remember one time at a Spice Network premiere party at the Mansion, as we were getting ready for a picture to be taken, Hef suddenly left to speak with someone. Seeing an opportunity, Marston stepped in and sat in the middle of the group in Hef's place. We all laughed, and the cameras went wild. The future of Playboy is bright indeed.

Hef has another grown son about whom many people don't seem to know anything: David Hefner, who is a couple of years younger than Christie. Some girls didn't even know he had an older son until he showed up at the

Playboy Jazz Festival. David seems reserved but has always been very nice to me, and I enjoyed seeing him at the festivals, during the holidays, and at other Playboy events.

Now eighty years old, Hef remains the company mascot: he continues to vigorously sell the magazine and the lifestyle associated with it by using his own life as the example. Those who see him on television making appearances to promote the magazine and his image as the ultimate playboy see a witty, gracious man. But only a few people get to see the other sides of Hef, the sides that living at the Playboy Mansion for two years slowly revealed to me: insecure and egotistical, controlling but naïve.

It is as difficult to label my relationship with Hef as it is to explain its nature. Hef was my boyfriend, my friend, and yet, at times, a stranger. When people asked if he was my boyfriend, I instinctively said no. Most of the time, the girls and I claimed that status only when we needed to—to pull rank and to assert ourselves for one reason or another. Initially he played the boyfriend role more than later on in the relationship. There were tender moments, real conversations, and genuine fondness. I remember shortly after I moved in and decorated my room, he came in and noticed my reproduction of a Dalí painting and my Picasso's *Guernica* tile. We discussed art and had real conversations, not just that phony baloney "Hi honey" or "Hi daddy" nonsense—we used to call Hef "honey" most of the time; sometimes we called him "Daddy" when being flirtatious and coy. I don't remember where the terminology came from, who invented it, but those were terms we all used. There were real moments with Hef at the beginning of our relationship, but they became increasingly rare as time went by.

When I met Hef, I admired him. I really saw him as an intelligent, accomplished man. And yes, I was attracted to him, not physically, but because he was a brilliant entrepreneur, social icon, and a one-of-a-kind individual. I looked forward to getting to know him better and learning from him; I really thought it would be a unique lesson in life to live with such a legend. My first impression of him was that he was kind and generous, a gentleman.

And that was the thing: it is easy to love him, but not in a sexual relationship. For an intimate relationship to exist, there must be lust and passion. As lovable and cute and sweet Hef was, it appeared to me that for most of us, there was never a physical attraction to him. There were moments when I looked at him and did not see age or physicality, when I saw only the man and his accomplishments, and that was a turn-on. But those moments alone were not enough for a true intimate relationship to exist.

After I lived with him for a while, I realized the limits of the relationship; it was shallow and superficial. We never had any one-on-one time with Hef, and when Holly moved into his bedroom, she made it impossible. There was no opportunity to bond or really get to know him. If there was, it was on his terms alone: watching old movies. But I think that's the way he likes it, eye candy who listen to him, admire him, and occasionally say something cute and funny.

No matter what he says about having seven Girlfriends, it is not a real, equal, and intimate relationship. It is simply impossible to be connected to seven girls at the same time. Though he did care for all of us, the feelings were superficial. The one thing that I found most puzzling about Hef was his perception of the relationship he had with the Girlfriends. Hef always used to tell us, "We are a family." That's the one thing Emma, Susan, and I would discuss to death: Did he really believe this is what family is? He didn't know that much about us. He knew the basics, our names, where we were from, and any distinguishing qualities. He would always say, "This is Izabella, she is from Poland and Canada, and she graduated from law school." He knew that Susan was also Canadian, and that Emma was British and had a son. He didn't know anything else really—our interests, our ambitions, our fears. He liked to keep things at a basic, uncomplicated level.

Because of that lack of intimacy, we didn't feel like real girlfriends and accordingly we didn't act like *real* girlfriends. We went out and flirted with boys, we went on dates, and most of us had boyfriends. But Hef doesn't believe things he does not want to believe. When he heard I was dating Gavin Maloof—co-owner of the NBA's Sacramento Kings and the Palms Casino &

Resort, among other things—he told me, "Oh, I know it's not true," before I even opened my mouth, even though it was partly true. If I were to tell him that Emma, who he knew was technically married, was spending time with her husband, he would get mad at me for ruining his image of love and family harmony. Yet he would be almost too shy or scared to ask her about it. It was the same with all of the girls; when he heard that some had boyfriends, he would put it out of his mind. That's the truly mind-boggling thing. I can't tell if he's that naïve or if he just pretends to be to make his life run more smoothly. They say rich men tend to believe in their own lies, and Hef must be an expert at it.

If you pay attention, you'll notice that he always says the very same things at interviews. I am surprised that his PR people have not caught on and pointed it out to him. He always says he is having the best time ever, and with every group of girls, he says this is the best group ever. Every Christmas was the best ever, every birthday or party was the best one ever. I think he doesn't want to let the truth in to protect himself from the pain it would bring, and it would shatter the sense of harmony he needs to feel. He lives in a bubble of his own creation—literally, Hefworld. People joke that when we get old we revert back to that childlike stage; maybe it's true. Why else would an eighty-year-old accomplished businessman get excited over his Girlfriends collecting Barbies and stuffed animals? Hef is Peter Pan, the boy who never grew up. He built a playground, and everyone came to play with him. He created his own world. Not just a magazine, not just a lifestyle, but truly a world of his own. He acknowledges that which he wants and ignores the rest.

I think the reason he believes all these lies is because of his ego, which will not allow him to believe that he, the original Playboy, is the one being played. Oh, but he was and he still is. The thing that got me was his arrogance: he still thinks he needs to say only, "Hi, my name is Hugh Hefner," and women will swoon. He actually thinks that women long to sleep with him, but he is fooling himself to a degree. Hef is not the irresistible Casanova he portrays himself as. Maybe that worked in previous decades, but it doesn't work anymore. In the months before I moved out, whenever he met a good-looking girl, she immediately wanted to know if he could make her a Playmate, and if not, how much money he would pay her to live with him? Women in Hollywood will not date a much older man just because he has lived an interesting life. So many of the older men in Hollywood believe that they are irresistible, but take away their money, and the girls would disappear. And it's okay as long as they realize it and don't pretend that the relationship is real. I often wondered why Hef bothered with the young girls. Why not get together with an elegant older lady? Because then Hef and Playboy would not get the attention and publicity that seven young blondes bring. The Girlfriends are there to feed other people's fantasies. Hef doesn't want a real relationship. Hef is giving people what they want and expect from him. I think his happiness is not derived from the relationships, but from the attention and publicity the relationships bring him.

I think Hef values women because they made his magazine and brought him the money and fame. He values them for the pleasure they can bring him. But he doesn't really value a woman for all that she is, all that she can be or is trying to become. He is not interested in strength or independence. He just wants girls to look pretty, sit beside him, and smile. He says *Playboy* brought sexual liberation for women because it told the world that nice girls like to have sex too. Hef likes to talk about how *Playboy* gave women freedom, freed them to be sexual. I think he means that it made it easier for guys to get laid.

Hef is a complex individual. There is the businessman, the creative genius, the man who is an icon and has been voted one of the most influential people of the century. There is the hopeless romantic, who is very charming and witty and still knows how to woo a girl; an eccentric hermit who is stuck in his ways; and a Peter Pan who refuses to grow up. But the bottom line is that I do, and always will, care about Hef. I think he makes a lot of mistakes as far as the girls are concerned, but he is a good person. I got to see things that he didn't, or maybe that he doesn't want to see. But the time I spent living with him was a one-of-a-kind experience. I wish him all the best in life; most importantly, I wish him real love.

10 : Desperate Housemates ★

"People do not always argue because they misunderstand each other; they argue because they hold different goals."
— *William H. Whyte*

The two years I spent at the Playboy Mansion were full of adventure, partying, scandal, deceit, emptiness, betrayal, and yes, bone-rattling, brain-bending fun. We, the girls, created most of this intrigue. What can you expect when you put seven girls from completely different walks of life under one roof? The answer can be found in just three words: Drama. Drama. *Drama!* Everyone wanted to know if we got along. "Yes," and, "It's like a sorority," were the answers we gave *MTV Cribs*. Emma and I are jumping up and down on the bed, like at some ongoing slumber party. We lied. What were we supposed to say? "The group is totally divided, and the range of feeling goes from tolerance to pure hate?" No, we couldn't say that, it would shatter Hef's naïve quest for "harmony" in the group. It pains me to watch that segment to this day. "We are a family," Hef used to say. As my insides turned at the comment, I would mutter under my breath, "I have no trailer trash in my family." The relationship among all the girls was the worst thing about living at the Playboy Mansion. It was a place where everyone avoided the truth. The Mansion created an atmosphere of distrust and insecurity. It was what eventually drove us out.

When screenwriter Scott Silver (*8 Mile*) came out to interview us for Hef's biopic, I'm sure we sounded like the women in *The Stepford Wives*. We couldn't answer his questions truthfully; we couldn't tell him how we felt, what really went on at the Mansion. We thought that even if he didn't tell Hef what we said, someone might overhear us and, either way, Hef would find out and we would be in trouble. I remember feeling bad for Scott; he was going to write a screenplay based on what we wanted him to think and not the truth. I see Holly, Bridget, and Kendra on television promoting their new show, *The Girls Next Door*, and saying they all get along so well, but I don't believe it.

At the heart of my bunny life at the Playboy Mansion lay the complex network of relationships among the girls, which is key to understanding the whole experience. The tone was set right at the beginning of the new era, in early 2002, when Holly replaced Tina Jordan as Hef's main Girlfriend. Holly got that position because no one else wanted the job. It meant sharing a room with Hef and having a regular sexual relationship with him; it meant more than what one considers standard sex. Apparently that was the requirement. Most of us were there for a *good* time, not a long time and not to be Hef's chambermaid. We wanted to have fun, party, shop, flirt with boys, and have the least amount of supervision from Hef—we didn't have grand delusions about being put in Hef's will. But Holly eagerly wanted the position. To me, Hef did not appear to be excited about Holly moving into his room when Tina's essence was still in the air, but since no one else was interested and Holly was so devoted, he let her move in and eventually grew comfortable with the arrangement.

When Tina was the main Girlfriend, she was the mother hen of the group, and with the possible exception of Holly, we were all sad to see her leave. Perhaps because she was a mother to a beautiful little girl in real life, Tina was a caretaker. She always had good advice for us girls when she was there. She explained many things to us about how the relationship with Hef works, when we were still new and confused; she gave us good advice on how to talk to Hef and how to ask him for things. She encouraged us to get whatever we needed and was always optimistic. I don't know if she was like that with the other girls before us, or if she was just being nice because she was leaving and had nothing to lose. In any case, we really missed her when she left. With Holly in Tina's place, things changed drastically. Tina enjoyed sharing Hef, but I believe Holly wanted him all to herself. Tina stood up for the group, but I never saw Holly do that; she was hoping we would all leave the Mansion faster. On Sundays when we watched movies with Hef, Tina would sit on the end of the couch so that another girl could be on the other side of Hef. After Holly became the main Girlfriend, she made him sit on the end so that she was the only sitting next to him. When we would come into Hef's room to watch a movie with him, she rolled her eyes and made us feel awkward. It seemed like everyone was in Holly's way, and she created a situation that was uncomfortable for everyone.

Things were so bad we had to call an emergency meeting once. The goal was to get things out in the open, eradicate distrust, and get along better. We were all placed in this unique situation because of our connection to Hef; why not make the most of it? We went out of our way to assure Holly that we respected her desire to be with Hef and her position as his main Girlfriend. We told her none of us was after her position; none of us wanted to do what she does and couldn't even if we wanted to. We thought that if she knew that, she would stop trying to eliminate the other girls. After everyone left, Emma confided to me that she had recorded the whole conversation; she did it to have evidence of us trying to make peace with Holly and also of any confessions anyone might let slip. I thought it was a bit strange, but I wasn't going to say anything about it to Holly. We undermined our own relationships with Hef to make her comfortable. We stopped hanging out in his room as much, we stopped watching movies and TV with him, we sometimes even avoided saying good night to him just to stay out of her wrath. The issue for me was that Hef kept coming to us and complaining that we were becoming detached and didn't spend enough time with him. He sometimes asked us why we weren't as devoted as Holly. What a laugh that was, because we were the sacrificial lambs of Holly's devotion. The sad thing was that when we distanced ourselves from Hef to make her more comfortable, she would point out to him how we did not care for him. No matter what we said to reassure Holly, things went back to awkward and unpleasant in no time. I think it stemmed from Holly's own insecurities, and there was nothing we could do to make this girl happy.

One of the most ridiculous things about her behavior was that Holly celebrated their anniversary. Every year in August she made us all celebrate their "anniversary." We would go to Hef's favorite restaurant, Trader Vic's in Beverly Hills, and Holly or Bridget would have gone in before to decorate the table. Some girls would get them presents; Stacy Burke, who was forever trying to get into the group, named a star after them. But Emma, Susan, and I just laughed. As if we were going to get *our* boyfriend an anniversary present for him and another one of his seven girls. What about our anniversaries? We could have celebrated them too, but my guess is Holly would have flipped out. She constantly tried to do things to make herself the number one girl, to distinguish herself in whatever way she could.

Just like Hugh Hefner created his Playboy Hef persona, Holly worked hard to create a new image for herself. Like a chameleon, she adapts to suit the preferences of whomever she is trying to impress. Holly set about her own transformation into Hef's ideal companion by mirroring his tastes and habits, and I think Hef, a narcissist, is flattered by her efforts. First she got her nose done. She knew Hef loved Barbi Benton's nose, and that is what she asked the plastic surgeon for. The very day she got her cast off her nose she went to Jose Eber, where she dyed her hair as white as it could get, and got a haircut à la Marilyn Monroe, because Hef has a major Marilyn Monroe obsession (she was the first *Playboy* centerfold, and twenty years ago he bought the burial crypt right next to hers for $75,000). She had a makeup artist do her makeup like Marilyn, black liner and red lips, and had her nails done in '50s fashion. I saw her at the salon, and I thought she looked really pretty. But Holly's efforts backfired. When she got home, Hef asked if she was wearing a wig and told her to take off the red lipstick because it made her look like a harlot. It was a lesson for us all; Hef did not take to change very well. If he liked the way you looked, he did not want you to change. In time he got used to Holly's hair, but he always preferred long locks. She had the short hairstyle for a very long time, and people always commented that she looked the most mature, but Holly was in fact the youngest. She has very nice skin, so I think it was just the matronly hairdo that made her look older; it led Emma to coin the nickname "Helmet Head" for Holly because her hair was short, puffy, and did not move.

It seemed to me that Holly must have studied all of the ex-Girlfriends and tried to adopt the things Hef liked about them to become his perfect girl. She tried to get Barbi's nose, Buffy's breasts. She copied all of the party outfits that the former Girlfriends used to wear: the Viagra nurse like the Bentley twins, the cheerleader like Stephanie Heinrich. She also started getting dresses from Baracci like the Twins used to, even though Hef was in a lawsuit with Baracci and we weren't allowed to shop there. I think her obsession must have been so intense that she talked him into letting go of the conflict. She and Bridget immediately started getting their dresses there and they all looked alike.

Holly was very jealous of his previous relationships, particularly the women he was especially close to like Brande Roderick, Tina Jordan, and Barbi Benton. She usually put on a smile when they came up to greet Hef, but we could see her rolling her eyes and twirling her hair. She reminded me of Cathy Ames in John Steinbeck's *East of Eden*, the empty, cold look in her eyes. And she usually had something negative to say when they were gone. I think she has some deep-rooted insecurities, maybe because it took a while to get Hef to notice her. It looked to me like she constantly tried to measure up to ex-Girlfriends by looking more like them and trying to get what they got for her to feel legitimate. She admitted as much on *The Girls Next Door*, when she said that being featured in the magazine finally made her feel legitimate because Hef's previous Girlfriends had been in it.

Holly always wanted to match Hef to emphasize that she was his true counterpart. Whenever we went out Hef always wore the same thing, a black Armani suit and one of those custom shirts he has in every color with the white collar and cuffs. Holly wanted them to match when possible, so if he wore a red shirt, she would wear a red outfit. This theme was taken a step further at parties, where she particularly wanted to be acknowledged as his other half. For the Halloween party, if she was a jailbird, then he was a prisoner, if she was an angel, then he was the devil. As for the other parties, whatever color her outfit was, she made him put on matching silk pajamas. One of the weirder things she did was when she would show up for buffet dinners wearing silk pajamas or a silk robe. Some of Hef's buddies commented to us at dinner how strange it was. She asked him if she could have his vintage Mercedes Benz. It was like she was morphing into Hef. She came up with nicknames for them: Muffin and Puffin. Hef was the Puffin and Holly was the Muffin. I am fairly confident that I never addressed them in this manner, but Susan would often make coy remarks such as, "Oh, Puffin and Muffin, you're matching today," and Emma and I would choke down our laughter.

Not everyone disliked each other. Emma and I liked each other instantly, along with Lea. We were a trio. Hef called us the Andrews sisters. When Lea left, another Canadian, Susan, took her place. The three of us bonded and this time Hef called us the Three Muses. We were really like the Three Musketeers, only more like combat veterans, or trauma survivors. At the other end of the group, Bridget became what I thought of as Holly's ill-spirited sidekick. Only when she gained more security in the group did we begin to see a different side of her. She allied herself with Holly because none of us was really interested, and Holly did not have any close friends in the group either. But it became more than that. Being close to Hef's main girl provided her safety; she had a patron. I think she may have won Holly over by feeding into her insecurities, probably by saying bad things about the rest of us. As time passed and the relationship developed, we heard about their elaborate plans on how to get rid of the rest of us so that there would only be the two of them left. But I am sure Bridget knows that in Holly's master plan, even she would eventually have to go, until only Holly was left. Holly has admitted this much on national television. When Bridget first started stirring the pot, people seemed to notice. Even Mary, Hef's assistant, told me a couple of times that she was not fond of her. But eventually Bridget started to play cards with Mary and her friends at her house, and she won her over. Mary noticed that "Bridgy" was watching all of the movies with Hef and sleeping with him so she was a good girl, unlike the rest of us. And that was it. The group was divided. There was Holly and Bridget, and then there was Emma, Susan, and me. The other interchanging girls were neutral. Candy seemed to play both sides, but we never trusted her, and Roxy had her own things going on.

When I say we didn't get along, I don't mean that everyone, all the time, did not get along. Yes, we all had little squabbles with each other over small things. I even got into a fight twice; both times it was with Roxy. I think she is a nice person and I had many good times with her, but she used to irritate me. I had no patience for her. One incident was the spa receipts fiasco, and the second time it was about a phone call Holly received. Holly said she received a phone call from a friend of hers who was on the way to a party at the Mansion, and told her that there was a guy on the shuttle who said he was coming to see his girlfriend Roxy. His name was JT. Holly told all of us, and we thought it was interesting. We asked Roxy about it and she denied it. We were at our usual Friday-night hangout, Barfly, and I remember telling her that I didn't care if she had a boyfriend, I wasn't going to tell Hef. She got defensive, and started saying I had a boyfriend with whom I worked at Playboy and we were seen having coffee together. Oh no, not the Henry rumor *again!* I got upset and told her to shut up. She had gotten on my last nerve and I wanted to kick her ass. I don't know what would have happened if Hef had not intervened. The funny thing is I met JT after I left the

As a young girl in Krakow

With my dad at a seaside resort

Today (photo by James Creighton)

My high school graduation (2nd from left)

With my mom at my law school graduation

My first "Fun in the Sun" Sunday (2nd from left)

The Mansion pool

Chillin' on Hef's bed with some Girlfriends, dogs, and Pinky, the little monkey

In front of the Mansion

My mom in the Grotto

At Carmen Electra and Dave Navarro's Engagement Party

Hef and I

Bogart and Balbina on my bed in the Mansion

Early in our relationship

We always arrive in style!

My birthday

Pimp Daddy Hef

The gang gets wild at a club

Holly, Hef and I at one of Hef's many birthday parties

Dancing with my boyfriend

DJ HMH

Colin Farrell at the Mansion

Hanging with Snoop Dogg at the Mansion

With Mark McGrath of Sugar Ray

With rocker, Kid Rock, and fellow Canadian Pamela Anderson

The dashing Hef

Halloween (3rd from right)

Justin and I at a friend's wedding

The night of the final fallout (4th from right)

Me and my ex

Mansion. I actually think he is a nice guy and we are friends. I asked him about Roxy. He told me he really *was* her boyfriend. He told me he dated her for a year and a half, and that she almost got caught because of me. He told me she felt I made her life miserable. I never meant to make anyone's life miserable, I was just defending myself. He said she was the kind of girl who knew what she was doing and had managed to get what she wanted out of him. He confirmed many of my personal impressions, and I felt vindicated. Besides those two instances with Roxy, I never had any problems with anyone. The third fight I was ever in came at the very end of my stay at the Mansion.

Somewhere along the way the line had been drawn and the group was divided into two camps. Holly was the mark. It seemed to me she was always the start of any conflict because there was always someone on her hit list. She wanted everyone gone, but she always focused on one girl at a time. For example, first it was Tammy and then it was Emma. I don't think it was a coincidence that it was whichever girl had moved into bedroom two. It was Tammy's role to recruit new girls, an unspoken agreement she had with Hef. But new girls were the last thing Holly wanted in the group. Whenever a new girl came around, Holly would list all of the things that were wrong with her—her favorite was that she was a "drug addict." She would give girls dirty looks, and she and Bridget had a system at the clubs that when one left for the bathroom, the other had to guard Hef and make sure no new girls got close to him. They even asked me, to my sheer amusement, to "watch him" a couple of times.

When Tammy left, her big room became available. I didn't bother trying to get it because I knew it meant more involvement in the group than I wanted. Emma acted like she didn't want it either, but then I found out that she had promised Hef that she would do whatever it took to have the room. This was the first time I found out that Emma was not always honest with me, and though it didn't affect our friendship, I remembered that later and was a little guarded with her. In any case, because of her promises, Emma had to deliver, so she brought in new girls for Hef. Of course Holly noticed and began resenting Emma. But we realized that when Holly was waiting for Tina to leave, she was friendly with Tammy. When Tina left she began her battle with Tammy, and when Tammy left Emma preoccupied her schemes. *That room is cursed*, I thought. It was a lose-lose situation for Emma; if she brought new girls into the bedroom or into the group, Holly was angry. If she didn't, Hef was displeased. And so she brought girls in and expressly told us Hef asked her to. Holly then would run to Hef and ask him why he would tell Emma to bring so and so into the bedroom. Hef would deny it and then of course Holly called Emma a liar, and the vicious circle continued round and round.

Holly and I had a civil relationship. She didn't get in my face and I didn't get in hers. There were many times when we got along, and even times when I really liked her. I remember when she was organizing Hef's bedroom and came to my room to give me this Cuban sculpture of a woman because she knew I had a similar one from Cuba (I had visited Cuba a couple of times when I lived in Canada). She also came by to give me a beautiful scroll of a tiger print that Hef had received from a Chinese ambassador because she knew I liked tiger and dragon motifs. I thought that was very sweet of her, and I reciprocated those gestures when I could by giving her a new shirt I thought she would like or giving her treats for her dogs.

I knew she didn't want any of us there, and she knew I was good friends with the girls she wasn't fond of, but we were polite to each other and sometimes agreed on certain issues. We had a little unintended ritual: on the weekends when I took my dogs out on the front lawn, she would come down with her dogs and join me. We would have a short but honest conversation about some recent drama, and then move on to our opposing sides of the group—returning to status quo. Emma's room looked out directly onto the lawn, and she always got mad that I spoke with Holly. As soon as I got back to my room, the phone would ring.

"What did you and your new best friend talk about?"

I just laughed. "Now don't be jealous, Emma!"

But I didn't hate Holly like Emma did. I just didn't have anything in common with her. I really wished things had been different. I have seriously thought about why I wasn't better friends with the girl, but I realize it was impossible because we had such different goals and perspectives. The main reason the group was divided into two was because our tastes, interests, and personalities were so different. We could not be friends; we could be friendly, but not real friends. Holly and Bridget wanted to go see *Finding Nemo* when the rest of us wanted to see *8 Mile*. We wanted to stay out late at clubs; they wanted to come home early. We wanted to go out to cool Hollywood events; they wanted to go to Disneyland. On our Christmas wish list were designer purses and Jimmy Choo boots, and on theirs collectible Barbies and Department 56 items. It was impossible.

We were young women who wanted to go out, meet boys, and have a good time. In my eyes, the other two were like children. We couldn't understand it. Holly had an obsession with Disneyland. She and Ashley, her other friend besides Bridget, had annual passes and went all the time. Every year for her birthday, that is where she wanted to go. I could never figure out why Hef agreed to go so many times; at seventy-eight, it was a lot of walking around for him, and if he was going to make the effort shouldn't it be for his children, not his twenty-five- to thirty-year-old Girlfriends? I love Disneyland, and I enjoyed the times we went because we got special tours, but at twenty-eight, I didn't feel the need to be there every month. It was fantastic not to have to wait in line, and at the end of our trip, Hef would let us go to the stores and shop; I always picked out a bunch of stuff I would later give away to family and kids I knew, while Holly and Bridget decorated their rooms. I actually ended up spending one of my birthdays there because I happen to share it with Bridget. I could not for the life of me understand how Bridget, my least favorite person in the group, and I shared the same birthday. We were nothing alike. Nothing. Luckily, the one birthday we spent together was planned by me—although we did go to Disneyland right before it as a special treat. The next year I was out of town, and she celebrated it at Shakey's pizza parlor, while my idea of a birthday celebration was dinner at Asia de Cuba at the Mondrian hotel and then drinking and dancing.

Another thing about Holly and Bridget was that they collected Barbies, which I can understand as a lifelong hobby, but it wasn't like that with them. She and Bridget seemed to have a strange interest in toys and childish things. We always speculated that it was related to a deprived childhood; maybe they weren't able to have those things as children and so it brought them joy, even in their twenties—or thirties for Bridget—to finally have those toys. We heard that Holly came from a small town in Oregon, and she always spoke in unflattering terms about her family. Bridget apparently came from a town called Lodi in Northern California and grew up in a trailer. I never asked them about it; I figured it was a sensitive subject. But we thought that explained their fascination with toys and costumes. On a positive note, Bridget had a talent at decorating her room for the holidays—she was very good with themes. Also, she is the most creative present wrapper I have seen to date; every present from her came wrapped in a whimsical and original manner.

In general we wanted to stay out all day and hang out with boys, and they wanted to stay in and play Monopoly with Hef. I got talked into playing with them one Tuesday night, and the butlers made fun of me forever. Every Tuesday when I was out and about, the butlers would call me and say, "They are starting Monopoly early tonight. Hef is looking for you—he's pissed you're not here."

I was confused and disturbed. "Are you serious? What the hell . . ." *What had I gotten myself into?*

"Ha ha ha . . . we got you," they would say.

"That's it, I am getting all of your sorry asses fired when I get home," I would joke back.

Even if I wanted to play Monopoly again, I couldn't. It wasn't worth dealing with all of the butlers, not to mention Emma when she found out— she never let me forget that one time I played Monopoly. In the limo while we talked to Hef about a possible trip to Miami or about company news,

Bridget and Holly would talk about another trip to Disneyland.

But they were not the only ones who were immature. Because Holly appeared to be preoccupied with her breasts, Emma would always comment on how huge my or other girls' breasts were to irritate Holly. I was so mad at her. Emma was trying to get to Holly, but at the same time, she was involving me in a conflict I could do without. I did not care who had the biggest or best boobs in the group. We all had different bodies, looked differently, and made decisions that suited us, individually. But Emma could not pass up an opportunity to unnerve Holly, and sometimes even I served as the means to that end.

The division within the group grew stronger with time. And Hef did not help the situation. We heard that they were called the A group and we were the B group. The A group apparently were the nice girls who really loved him, while we in the B group were the rebels who had their own agendas. Holly put this idea in Hef's head and tried to make it a fact by doing a little article in the *Globe*. But as much as he liked the good girls, Hef also like the "bad" girls. Men are always drawn to what they can't have. And even though we lived in his house, he did not "have" us. We were not devoted to him the way Holly and Bridget were. We reminded him of other girls, the ones that had fun and split. He could never make us Playmates, because he knew as soon as he did we would be gone. We were more fun; we had interesting ideas. We were the ones that always got all of the attention from boys and men. And Hef always gave us whatever we asked for.

There was a constant battle between the two sides; in our eyes it was a battle between good and evil. Some would say it was a battle for power, but for me, it wasn't about power. For me it was about getting what we deserved and staying under Hef's radar. For the other girls, it was about making us miserable, making sure we didn't get our way, and ultimately, getting rid of us. It was like *Survivor: The Playboy Mansion*, with every girl scheming behind the others' backs, trying to build the strongest alliance to make sure she wouldn't get voted off. At one of the Mansion parties, I actually saw Jeff Probst, the host of *Survivor*, standing at the bar, and I decided to speak with him. I introduced myself and told him I wanted to try out for the show. He told me I had no chance of surviving, but I begged to differ. "I have lived here for over a year, Jeff, and have battled many beasts, and that doesn't even include the animals. I can handle mental torture; I still live here after all. And I am used to the wildlife. . . . We have monkeys, fish, African cranes that like to chase us around. . . . I can do it." Entertained but unconvinced, Jeff told me to send a tape in, but I never did. I have become friends with Tommy Lee lookalike *Survivor* alum Robb Z, and he told me that it was much more difficult than it appears on television. I took his word for it and resigned myself to simply watching the show.

There were the rare times when we all got along, when we actually had fun as a group. Usually it involved doing a project we were all excited about like when we did a photo shoot for Italian *Vogue* or *Paris Match*. It was glamorous and exciting, and we all had fun with it. And there were tender moments such as when we all went to see the decorated houses on Candy Cane Lane. It was all of us girls, Hef's sons Marston and Cooper, and even Roxy's daughter and Emma's son came along. We had hot chocolate and cookies and a lot of Christmas spirit. We stuck our heads out of the limo rooftop and cheered for the houses we liked the most. Those times were special and I treasure them, but they were few and far between. By and large, the relationship among the girls was so ridiculous and emotional and crazy that it would have made for the best reality show ever, a *real* reality show, not something packaged. It was by far the worst thing about living inside that demented bubble.

I would like nothing more than to believe that Holly's feelings for Hef are genuine and not motivated by money. However, I have reservations. I know Holly admires and loves everything about *Playboy* magazine, and she is dedicated to Hef inasmuch as she spends her time with him and does whatever he wants her to. But I specifically remember when I first moved in she talked about not wanting more girls to move into the Mansion, because it affected the amount of things she received from Hef. She said she used to get more when there were fewer girls and wanted to make sure that new girls did not move in so that this would continue. She cited specific possessions that led me to believe that she was very much aware and very focused on the material aspects of the relationship. There was also a rumor that she was going to stop taking the spending allowance, supposedly to prove that she was there for Hef and not the money. In my opinion, the motivation behind that was getting rid of us; if Hef really stopped giving us an allowance he would see who was there for the "right" reasons. She continuously repeated to me and the other girls that she was not going to leave, ever. "What am I going to do, go back to Hooters?" she said. She found her gravy train, and she was not getting off. In the meantime, it looked like she intended to make the ride bumpy for everyone else.

11 ⋆ In Da Clubs

⋆

"I drink to make other people interesting."
— *George Jean Nathan*

W hy, you may ask, does a seventy-eight-year-old accomplished businessman want to go out every other night to nightclubs with people a third,
or even a quarter, of his age? Why would this inveterate jazz fan, who actually
launched the Chicago Jazz Festival, subject himself to blaring, pounding hip-
hop music made by people he's never heard of? How can he possibly get any
satisfaction or pleasure out of this? Sure there's the self-promotion angle—
Hef is the living, breathing embodiment of the Playboy brand. Publicity is one
of the main reasons he continues to go out. Everybody likes to be seen and
noticed and catered to. But there is another motivation for going out: girls.

Out in the clubs is where Hef can meet new Girlfriends—and he's
always looking. Outside of Holly and Bridget, he wasn't really getting much
action at the Mansion. And if he went out, then he could have an after-party
in his room and invite girls back. And you'd be surprised how many girls we
met who, inside of two minutes, would want to come home with us. They
wanted to ride in the limo, go to the Mansion and drink champagne, and have
sex with Hef. Most of those girls had the illusion that he'd make them
Playmates if they slept with him. Many others wanted to become Girlfriends,

but there were some who simply wanted to sleep with an icon or were just curious and sexually adventurous. And so it is not a coincidence that the two nights a week that we went out, usually Wednesdays and Fridays, were also the two "sex nights."

The night would start off with all of us meeting downstairs in the great hall. Most of the time, it was the seven steady Girlfriends (if we didn't have seven official Girlfriends, then there were usually "potential Girlfriends"), as well as guests such as the girls who came to test for *Playboy* or girls shooting their Playmate centerfolds. The girls who came to shoot their centerfolds usually stayed in the guesthouse for a couple of weeks and were always invited to go out with us, and many times they ended up coming to the bedroom as well. Sometimes other Playmates came out with us; after her very public divorce, Shauna Sand came out with us regularly. I think she just needed to be cheered up.

When we were all gathered and after taking pictures (the first of *many* pictures taken throughout the night), we would hop in our limo, where Hef would take pictures again. Our limo was awesome, a white Hummer with spinners, leopard-print interior with Playboy bunny logos sewn into the seats, Dom Pérignon champagne, apple martinis, and a booming stereo system. In the limo, Hef would also hand out Quaaludes to whichever Girlfriends wanted them; he always broke them in half so that the girls didn't get too rowdy. Quaaludes were supposed to give you a nice buzz—make you feel like you had a couple of drinks without the bloating. The problem was that some of the girls would also drink, and the combination was toxic. I would always accept one from him because I didn't want to seem like a party pooper, but I very rarely took them, and to this day I have some left over. Hef confessed to me once that they used to call them "leg-openers" back in the day, because they made girls feel horny. That explained a lot. On the ride to the club, things were usually tame in the limo; we were just listening to the music and having a drink, getting warmed up for the club.

When we arrived and got out of the limo, an on-staff photographer and sometimes paparazzi would be there waiting and we would pose for pictures again. In the club, we would make our way to our usual roped-off area. We ordered drinks and scoped out the scene. I would laugh at Bridget and Holly's dancing. I can't tell you how many times girls came up to Emma and I and asked why, with all his millions, has Hef not paid for dance classes for Holly. The funny thing is that he did, but I think she took '50s dancing (part of her plan to turn herself into Marilyn Monroe). Then there was Hef, so endearing doing the sprinkler and the shuffle, or pumping his elbows to the sounds of Eminem.

Hef had a lot more energy than all of us when it came to going out frequently and staying up late. It was always us who complained about being tired and feeling run-down, never him. Going out to clubs was a blessing and a curse. If we did not go out to clubs, we would not see the world as it existed after 9 p.m. That is a weird thing for anyone, let alone young women who crave attention. On the other hand, the fact that we *had to* go out, *always* on the same nights and to the *same* clubs, did get a little tiring. There were certain clubs we went to that were cheesy Hollywood clichés—the ones that attracted the rich older men crowd, the men who thought that their money could buy them young girls, and often it did. The girls who attended these clubs were suited to these expectations. Then there were clubs like Las Palmas or Concord, which had hot, funky young crowds and cute guys. This was where we thrived. From behind the velvet ropes, we flirted as much as we could. However anticlimactic the situation might have been, it was all we could do, and it got us by.

The thing that sucks about going out to clubs with Hef is that he gets comfortable with going to the same places for as long as they are operational. When I started out, it was Las Palmas on Wednesdays and Barfly on Fridays. After Las Palmas closed down, we alternated between Purple Lounge at the Standard, Ivar, and finally the Concorde when it opened. By the time Barfly closed, we were so sick of it. But Hef loved his Barfly. It was usually Emma who sat to the left of Hef, and then next it would be me and then Susan on my other side. We liked sitting on his left side because his left ear is the good ear, so it made talking to him much easier. Most people don't know that he is deaf in his right ear, and there were many awkward times when he would turn his head so that they could talk into his left ear, but they didn't get the hint and kept speaking in to his right; he would get frustrated and just yell, "I can't hear you!" We always ordered this delicious thin-crust cheese pizza at Barfly (besides the previously mentioned edamame, it was the only thing he ever ate that was not prepared at home), and he always insisted on eating it and talking at the same time. Emma used to complain that he would spit little bits of pizza on her and, in fact, when I looked at her black outfit, I saw little bits everywhere. I laughed so hard. Next she noticed that her face would break out on the same side that he was sitting on and spoke to her from. Every time thereafter, when he started eating his pizza and turned to her to speak, we would just burst out laughing. She learned to quickly get up and dance. Needless to say, when Barfly closed down, Hef was disappointed. We started going to Bliss, but he would still reminisce about the pizza. Emma didn't miss it.

Most people think it's cool to be in a VIP area, so exclusive that it must be marked off with that crimson velvet rope—we didn't. Oftentimes, we felt isolated, and we took every opportunity we could to go walk around; Emma even pretended to take up smoking. We wanted to mingle, we wanted to flirt with the cute boys that would be staring at us from afar, we wanted to be young and wild. Eventually Emma did take up smoking at the clubs so that she could have an excuse to get away from the table and go outside to the smoking area, and of course Susan and I would join her. Or we kept going to the bathroom every half an hour and we would walk through the whole club to get there. That was our time to talk to guys and exchange numbers or make plans or whatever. And while our/Hef's security was constantly at our side, waiting for us outside of the bathroom doors, they never reported to Hef that we talked to guys, and if they did, he never did a thing about it.

Though it was nice to have the security most of the time, sometimes it was just too much. They were all cool guys, but we had too many with us all the time. Sometimes we would go to these small clubs and sit at the corner table or booth and they would line up around us like a wall. We couldn't see a damn thing; people-watching was the reason we liked to go to clubs in the first place. Instead, on many nights we just sat there and stared at the backs of men in black suits. Wild times with Hef! It was ridiculous; you'd think the president was there instead of Hef. I couldn't figure out the reason: was Hef in danger? If so, I would have liked to know about it.

But who would hurt cute, little, aged Hef? All of the men who saw him high-fived him and thanked him for years of good articles in the magazine. (Yeah, right.) It was always the same story: the son found the magazine under the father's bed and then started his own collection, and of course *Playboy* was the first magazine that they all pleasured themselves to—or another heart-warming story like that. Out-of-towners and celebrity fanatics oohed and ahhed over Hef and the Girlfriends, asking him to pose for pictures, and sometimes an autograph, while security held them back. So if Hef was not in danger, why all the security? To keep an eye on the girls, of course.

Ironically the only time the girls got into a fight, the guards stood out-side of the ladies bathroom and did nothing. I did not go out that night because I had a cold, but apparently four of the Girlfriends went into the bathroom and some of the other club-goers—you know, the bunny-blonde haters—in there started provoking them, and they pushed one of the girls. So Holly and Tammy hid in their stalls while Emma and Susan kicked some ass. Security was nowhere to be seen. But thanks for coming out, guys! A couple of times, security did get into an altercation, which usually happened when some guy was trying to come past our velvet ropes, and the few times it hap-pened, security got too rough. There were so many of them, and they are all strong and bored, so when a fight came their way they made sure to each get a punch in there. One time in particular, I remember we had a talk with Hef about the security being too violent. I don't recall the details, but I remember one of the girls was crying because what she saw disturbed her so much.

At around midnight, Hef would take his Viagra; it was always wrapped in a crumpled Kleenex (although Holly bought him a nice Tiffany pillbox once, he always stuck to his habits). After that he would constantly check his watch to make sure we left at the right time because if we didn't or the timing got messed up, he wouldn't be able to perform later. We would leave between 12:30 and 1 a.m. This caused tension among Emma and Hef and Holly. Emma, along with Susan and I, wanted to stay and have a good time instead of leaving when the party was just beginning. Many times, we saw celebrities (usually the hot male ones) arriving as we were leaving, and we resented it. So many times actors or singers came into our area to say hello to Hef and to us, and then they would stick around and start dancing or talking to the girls (*gasp*). I would immediately notice Hef getting antsy and staring at them. "Oh no, he's getting pissed," we would say to each other. I thought he was so insecure and jealous about other men that he needed to be the only one with a penis in his zone to feel comfortable. When he could handle it no longer, we would hear him yell at his main security man, "Mark! Mark! What the fuck is so-and-so doing? Get him out of here!" And we would stand there mortified that the celebrity had heard and would realize how rude Hef was being. There were many incidents like that over the years. He would also get pissy when we were leaving a club. We had to line up like geese and follow each other out, but eventually, some girl along the way would stop and say bye to someone she knew and halt the line. Hef is known to push and poke the girls forcibly. I remember several girls being upset and embarrassed that he pushed them like that in public. When he didn't get his way, things would quickly get ugly.

Sometimes things got rowdy when we got back into our limo, depending on how drunk everyone was. Usually the girls who were testing for *Playboy* or the ones trying to become Hef's new Girlfriends would take their tops off and Hef would take photos. They would start dancing, or giving other girls lap dances, which usually escalated into the girls kissing and fondling each other, to Hef's delight. I didn't participate in the debauchery; after the first few months at the Mansion, I never got drunk enough to do things like that.

I was the jaded Girlfriend who had earned her right to just sit there and be entertained. And it was entertaining. Back in the early party posse days, it would go even further than that—the main Girlfriend would unzip Hef's pants and pleasure him orally while the one sitting on the other side sucked on his nipple. I saw this a couple of times when I first went out with Hef, before I ever became a Girlfriend. I remember being stunned and feeling awkward, and some of the other new girls or girls testing for *Playboy* were completely disturbed. Sometimes we would get home before Hef and the participants realized it, and Hef would be zipping up his pants as security opened the back door. Eventually, I got used to it all and thought it was funny; I sat at the other end of the limo so I never got dragged into it.

Another funny thing about the limo ride home was the selection of music. Sometimes at Hef's request, Holly would play the "Face down, ass up, that's the way we like to fuck" song just to get everyone in the mood. I think it was done to set the tone with the new girls. I was sick of that song after months of continuous play. I was tired of the lyrics and hated the beat to begin with—to have to listen to it all the time was painful.

When we got to the Mansion, the Girlfriends would go to their own rooms to change into something more comfortable, while Holly would run a bath. Bridget usually "guided" whatever new girls came home with us, telling them what to do and how the night would unfold. Hef always asked Emma or Bridget to coach the new girls and encourage them to join him in the bedroom. The bedroom would always be prepared by Holly before we even went out to the clubs. She would lay out certain paraphernalia on the bed—toys, handcuffs, lubricants, whatever he had asked for or might come in handy. There would be porn on two screens the whole time—never unconventional or gay porn, contrary to one popular rumor I've heard many times. Maybe there was a time in the overindulgent, promiscuous '70s when that happened and that is why the rumor persists, I don't know, but I never saw any gay porn at the Mansion in the two and a half years I was there. Also, Hef never brought any men into the bedroom during the time I was there. It was only him and the girls.

We would all meet up in Hef's bedroom. The room is beautiful architecturally—all wood with carved naked nymphs. The bed is very large and sturdy, practically built into the wall. There is a back shelf (which holds many "toys"), a big mirror behind the bed, and one on the ceiling, and there are bookshelves and a magazine rack in front of the bed with the latest copy of a variety of magazines, everything from business to entertainment to tabloids. In front of the bed, there are two huge TV/projection screens side by side. There are pictures of Hef, his wife Kimberly and the kids, and all of his past Girlfriends covering the main wall (although right before I moved out, Hef said he was going to take down all of the family photos and put up pictures of the Girlfriends). There is a couch with stuffed animals—he loves stuffed animals—in front of a fireplace. There is also a winding staircase that leads upstairs to his office/scrapbook room and connects with the movie room and the video department. And last but not least, there was clutter everywhere: hundreds of videotapes, magazines, books, and gifts from people all over the world.

This is the place where people think Hef's deepest fantasies are played out. They imagine we're all swingers and do all these wild things. That could not be further from the truth. First of all, I guarantee more scandalous and wild things happen at college parties than in Hef's bedroom. I certainly had way more fun and learned much more in college than at the Playboy Mansion. Secondly, it's not a free, uninhibited environment where anything can happen—regardless of what Hef thinks. It is a very structured setup. But you probably want details, don't you?

12 ∗ How to Make Love like a Rabbit

> "Here am I: at one stroke incestuous, adulteress, sodomite, and all that in a girl who only lost her maidenhead today! What progress, my friends . . . with what rapidity I advance along the thorny road of vice!"
>
> —*Marquis de Sade*

The question that is on everyone's mind: Does Hef really have sex with all those girls? Yes. Yes and no. All the crazy things that you think happen there do happen there. There's just so much more to it. Everyone knows that Hef is the self-proclaimed King of Viagra. Hef was introduced to "Vitamin V" one year on his birthday when he received a gift-wrapped goodie bag from his doctor at his annual Mansion birthday party—one of the first prescriptions written for Viagra in Hollywood. And the little blue pill does its job when duty calls, meaning it does get the penis hard. Hef can and often has had sex with several girls in a row. How do I know? I have seen it many times, too many for my liking. But while I lived there, Hef was in his late seventies, and Viagra isn't magic; it's not like you take the pill and you all of a sudden become the world's greatest lover. First of all, timing is everything. If the pill was not taken at an exact time in advance of the expected "performance," then he would not be able to perform. Also, whenever there was stress or drama in the group (and trust me, this happened *a lot*), the blue pill could not do its trick; angry and frustrated, Hef would kick everyone out of the room.

When Viagra did work, it didn't work alone. The bedroom encounters all started off the same way: Hef would lie on his back in the middle of the bed, and as some of us were getting stoned or drinking Dom, he would cover himself in baby oil. Many of the girls he slept with would get yeast infections, which they blamed on the baby oil. (To this day, the smell of baby oil makes me gag.) Holly would start off the festivities by orally pleasuring Hef until he became erect. It seemed to me as if she never wanted to let other girls do it; I assumed it was a part of her plan of sexual monopoly over Hef, which was quite *okay* with all present. As soon as she got him hard, some new girl would be ready to have sex with him. That was the thing about Hef; he was always on his back, so whoever had sex with him would have to get on top. I guess this was good because the girl was always able to control the length and the involvement of the encounter. Occasionally he would get up and get on top of a girl. It's sad to say, but this usually happened when he wanted to have sex with some new girl who was shy or hesitant to have sex with him. He knew he would have to get up to get any action. This was rare, and though it used to crack me and my friends up, Holly's blood boiled when this happened. She was jealous that he made an effort for anyone other then her, because the only other time Hef physically moved to have sex was for a particular scenario, and that scenario involved only her.

After the first girl had her brief session with Hef, there was a second and a third . . . and sometimes even a fourth would do the same. Finally, when it was confirmed that no one else wanted to "go," it would be Holly's turn to assume the position. However, by that time Hef was already limp and Holly would have to orally excite him and get him going again. I think it gave her a sense of power to always be the one to get him hard. Frankly, I thought it was disgusting that she would do that after all those girls (even if it was just one) were with him. Most of the time they would do a 69er; I think it was for show, but it was the only thing that would get him hard again. Finally Hef and Holly would have sex, in any position. (That appeared to me to be the distinguishing mark of the number one Girlfriend—not only was she the only one who had sex with him regularly, but she was the only girl that ever had that particular kind of sex with Hef.) Holly was always quick and full of moans and groans and "Oh daddy" shout-outs. This from a girl who would tell Hef that everyone else fakes it in the bedroom, and here she was, to me, the biggest faker of all. After that came (no pun intended) the grand finale: Hef masturbated while watching the porn, and Holly sucked on his nipple, trying to spread herself all over him so that no one else had physical contact with him during the moment of his ultimate ecstasy. I never saw him come while having sex with anyone; he *always* masturbated. And it was always the same: too much baby oil, his hand, and the visual support of porn or the better alternative of a couple of the girls making out. It was all over with the loud, dramatic "God damn it . . . wow." Lines we knew so well that we would laughingly mimic them exactly when they were being voiced. At this time, Holly would climb on top of Hef to snuggle and do some post-coital bonding to the exclusion of everyone (again, part of her plan of domination).

Even though Hef might have sex with three or four, or sometimes even more girls, it is important to realize that each of these experiences was brief. So truly and honestly to all the envious men out there: It all lasted as long as the time you spend (or *should* spend!) with just one woman. There are many people out there who think Hef has sex with several girls the way that they have sex with their sole partner, but it is not like that. The experiences are brief and uneventful—it's almost as if he is doing it for show and for his ego. It is all an illusion; an illusion that he is still a swinger, a man with many women in his bed, a crazy orgiastic experience. It is just not so in reality. Many of the girls said he kept track of the number of girls and who he slept with every time. I thought it was ridiculous, but considering his egotistical obsession, it may just be the truth.

I remember being curious to see if Hef was a good lover; age aside, I wanted to see if this experienced King of Sexdom knew anything the rest of us did not. As all women know, a man's sexual ability is best judged by the way he moves his body, whether on top of you or around you, the way he moves his hips, the way he lifts and moves your body. It is judged by the amount of time he spends pleasing you, his touch, his intensity, and his patience. Those things did not exist with Hef. It seemed to me he just laid there like a dead fish. Never thought I would say that about the icon of sexuality! In my opinion, Hef was not a good lover. No passion, no physical abilities, never a moment where I thought, *Wow*. Besides the lack of skill, there were also technical difficulties. He had a hard time getting hard. When he did, it didn't last long. Many poor girls had to revive his extinguished flame as it died in the middle of their time with him; such awkward moments killed the spark even if there was one to start off with.

We often wondered why he did it at all. Why bother with this whole charade? The words of former President Bill Clinton come to mind: "Because I could." Hef has the money and influence and charm to get this show to go on, but he must know deep down inside that it is just a show. Hef is trying to live out this fantasy he has been selling to people since 1954. He wants to live up to the Playboy image he created and the expectations people have of him; it wouldn't be as cool if he slept with only one girl once every few months, like all the other eighty-year-olds. Without the magazine and the wealth, Hef would not be able to attract all of these women, and without the Viagra, there would be no sex nights. In my opinion, Hef is not exactly the irresistible Casanova that he portrays himself to be.

I never saw Hef use condoms. Period. He wiped himself off with a wet bath towel prepared by Holly in advance after he had sex with each girl and before the next; no there was no germicide or anything but warm water on those towels! Doesn't everyone worry about sexually transmitted diseases? Of course; that is one of the reasons I, and some of the other girls, never wanted to be intimate with Hef after we learned there was no protection. I can honestly say I have never had an STD in my life, but I know some of the girls at the Mansion did, and do, have baggage for life, so to speak.

The thing about the bedroom is, you're not seduced, and you're not always there by choice. You're there because it's a rule—an unspoken rule. I didn't go in there for a long time initially because I wasn't ready to confront whatever awaited me. Hef was always cool and understanding and always repeated, "You're more than welcome to come along, and you don't have to do anything you don't want to do. All the girls are clean, and we just have a good time." The girls assured me that if I didn't want to do anything I should just keep my panties on (that was a longstanding rule). Eventually my curiosity and drunkenness won and I went in. I kept my panties on for weeks and didn't have to do anything but watch what was going on in this bizarre, wild, yet peculiarly structured world that was Hef's bedroom.

The general atmosphere at the Mansion was sexually liberating. By the simple fact that I was living at the Playboy Mansion, I became freer. The walls of that house are greased with sex, the air smells like sex, and sex is always on the menu. There is this mystique, this aura of sexuality. It's like the house fondly remembers the '70s, when sex ruled, and it tries to seduce you back into the swing of things. Even if a person is not that sexually open-minded, at the Playboy Mansion he or she can pretend to be. When in Rome, do as the Romans do. We all explored the sexual side of ourselves; we played the role of sexy girls who love sex even though in reality that was not the case for some of the girls. Although fairly traditional, I am comfortable with my sexuality. I always have been. I think I am innately more lustful than romantic. It seems like lust is a natural aspect of being human, while romance is an engineered process, an enlightened and polite way of unleashing the lust. At the Mansion more than any place in the world, you can explore that part of your nature. But things are not nearly as wild as people imagine them to be, unless you consider two nights a week of structured sex to be wild and exciting.

Some sort of a sexual relationship with Hef was inevitable for all of us. And the day my time came, I was ready. I was also drunk, horny, and curious. This man was sex personified; of course I had a desire to know what it is like to sleep with a man regarded as an icon of sexual freedom. But that inquisitiveness was pretty much over with the first experience. The few times I slept with Hef, it was always brief and always the same. After a while, I didn't bother. And the great thing was that he never brought it up to me like he did with some of the other girls. In my opinion, every girl played a different role in the relationship: Susan was needy and Hef liked that, Emma was fun and outrageous, Bridget had the same likes as Hef, Holly was totally devoted to him, Candy was easygoing, and I was the sensible one with whom he could talk about anything. Living at the Mansion was not about having sex with Hef. If it was, I would not have moved in, nor would I have lasted long after I did. My relationship with him was not based on that. He had a certain respect for me that allowed me to stay in the relationship without being intimate with him. I was the token "brain," the token smart girl that validated the group in an intellectual way.

Why did I have sex with Hef? The main reason, if there must be a reason, was the fact that I did have a relationship with this man. And there were many times when I had real feelings toward him. Besides the feelings of gratitude, there was also appreciation, respect, and a certain type of love. Not love in the raw sense of true, complete, infinite love. But a love in the sense that you care about someone and what happens to him. There were times when he and I would discuss business or world events and I appreciated his perspective. I loved hearing about the early days of *Playboy* magazine, his trials and tribulations and successes. I tried to learn what I could from him. More than anything I liked when he joked around, when he was silly, especially when he did his dolphin sounds. He was human then, he was lovable. I was also proud of him; I remember when an African-American jazz musician spoke about what Hef did for him and other musicians by having them perform on *Playboy After Dark* and at the Jazz Festival, I could not help but feel pride and joy to be associated with this man. These were the times that I recalled my initial fascination with him—the man who founded *Playboy* magazine and revolutionized sexuality. I looked up to him, and there were times when I felt connected to him.

The problem with the relationship was that there was no intimacy. There was no alone time with Hef; therefore, nothing felt personal. And the sex, more than anything, was impersonal. The few times it did occur, it was in front of an audience and it was brief, no longer than a minute. We never really kissed Hef either; most of the time, it was just a peck on the cheek or a goodnight kiss on the lips, which is not a big deal considering everyone kisses Hef on the lips—female friends, Playmates, any female acquaintance. French kissing between Hef and his Girlfriends was rare; if it occurred, it was mostly in the bedroom. I love kissing; it is my favorite thing to do, and it was just another thing that never happened in my relationship with Hef, and that contributed to my lack of intimate feelings toward him. While I lived there, he never came to our rooms to spend time with us alone, one-on-one. It is unbelievable to think that in two years of living at the Mansion, I shared less than fifteen intimate minutes with Hef. But it is true. And so even if the feelings going into it were genuine, the experience did not feel like it was. Maybe because having sex with Hef was part of the unspoken rules. It was almost as if we had to do it in return for all of the things we had, for sharing his life at the Mansion. I think in his eyes, it was the only way we had of showing our gratitude for all that he did for us. But expectation becomes an obligation, and obligations are not performed out of desire but out of duty. And when I look at it that way, it makes me resentful and makes the whole thing ugly and meaningless. In the end, it always left me with conflicted emotions.

I don't believe that many of the regular Girlfriends really wanted to have sex with Hef. Some of us always kept our panties on: in fact, we quickly adopted boy-shorts to make things even less intimate. We always had excuses; we had periods that went on for months, and when that excuse got old, we would suddenly get yeast infections. For all the people that speculate and wonder about how the girls feel, I think it's quite simple really: I just don't think many were attracted to Hef sexually.

Physically, Hef looks great for his age. His skin is surprisingly soft and supple and so white that he glows in the dark. He doesn't have any weird veins or skin discoloration, and I would say he looks much younger than he is. All those years of being an eccentric hermit and workaholic, cooped up in his Mansion, has paid off for his skin. But for me, it wasn't about the way he looked. I just did not have that close, passionate relationship with him, and so I did not want to have sex with him. That is the basic truth. But there were exceptions. Whenever any of the Girlfriends wanted something, he would use it as a major weapon: "You know, you girls never do anything in the bedroom." He never mentioned it to me, but I would hear about it. It certainly contradicted what he told me in the beginning of our relationship, which was that there was no pressure to participate in anything in the bedroom. Sometimes Emma and I pointed that out to him: "We thought the relationship wasn't about sex, Hef?" He would get all defensive and say it wasn't. But we knew what he really wanted. Whenever a Girlfriend wanted something, she would have to participate more in the bedroom. Sex was a weapon, and it was skillfully used by both sides.

The majority of the time we were in the bedroom, it was not that exciting. We were there to unwind after a night out, to hang out while our alcohol buzz wore off, to see what new drama was bound to arise, and to meet his numerical presence requirements. We ordered drinks and snacks while he did his thing. When we were there, we would dance around on the bed and cheer him on as he had sex with whomever, or we did the pseudo-lesbian thing. We got a kick out of making him think we really did it with each other, but mainly it would be Emma plopping down on me and tickling me until I pushed her off me and pinned her down on the bed, or playfully smacked her around with one of the toys. We would get silly. Hef really got excited by watching two girls make out, and so to get a rise out of him, we would pretend sometimes.

Don't get me wrong, there were times when the sexual vibe was real and strong. We would come home after a night of drinking and dancing, and all that sexual energy needed an outlet. When you have gorgeous young women who are comfortable in their own skin, with bottles of champagne, and surrounded by the mystique of the Playboy Mansion, magical things happen. Many times the other girls who would come up to the bedroom, in addition to the Girlfriends, were models and current Playmates who truly are into girls. When a beautiful Playmate of the Year is trying to climb on top of you and kiss you, and you're already in that kind of environment, sometimes you go with the flow. It is a very sensual experience to be seduced by a beautiful woman.

I noticed that several times when a truly hot girl came up with us, it was because she wanted to be with the women, not with Hef. And that was fine with Hef. But he did get plenty of action from other girls. One time these two knockouts showed up from Australia, a married girl and her lesbian lover. They basically rocked his world—did all kinds of kinky things with him and had sex with each other so that he could watch. He seemed to become obsessed with them and their blatant sexuality; he eventually made one of them a Playmate and would have made her a Girlfriend, but then he found out they were also sleeping with one of the butlers and they got kicked out.

I remember a time when one of the Girlfriends started to caress me and kiss me and told me to remove my panties. I told her they were on for a reason, but she continued to try to remove them. I finally just said no in a blunt way, and she stopped. After the night's activities were done and I was walking to my bedroom, she ran after me and started screaming that she was not a lesbian, that she was just trying to be nice and could not believe I was being so mean to her. I was dumbfounded, but wrote it off as her being drunk and high and continued to my room. Next thing I know Hef was in my room to have a "talk" with me because she went to him crying that I rejected her. Now I was in total disbelief. A painful reality check: here I was a law school graduate, getting a talk from my "boyfriend," because one of his other Girlfriends was hurt that I did to allow her to pleasure me. I could have cried, but I started laughing. It was all so ridiculously absurd that it was actually hilarious. I told him I had my period, had my panties on—as per the obvious rules— and I wasn't in the mood. Heaven forbid someone not be in the mood at the

Playboy Mansion! The truth was she and I had fooled around on other occasions, and I was attracted to her in as much as I can be attracted to a girl. I let her suck my toes a few days later, and she got over the rejection. She was the only Girlfriend I ever did anything with.

Months later, a new girl joined the group who also seemed legitimately interested in girls and she had a thing for me for the longest time, always telling me how she was going to "get me." Emma and Susan thought it was funny and kept telling her I was ready for her, which of course was not true, so then I had to hide and avoid the girl. I did not think she was an attractive girl in any way; in fact, I was surprised she became part of the group. But she was one of those quiet, nice girls who didn't ruffle anyone's feathers, and Hef let her stick around. One night when I was really drunk, I let her kiss me and it was terrible—sloppy and gross. That was it for me. I had my few experences with gorgeous models, and I had to close the chapter on experimentation with girls while the memories were still pleasant and erotic.

The Mansion has the aura of being this free, uninhibited place, where you are more than welcome to expose your sexuality. You are free to be your true sexual being. And maybe it was like that in the '70s and '80s before Hef got married. But it is not so anymore. There are too many unwritten rules, too many power plays, and everyone acts.

13: Boys, Boys, Boys

"Ten men waiting for me at the door? Send one of them home, I'm tired."
— *Mae West*

Since no satisfaction was to be gotten in the bedroom or anywhere in the house and since the gates were locked at 9 p.m., our options were limited. But where there is a will there is a way. Like rebellious children, the Girlfriends spent a great deal of time figuring out how to break the rules. With the exception of Holly, who in my opinion was unhealthily obsessed with Hef, most of us had our secret lives and our little flings. That was always one of the most common questions people asked us: Are you allowed to have boyfriends? The answer was no, we were not allowed to have boyfriends—Hef was our "boyfriend." In most relationships it is implied that you and your partner are monogamous—you do not date others. But because this was not a traditional relationship in any sense, and because I think we were *really* there as publicity props, it was not obvious to us that we should not see anyone else. Hef had to make it an actual rule after a couple of embarrassing situations. Girls "cheated" from the very beginning: the Bentley twins were known to have boyfriends in Las Vegas and were rumored to have dalliances with the staff. As they left and the party posse era began, it got even worse. One of Hef's favorite ex-Girlfriends, who was also a Playmate, supposedly went on tour with a rock star for a while, and was also involved with a butler. Another had an affair with an actor, which ended up in the tabloids. Girls were seen driving around with their boyfriends in cars that Hef bought them, and countless quickies supposedly occurred between Girlfriends and Mansion staff. And then there was Hef, the self-proclaimed Mr. Romance, praising his relationships in interviews and all the while being made a fool of behind his back. And so it became a definite rule: *No boyfriends*.

Most of us understood that to be the case when we began hanging out with Hef and then moved into the Mansion, but it was the ex-Girlfriends and the girls who were leaving as we were arriving who taught us that it was okay to break the rules. Tina confided in us that she was leaving for a man she met while with Hef in Las Vegas. I remember one night we went out to Myiagi's on Sunset Boulevard for some sushi, and a few minutes into the dinner, Tina received a phone call that her daughter had a high fever, so she had to leave. She later told us that she caught a 9 p.m. flight to New York to see her man. She stayed several days, and the day she got back was the same day we went on our first trip to New York City. She was cracking up on the plane because she had just returned from there. As time went on we learned that practically everyone had a relationship outside of the Mansion.

Being locked in at night was tough; it was like wasted youth. Some of the girls entertained themselves by having relationships with the butlers. One of the Girlfriends fooled around with a security guy right there in the movie theater, with Hef a couple of seats over. They would also sneak into the game room or somewhere out on the grounds for a moment of pleasure. Personally, I was never interested in the staff. There was one time when Hef and the girls went out and I stayed in because I had just had my boobs done, and one of the cute young butlers asked if there was anything I needed and I joked that I needed a boob massage. He came to my room and sat on my bed, making it obvious that he was up for anything I wanted, but I started giggling nervously and asked him to leave. I never did anything with anyone that worked for Hef. It wasn't my thing. No matter what I thought or didn't think of Hef, I couldn't be that disrespectful. The man was paying my bills, and I was living in his house. I had to draw boundaries.

We were not nearly as insolent as some of the previous Girlfriends had been, but most of us were also involved with people outside of the Mansion. Emma was married, and although Hef knew it, he thought they were separated and did not know they shared an apartment. Under the pretext of spending "quality time" with her eleven-year-old son, she told Hef she needed to spend Sunday nights at her apartment. Of course she would go home and spend quality time with her husband instead. Every time Hef challenged her about why she still kept an apartment and needed Sundays off, she would overwhelm him with a speech about children's needs, in turn, I think, making him feel guilty about his own shortcomings as a parent; he backed off. However, he must have realized that when she went home on Sunday night at 9 and her son had to be up for school the next morning, it was not about doing homework together. In addition to her changing local boyfriends, Emma also visited a former love in England. She would go on these trips to see him and show me pictures of him upon returning to the Mansion. She used to make me laugh so much with all of her scandals and intrigue.

Soon after she became a Girlfriend, it came out that Bridget was also married. Apparently her husband still lived in Lodi and had supported her move to L.A. She was to have one year to "make it" in the entertainment industry, and he supported her financially during that time. We thought it was weird that she had dated Ray Manzella and now was sleeping with Hef, considering she was married, but as long as she stayed out of my business, I stayed out of hers. Besides, Emma didn't want that to become an issue with Hef, as it would bring her situation to light as well. I found it ironic that Bridget, the girl who spent her time gossiping about the rest of us and trying to get us in trouble by finding out what she could about our lives, had some things to hide. But I wonder how her husband is still tolerating her presence at the Mansion as she admits to having sex with Hef on national television to promote the reality show.

Though Emma and Bridget were the only married ones, Roxy also had her boyfriend, Susan was seeing a couple of different guys, and even Candy, who always seemed so innocent, had some football player boyfriend. It seemed like everyone besides Holly (at least as far as I know) had a relationship with a man or men outside of the Mansion when we lived there.

I was still hanging out with Justin regularly, even though we were not in a relationship. We still had feelings for each other that continued to grow throughout the time I lived at the Mansion. We spoke on the phone several times a day, and we saw each other as much as we could. I even managed to get him into a couple of parties at the Mansion. We all did that; Hef allowed each Girlfriend to invite a few people to the parties. To get boys that we liked into the parties, we usually matched them up with other female friends on our list and presented them as couples to divert suspicion.

The famous Playboy Mansion parties were a great way to meet new boys. We could not wait to walk away from the table we had to sit at with Hef; we constantly made excuses to go to the bathroom, to get food, and whatever else we could think of so that we could get up from the table and go walk around and mingle. I met Stephen Dorff at Hef's birthday party. We made eye contact and kept flirting with each other, but because my duty was to sit at the table with Hef all night, nothing more came of the flirtation. The next morning, I heard Stephen had gotten caught with some other girl in the guesthouse, and at the time he was actually going out with the Playmate of the Year. There were so many casual encounters like that. One night when we were having dinner at Morton's, Emma and I managed to exchange numbers with Warren G by shaking hands right in front of Hef, without him knowing. And there were lots of late-night calls on my cell from Ja Rule, trying to hook up. But I never did anything about it.

My favorite story involves meeting a rock star I had a crush on for years. It was just another Wednesday night, and we made our way to the Purple Lounge at the Standard. I was totally bored, scanning the room for anything interesting, when a hot guy dressed in all black walked through the door and drew my attention. I checked him out and thought he was cute. There was something strangely familiar about him, and in a light bulb moment I realized it was a rock star guitarist I had had a crush on for three years! Wow. There he was, he whom I considered to be one of the hottest men on earth. A guy I never thought I would meet, particularly since I knew he lived on the East Coast. He joined a group of guys sitting a few feet away from us. I turned to look at him to make sure I didn't just imagine this; our eyes met, it was him. I had to do something. I had to go meet him, just to say hi, anything. I needed a reason though. Just then Hef was getting antsy and wanted to leave. I had to think fast. I was totally embarrassed, but I asked Hef for his camera, and went to say hi to him and told him I was a fan and I would like a picture. He was sweet and gracious and posed with me. Hef then wanted to know who it was and of course wanted in on the action so we took another photo with him. He told me that he would be back in town in a few days for the KROQ All Acoustic Christmas concert. He told me I should go and, trying to act nonchalant, I said that sounded cool. I gave my phone number to one of his guys. He called me a couple days later and told me they would have tickets for me at the box office. I was ecstatic. But how would I get out of the house?

The concert fell on a Sunday night, a day Emma was allowed to go home and spend time with her son. Emma and I came up with a plan: We would tell Hef that I had to go over to her apartment so that we could work on a Christmas present for him. It was the perfect solution; it was for him, and it was a secret so we didn't have to say too much. That Sunday afternoon I went to talk to Hef. He wasn't thrilled about it and acted slightly suspicious, but after some moaning and mumbling, he acquiesced. I got ready and jumped in my car, following Emma out of the Mansion. I went to pick up my friend Lea, a former Girlfriend of Hef, and we headed to the Universal Amphitheater. When we got to the concert venue, we picked up our tickets and passes, and we went backstage to hang out with the musicians. Lea knew a couple of guys from Good Charlotte, so we hung out with them. Then my rock star came out right before the show began to say hi. We went in to watch the show. We were up against the stage watching him perform. When he was on the stage we made eye contact, and he smiled at me—I was in heaven.

Afterward, we went backstage and met them at the dressing room. From there, we all headed over to their tour bus. We hung out until 3 a.m.; they played music and sang and we talked. Yes, *talked.* It was all so amazing I never even thought of initiating anything sexually. Then the bus driver suddenly announced that they had to leave—they were heading to Vegas for the American Music Awards. He walked me to my car to say goodbye, and we kissed. It was amazing.

He got married five days later.

Hef never asked me why I got home so late or any other questions regarding that night. I was prepared to tell Hef that I drank too much wine at Emma's and had to sober up before I could drive home; fortunately, I never had to lie. A couple of months after the concert, a picture of us that Hef had taken at the Standard showed up in the "Hanging with Hef" section of the magazine. I smirked when I saw it. *If Hef only knew.*

There were other times when men we had crushes on came right to our doorstep, literally. Like the time Nelly and Justin Timberlake shot a video for "Work It" at the Playboy Mansion. When we heard that we were going to be in the video we were psyched, all being fans of Nelly and Justin. The shoot took two days, and we got to hang out with the guys a few times; both were friendly and fun. The video was released in Europe and Asia but not in North America because of some sexual content. We didn't even know until we saw it a couple months later. There was a scene on the Mansion's tennis court with these two models playing and every time the ball hits them, a part of their clothing falls off, eventually leaving them "nekkid." The video is actually a really cool, concept: Justin and Nelly play two Mansion gardeners who decide to take over the Mansion and have a party while Hef and the Girlfriends are out of town.

After that Justin became our buddy, inviting us to his white-trash-themed birthday party at Dublin's on Sunset Boulevard. There were newspapers on the tables with KFC buckets with forties and Spam in them. His lady friend at the time, Alyssa Milano, was there and his ex, Britney Spears, ended up coming later on in the night. Other guests included Olivier

Martinez, who was *so* sexy in his role in *Unfaithful* with Diane Lane, as well as Pink, Nick Lachey and Jessica Simpson—who did not seem happy that all of the blonde Playboy bunnies were sitting next to them. Some time later, Justin came to Hef's birthday party wearing a "Who's afraid of a little pussy" shirt, with a cute kitty cat underneath the words. A slightly awkward moment ensued when Justin saw Fred Durst across the room and then Britney made her quick appearance in the same room.

We hung out with Justin's best friend, Trace, who wanted to get into the grotto. We were all for it, except we had to make the grand exit with Hef and then sneak back down again. When we did, we saw Trace in the grotto with some girl but couldn't find Justin. Of course we would have gotten in so much trouble if Hef found out that we went into the grotto with boys, but at the time we weren't thinking about the consequences—we were living for the moment. Unfortunately we did not even have an opportunity to get in trouble.

There was never a shortage of men or intrigue. The weirdest thing happened to me one night as I lay in bed with the flu while Hef and the Girlfriends went out to a club. I was watching television, and I got a call on my cell phone from the manager of the rock band Creed, who wanted to know if I could help the lead singer, Scott Stapp, get into the Playboy Super Bowl party in San Diego in two days. I told him I would see what I could do and told the guy that Scott was free to call me if he didn't hear from me before the party. A few minutes later, the phone in my room rang. The butler told me it was Scott Stapp! I was stunned—the lead singer of a band I had been a fan of for years was calling me. *This should be interesting*, I thought. I told the butler to put him through. He said hi and asked about the party. I told him I would do whatever I could to get him in. He gave me his phone numbers and I told him I would call him the next day. I hung up and thought, *That was a cool, random, little experience.* Fifteen minutes later, my phone rang again, and the butler told me it was Scott Stapp. I could tell from the butler's tone that he was wondering why this rock star was calling me again, but I didn't know myself. The Girlfriends are not allowed to receive calls to their bedrooms directly; all of the phone calls go through the butlers. But of course I took the call. Scott tells me he is in Carlsbad at some hotel and he has a cabana. He doesn't know if he is going out that night yet, but he enjoyed talking to me earlier and was wondering if we could chat. Intrigued, I say yes. We ended up talking for about five hours! He told me about his childhood, his father, and his sisters. He talked about his heartbreak and also about how much he loved his son. He also talked about the band. He told me that the other guys were total band geeks, but that he never really wanted to be a rock star; he wanted to be a baseball player. He said the band thing just fell into his lap and it was so easy to be a singer, to be a rock star. I thought he was ungrateful. I have so many friends who are musicians and wish they had the opportunities that he had. Scott was lucky and did not realize it.

Nevertheless, I enjoyed the thoughts and experiences he shared with me. He seemed like he was a little lost, like he needed a friend and I was happy to be there for him. Toward the end of our conversation, around 1 a.m., he announced that he was coming to get me in his limo. He was going to get a driver and come pick me up at the Mansion. I thought it was charming even though I knew there was no way in hell I could ever get out of the house past nine, let alone in the middle of the night with a rock star. I can just imagine the conversation with Hef, "Honey, I know I didn't go out with you tonight because I wasn't feeling well, but Scott Stapp is coming to pick me up in his limo and we are going to go to a few pre-Super Bowl parties in San Diego. Sleep well." My stuff would be packed up and left on the curb before I even got out of L.A. But I was too embarrassed to explain to Scott the whole curfew thing and the rules I was living under, so I just told him that it would take him two hours to get here and then two hours to drive back, and it would be way too late to go anywhere. Plus, I was sick. He gave up eventually.

The day of the party, I called Scott and left a message saying he would get in, and if there was a problem to call me when he was at the door and I would come out and make sure he got in. I did not see Scott at the Super Bowl party. He called me and I called him back, but somehow we missed each other. Maybe because we always left a party before it got any good. It sucked! We chartered a private jet to take us to San Diego from Los Angeles. We were met at the airport by our security as well as several police cars, which escorted us to the Super Bowl party. I had never had a police escort before, with traffic stopped and streets blocked off; we felt like superstars—it was awesome. The party was a lot of fun, but even at our own party, we were roped off in our separate area and unable to mingle with guests. There was also a burlesque dance performance by Dita Von Teese, now married to rocker Marilyn Manson, which was great, though we were not thrilled by it because we had seen it so many times. And just as celebrities began arriving, we had to leave. Hef said it was because of the jet we chartered—we had to fly it back by a certain time. But why couldn't we have just stayed at a hotel? We could have gone to the Super Bowl the next day and left afterward. Hef disliked traveling; he wanted to be home and that was that. So we, the hosts, were the first to leave our own party, and I never saw Scott Stapp that night. We got to do all of these cool things, but since they are always cut short, they were so anti-climactic. I later heard that Scott was at the party. It was another case of missed opportunity.

Even though sometimes we resented going out to the same clubs on the same days of the week, every week for months at a time, it was still the only way we could go out at all. I met Nicolas Cage at Concorde on our usual night out. I saw him checking me out as I walked by, and I smiled. He motioned for me to come over and sit with him. I did, but I immediately told him I was there with Hef. After some small talk, he asked for my cell phone number and I gave it to him, because there was something very interesting about him. He called me the next night; it was late and he was tired. He told me he was filming a movie called *National Treasure*, and he wanted me to come to a Christmas party he was having in a few days. I told him that I would love to, but I had a curfew (damn curfew was ruining my social life!). He mentioned that he could invite Hef and then we could all come. The next day Hef proudly announced that we had been invited to Nicolas Cage's Christmas party that Saturday. I smiled. *If Hef only knew.* Nicolas called me a few more times before the party, but it was always late and he seemed tired. I thought he was very enigmatic. There was something about him that made me very interested although somewhat intimidated (maybe it was the Oscar?).

As we arrived at his house, I felt a little nervous but excited to see him. Ever the gentleman, he greeted Hef, said hello to all the girls, and gave me a kiss on the cheek. The décor was absolutely beautiful. A winter wonderland. As you walked out of the house into the backyard tent, you were surrounded by white and silver. There were many beautiful ice sculptures. In contrast, his house was dark and warm: dark wood, earthy tones, just what I like. One thing that stuck in my mind was a beautiful carved red dragon he had over the fireplace. I decided I wanted something like that for my own home, but I have not been able to find a dragon like his. After getting acquainted with our sur- roundings, we proceeded to find a place to sit in the tent. Most of the tables situated in front of the dance floor were already taken, so Hef decided that we should sit right behind the dance floor on a white couch. Once again, we were isolated—we were seated by a dance floor away from everybody else. I was mad. Why go to these beautiful parties where interesting people were and be seated so that no one could talk to you? Of course I made countless excuses to go to the bathroom so that I could walk around. At one point Hef, some of the Girlfriends, and I started to dance, and Nicolas came over and danced with us for a while. I saw him looking in my direction several times. It was frustrating not to talk to him.

The other guests included Demi Moore and Ashton Kutcher with all of her daughters; Bruce Willis was also there with Brooke Burns and she was very friendly. She smiled as we all walked by, which I thought was very cool since most women, particularly at the side of a famous man, tend to snicker. I concluded that she was a happy, confident woman, as she should be. Of course we weren't there too long before Hef decided it was time to go home. I didn't mind; it's not like I was allowed to have any fun so we might as well go home. As we were walking out, I saw Nicolas and made eye contact. He quickly came over and asked if we were leaving, and I nodded. We said goodbye. I was sad to leave. As we were walking out, Hef stopped to talk to Stephen Bing, who was formerly linked to Nicole Kidman and is the father of Elizabeth Hurley's son. While we waited for Hef, we noticed Jack Nicholson standing by. Emma and I chatted with him for a while; he was witty, sharp, and charming. It's so nice when someone you are a fan of turns out to be a cool person. After that night, Nicolas called me and invited me to dinner on Christmas Day. Not only was I sick with a cold, but my parents were also visiting from Canada. I didn't call back immediately and by the time I was able to, it was too late. He had married some waitress he met. Although I wish him all the best, I regret not having dinner with him. There was just something about him. I guess it will have to remain a mystery.

While I lived at the Playboy Mansion, there was one person that I did actually care for other than Justin. I met Gavin Maloof at my friend Jason Davis' birthday party at the Beverly Hills restaurant Trader Vic's. Jason called me all the time, asking me to come to lunch, coffee, or anything, but most of the time I couldn't because of Mansion obligations. But for his birthday I wanted to make an effort, so Emma and I went over at 8 p.m., knowing full well that we had to be home in an hour. By the time all of the guests arrived, it was time for us to go home. But I just didn't want to leave; Jason was so happy that we came, and we were actually having fun, so I decided we should stay for the appetizers and deal with the consequences later. When we were seated, I was beside Jason, Emma next to me, and George Maloof next to her. We had met George during the fiftieth anniversary of *Playboy* celebration at the Palms. As the owner of the Palms Casino Resort, he was our host, so we reminisced about the weekend. As we sat down, Jason started opening his gifts. He opened one that was a basketball signed by the Sacramento Kings and a Kings warm-up suit; besides the Palms, the Maloofs own the Sacramento Kings, among other things. Emma and I thought the suit was very nice, and I said something about wanting one. The person who gave him the gift, George's brother, Gavin, immediately took notice and asked me to write down our address and he would have something sent to us. I wrote down our Mansion address but did not really think we would hear from him. A few days later a package arrived from the Kings with a couple of hats and two tracksuits. I was pleasantly surprised. Gavin called to make sure we got it. We chatted briefly, and he said he wanted to have dinner next time he was in town. For the next year and a half, Gavin and I saw each other occasionally, mostly for dinner. I never worried about getting "caught" because I was not sleeping with him. I was simply having dinner with a man I found to be interesting and kind. One night we were having dinner at Koi when I saw Playmate Jennifer Walcott at the table next to us. I also found out that Gavin's brother Joe went on a date with another Playmate, so I knew it was just a matter of time before rumors began circulating.

In February 2004, Emma told me she wanted to go work as a model at the Magic Clothing Convention in Las Vegas. She told me I could work with her, but first we had to get Hef to agree to let us go. I thought it would be a great opportunity to see Gavin, who had invited me to Vegas countless times. We had to get psyched up to go ask Hef; it was a big deal because he hated to let Girlfriends go out of town for any reason and rarely agreed to it. We told him that it was a clothing convention and we would be modeling and that our flight and room was paid for—which was true. Hef looked at us with suspicion, and then told me that he heard I was dating one of the Maloof brothers but that of course he did not believe it was true. I thought it was strange that if he heard it previously, he never came to ask me about it. But I guess he felt it was appropriate to bring it up now since we were going to Vegas and the Maloofs owned a casino resort there. It was his way of asking if I was going to stay at the Palms and see Gavin. I reassured Hef that nothing was going on, and he very reluctantly agreed to let us go. We could not believe it.

When we arrived in Vegas, we went straight to the convention. To my surprise, Emma's modeling job was with Hustler clothing. Oh my God! I couldn't believe she failed to mention that important detail to me. I also found out that she had worked with Hustler before. *Hef would die if he saw her donning Hustler gear,* I thought. I had no choice but to hang out, so I put a

Hustler tank top on and stood there looking pretty for three hours. Don't get me wrong, everyone from Hustler was very nice and friendly, and we did not discuss our Playboy connection, but I was sure Hef would freak out if he knew, so it made me very uncomfortable the whole time. While Emma worked at the convention over the next two days with another of Hef's ex-Girlfriends, Lea, I stayed at the hotel. I just couldn't betray Hef to that degree.

The first night when we went to the Hard Rock hotel to check in, we found out that they had already given our room away because we arrived late. I called Gavin, who immediately sent a limo to pick us up and told me to go to the VIP check-in at the Venetian and they would take care of us. We got our room key and entered the most beautiful room I had ever stayed at, even when we traveled with Hef. It was a two-bedroom high-roller suite, and it was stunning. I had my own huge bedroom with two bathrooms and a gym, and Emma—and Lea, who came with us—had their own two-bed luxurious bed-room. It was amazing. We ordered dinner and ate in our dining room and met Gavin afterward. He took us to see Eminem, whom Emma and I both love, at a private show, and then we partied into the wee hours of the morning at Ghostbar at the Palms, where Eminem later showed up. He got on the bar and started spraying people with alcohol. Gavin told me Eminem was staying at the Real World suite at the Palms, so named because that is where the Las Vegas season of MTV's *The Real World* was filmed. It was a wild night! The next night I ended up going gambling with Gavin; he taught me how to play Baccarat and gave me some chips to play with, though he was making all of the decisions. I ended up winning $7,500! We cashed in our chips, and I turned to give him the money, but he told me to keep it because I had won it. I could not believe his generosity! That was the equivalent of seven and a half weeks at the Mansion! We had to fight with Hef to get our allowance some-times, and here was Gavin giving me all of this money and expecting nothing in return. Though I was attracted to Gavin, nothing happened between us other than a kiss. He dropped me off at the Venetian, and I ran up to see the other girls. I didn't tell them about the money because I didn't want them to feel bad that they did not have the same luck.

When we got back to the Mansion, we got in trouble. Hef called us in and asked how we could afford to stay in a room that was thousands of dollars per night. Apparently he already knew that Gavin was taking care of the room. We had told Hef before we left that we were staying at the Hard Rock hotel, and that it would be paid for by the company we would be working for. But when we could not stay at the Hard Rock, we called him to tell him we got a room at the Venetian instead, but we certainly never gave him any details of which room or who took care of it for us. I don't know how he found out, but I guess a little birdie called the Venetian and asked about our room. *Hmm, who could it be?* I didn't care either way. If he kicked me out for it, it still would have been worth it. Though Hef was generous with some things, Gavin's kindness, without any strings, changed the way I viewed Hef. He bought us boobs, which we wanted, but never really did anything that would have a permanent, positive impact on our lives. It was a matter of weeks before I would leave the Mansion.

Despite the fact that I constantly was hit on and met many men, and despite the fact that I had lunch or dinner with several people, I never slept with any of them. Not one. Justin and I hooked up a couple of times, but I wanted to wait to be intimate with him again until after I moved out of the Mansion. I wanted to see what happened between us when I left, whether we were going to give a relationship another chance or we would just remain best friends. And the only other person I had been intimate with a few times, as previously explained, was Hef. That was it. It is so strange and ironic to realize that the two years I lived at the Playboy Mansion were the years I had the least sex ever. I think I just did not want to complicate my life any more than it already was. I was living with one man, I still loved another, and while I was intrigued with Nicolas Cage and cared for Gavin, neither of these relationships had a chance to develop. Other than my amazing night out with the rock star, I didn't even kiss any other boys! Wild and crazy Playboy Mansion? Yeah, *right!* I may as well have lived in a convent.

14: What Happens in the Grotto...

"When a fantasy turns you on, you're obligated to God and nature to start doing it right away."
— *Stewart Brand*

What happens in the Grotto does *not* stay in the Grotto; it ends up on these pages. With that promising introduction, I now must tell you that not much happened in the Grotto during the two and a half years I was at the Mansion. I think the Grotto's finest memories come from the swinging '70s, and thankfully the water has been changed since then. I always hoped that the Grotto would live up to its reputation and get some worthy action during the parties, but all that would happen was a bunch of naked guys would get in and hope for the girls to follow. And these were usually the same guys that by some stroke of luck had gotten on the party list and knew this probably would not happen ever again, so for bragging rights, they had to get in the Grotto just so they could say they did and maybe, just maybe, some drunken hottie would get in and make their fantasies come true. I understand their hopes. Oftentimes toward the end of the parties (and yes, we checked regularly on the progress), a couple of girls would find themselves in there and make out with some willing guy. But there was never an orgy or any blatant sexual activity. Perhaps there could have been, but by the time people were ready for that kind of licentiousness, security would ask everyone to leave.

As for celebrities, I have seen many go in and ogle but not dare get in. I can't blame them; as soon as they dip their big toe in the water, the tabloids will be reporting the wild orgy they participated in. And this I know from experience. When Emma visited her mother country—jolly old England, where I am told they love the gossip—she decided to make some pocket change and gave an interview about life at the Mansion. She told the story of how Justin Timberlake got into the Grotto and partied with several naked girls as Cameron Diaz watched. The real story—as I mentioned previously—is quite different. Let me begin by saying that Cameron Diaz was not even there when he was, and this was before they started dating. Emma had a major crush on Mr. JT, so all night we talked to him and his pal, who suggested we all go in the Grotto. Of course we pursued the idea; hey, if there was any chance of getting JT in the Grotto, we were going to try. As the night progressed, JT's pal did end up going to the Grotto with a couple of girls, but Mr. JT remained fully clothed in his memorable "Who's afraid of a little pussy" T-shirt. If my own gal pal can exaggerate the truth, many more can and do. Emma's tabloid feature led to a major fight within the group, and Emma almost got kicked out. After being pressured by Holly to kick her out, Hef came to me and asked me what I thought he should do about Emma, and I saved her butt. I told him it was something we could move past, and hopefully she wouldn't do anything like that in the future.

My own personal experiences in the Grotto left much to be desired. There I was, a twenty-six-year-old red-blooded American (well, Canadian) girl who enjoyed sex. And the Playboy Mansion, more than anywhere else, is the House that Sex Built. The Grotto for me was Emma, myself, and a few Coronas on a regular week night . . . fantasizing about what we would love to do in the Grotto. It's really sad if you think about it: two young girls, getting drunk, wishing there were some boys around. When we got desperate for male attention, we would call the pantry and order more drinks to be delivered to the Grotto just so we could splash and tease the butler. Desperate times called for desperate measures!

During the entire time I lived at the Mansion, Hef went to the Grotto three times. And unfortunately, or fortunately, for me, I missed all three of those times. The first time, after the usual Friday night out (I stayed in sick) and heavy drinking, the girls managed to convince Hef to go to the Grotto. According to the report I received in the morning, Hef remained sitting while having sex with Holly and Bridget, as the other girls provided visual stimulation by splashing around and touching themselves and each other. It was short-lived; I don't think Hef can remain in the hot waters of the Grotto for too long because of his heart (he had a stroke in the 1980s), and that is why the Grotto excursions were so infrequent. The other two times happened right before we (Emma, Susan, and I) left the Mansion. It was part of Holly and Bridget's master plan to exclude us and show Hef what a wild time they could give him without us. So along with the new recruit, eighteen-year-old Kendra, they snuck down there and did what they did.

For me, though, the Grotto remains an elusive fantasy.

15: House Parties

"No party is any fun unless seasoned with folly."
— *Desiderius Erasmus*

Who doesn't like a good party? Parties at the Playboy Mansion were a lot of fun. Hef spends more than a million dollars a year to entertain his guests and himself. The Mansion was always transformed into a magical place according to the theme of the party. Many people would work day and night to get the place ready, and the transformation was incredible. The Mansion also has a self-contained kitchen that provides food for more than a thousand guests; the Mansion chef does all of the catering at the parties. A great pad, fresh food, unlimited drinks, a gracious host, and beautiful guests—that was the standard.

There are five annual parties at the Mansion, starting off with the New Year's Eve bash, then the Mardi Gras party in February, followed by Hef's birthday party in April, then the famous Midsummer Night's Dream party in August, and finally, the most elaborate of them all, the Halloween party. Hef is a very generous and welcoming host. I think his first and foremost reason for hosting these parties is, as with everything else in his life, to promote the Playboy brand and to continue to live life according to the

Playboy philosophy. The secondary reason is that Hef liked to invite hot young girls not only to enjoy as eye candy and hook up his aging friends but also to enjoy their gracious flirtations and to possibly recruit new members.

Celebrities are a staple at Hef's parties. Without the celebrities, the parties start to look like a gathering of Hef's cronies trying to pick up girls who are way too young for them. The truth is, the girls come to meet the celebrities. The celebrities come because it's a fun party where you know you are the center of attention and can have your pick of beautiful, accessible women. The other guys come because they know there will be only a few celebs, so most girls will have to settle for less. Some of the girls come for other girls. Many of the girls come to be noticed by Hef and become a Girlfriend or a Playmate. And everyone comes for the experience itself: to see and be seen, to say you were there, and to have fun.

We, the Girlfriends, liked having the parties because we felt like it was *our* party. I loved the convenience of being able to go up to my room anytime there was a wardrobe malfunction or to fix my makeup. As soon as one party ended, we would begin thinking about what we would wear to the next one. There was extra pressure for Hef's girls to wear spectacular, one-of-a-kind outfits, so we had to plan early. But we had fun with it; when sky is the limit, you can really allow yourself to be creative. As the Girlfriends, we felt obligated to have the best outfits. It is hard to keep things exciting and original, but we always had to set the standard. Usually we would begin by choosing a color or a theme: *Moulin Rouge*, Pussycat Dolls, or the like. From there, we would go about putting together the outfit. I always started with shoes. . . . What shoes do I want to wear all night as I walk over the pool area stones? Boots were usually the most comfortable, so I tried to build an outfit around boots. That usually meant something bad-girlish and sexy versus cute and sweet or angelic. It was so much fun. The only limitations to what we could be were our own imaginations. There is a certain freedom about dressing a part and acting out your fantasy.

In the beginning we used to go out the night before the party, since Friday was our club night and the parties were always on Saturdays. Eventually we convinced Hef that going out the night before the party drained us of energy, and it became a tradition to stay in. The day of the party, we would take all day to get ready. It was a ritual: sleep in late, relax, have your hair and make-up done, get dressed. It was always exciting to see what the other girls were wearing. We would all meet in Hef's room and make our big entrance downstairs. One after another we walked down the curved staircase, hoping not to trip and fall as the flashing light of the cameras and all the guests' eyes were focused on us. We would then pose in the great hall for the official group party shot. Our arrival meant that the party had officially begun. We then made a second grand entrance, into the party tent, followed by a ceremonious walk to our table. We then sat in our hierarchical order, and that was supposed to be our basic station for the night.

But where there is a will there is a way, and when the boys show up, the girls will play. At the beginning of a party we sat there dutifully smiling and posing for pictures, all the while keenly aware of which guests were arriving at the party. We sat there as the ever-gracious hostesses and made goo-goo eyes with hot male celebrities. And as soon as the party was rowdy enough for Hef to be distracted, we would excuse ourselves to go to the bathroom, taking the longest possible route to get there. Our next excuse was to go get food, and after flirting and chatting with the guests, we always made sure to grab a plate of food on our way back to the table and announce to Hef how happening the party was and how we had to wait in line. After that, when everyone had a few drinks in them, we would basically sneak away as soon as Hef turned his head. He would always leave the party early. This was good and bad—bad because we wanted to stay longer, and good because we figured the sooner he went to bed, the sooner we could sneak back down and hang out freely by ourselves.

Let's take a closer look at the five annual Playboy Mansion parties.

New Year's Eve Party

The party calendar began with the New Year's Eve party, my least favorite of the year. The reason is not because of the décor or the food or a lack of festive spirit, but because the odd mix of guests lacks the usual energy associated with Mansion parties.

It is simply that most people like to spend New Year's Eve with their significant others, and since Hef is so strict about not inviting men, many girls do not want to show up solo. According to Hef, "a good party has more good-looking women than men," but most women want to spend New Year's Eve with a date. Also, it is a time when people are usually with close friends and family, and Hef does not usually permit his guests, other than the Girlfriends and his close friends, to bring more than one friend to the party. As a result, a lot of celebrities and hot, fun people do not attend the New Year's Eve party. It is a random mix of Hef's older friends, a handful of celebrities, and mostly female singles. The Mansion is a good place to go on New Year's Eve only if you are single and at least a couple of your friends are also invited to the party.

The New Year's Eve party is more elegant and subdued than all of the others. The décor is usually black, white, and sparkly: white flower center-pieces, silver chairs, black sparkly tablecloths, a black-and-white checkered dance floor. There is also a greater contrast in what the guests wear; a lot more women in dresses and men in suits, unlike at the other parties, which are all lingerie. As time went on, even the Girlfriends started to wear more clothes for that party. The last year I lived at the Mansion, Emma, Susan and I all wore short black dresses, Holly wore a silver sparkly flapper dress, and Bridget wore some bizarre gold get-up.

The New Year's Eve party was not only mellower in terms of décor but also in terms of the shenanigans that went on. Nothing much happened, despite our efforts to create fun. One year, Emma invited some guy she knew from the East Coast and his brother. She got them on the list because they were musicians. She kept sneaking off to the game house to smooch with this guy, and I would go with her to make sure she didn't get caught. I think she did it out of boredom, and her idea was that I would hook up with the brother, but it wasn't my thing. I wasn't bored enough to hook up with random people, despite my occasional Grotto fantasies. There was also a big movie star at the party who hooked up with Susan's friend, whom Susan invited to the party as her guest. I was shocked to see it happen because I had just watched a TV special about him, how he met his wife, and I remember thinking what a great relationship they had. *Typical Hollywood illusion*, I thought.

The last New Year's Eve party I attended as Hef's Girlfriend was in 2004, the year I moved out of the Mansion. After doing Vegas and taking Manhattan, we capped off a trio of *Playboy* fiftieth anniversary bashes with a blowout New Year's Eve spectacular at the Mansion. Minutes before the New Year arrived, we gathered on the dance floor, where we were swarmed by dozens of women hoping to kiss Hef, pushing and shoving, as balloons fell from the ceiling and engulfed the party. It was a fun way to bring in 2004 and a fitting way to celebrate the golden anniversary of the magazine.

The only time I really enjoyed the New Year's Eve party was when my parents were visiting me for Christmas and they came to the party for a couple of hours. It was nice to share the experience with my parents, who had never been to a Mansion party; after all, this was the classiest party as far as the dress code and behavior went. My mom was excited to meet some actors from the soap opera she watches. My father was just mesmerized. Unfortunately there were not too many celebs other than ESPN's Dan Patrick and Blink-182 drummer Travis Barker, who rang in the New Year in style alongside dozens of sexy Playmates. Because of my mom's back condition, they weren't able to stay too long, so I called Justin to pick them up at the back gate of the Mansion. I walked my parents out, and they got into his car. It was so hard to see him there on New Year's Eve and not be able to walk him into the party. He wasn't doing anything that night. He took my parents back to my apartment and hung out with them. It was things like that that made me appreciate him and really consider a future together when I left the Mansion.

Mardi Gras Party

A month and a half into the new year, we celebrated Mardi Gras. When I was first invited to the Mansion, this party was the Valentine's Day party, but that concept wasn't very successful. Playboy parties are mostly girls, and on Valentine's Day, you are either with your partner or you are looking for one. On Valentine's Day, Hef took us out for dinner and—as I said before—gave us a small gift, usually Playboy paraphernalia such as panties and tops. No diamonds or pearls like everyone imagined we got from our wealthy and famous boyfriend. Anyway, the party was then renamed the Mardi Gras party—a fun, provocative theme.

The Mansion was decorated in bright colors, and hundreds of beads were handed out. It seemed that more guys were invited and the party was a success. Some of the guests included Justin Timberlake, George and Geoff Stultz, AJ McClean, Matt Cedano, Seth Green, Wilmer Valderrama, and more. The sexual dynamic was increased—the men used the beads to get women to take off the very little clothing they had on to begin with. It was a fun, carefree party. The wild theme of the party allowed the guests to get even more creative with their outfits; many went topless, and outrageous feather and fur hats were seen everywhere. The Girlfriends wore whatever we could come up with. I remember one year Emma and I got matching little outfits: a frilly bra top and see-through pants (her lace was red; mine was pink). We were in Emma's room and we were just about to go downstairs to the party when a girl that was hanging out with us arrived: she was wearing the same outfit as Emma. Normally, if another girl is wearing the same thing it is not more than mildly annoying. But this time was different because this girl was sleeping with Hef and hanging out with Hef and was therefore invited to sit at our table. We could not have two girls at the table wearing the same thing unless it was preplanned. I could see Emma was upset and didn't know what to do. So I had to step up. I told the girl that she had to change her outfit. Emma and I were Hef's Girlfriends, and we had planned for days to wear matching outfits, and I said I was sorry, but if she wanted to sit at our table, she would have to change. I then told Emma to show the girl some alternative outfits. Eventually she ended up putting on some psychedelic one-piece suit. She later complained that I bullied her. But I had to protect my friend's interests, and I would have done that for any girl in the group. Despite our differences and internal problems, we were bonded. This girl was just a passer-through, some girl Hef slept with occasionally but was not interested in and would never be a Girlfriend.

Hef's Birthday Party

In April we celebrated Hef's birthday all month long. Whatever clubs we attended on a regular basis would each hold a party for Hef—sometimes we attended three birthday bashes a week! They all tried to outdo each other with the cakes: Hef as a Simpsons character, a caricature of Hef, Hef with the girls. But the main event was, of course, Hef's birthday party at the Mansion, which was my second favorite of all of the parties. I find that a lot of interesting people tend to show up to wish Hef a happy birthday, including celebrities who do not attend our other parties. In addition, Hef's birthday party is one of the two annual parties that are limited to 500 people, and it feels more intimate. Our table is located right at the entrance, so we get to see everyone who comes in.

As for the décor, it varies. For Hef's seventy-sixth birthday pajama party, the Mansion was transformed into an art deco old Hollywood, where new Hollywood players Snoop Dogg, Drew Barrymore, David Schwimmer, Matthew Perry, Gavin Rossdale, and Kiefer Sutherland mingled with scantily clad women. After an early-evening screening of the James Cagney movie *Footlight Parade* with fifty of his closest friends, Hef emerged from the Mansion's screening room to join the beautiful crowd with us by his side.

My favorite was when Snoop Dogg showed up at the party with the pimp Don Magic Juan. They had on their pimpest outfits and carried their own blinged-out chalices. Emma and I snuck away from our table the first chance we had to look for Snoop, and we found him outside sitting at one of the tables.

"What's up Snoop? Welcome to our house!" we said.

"Wuz up, baby girl!"

Snoop then asked us if we cared for a smoke, and of course we said yes. He then proceeded to roll and pass over what looked like a cigar. Emma and I giggled before we even took a puff. Snoop ruled. He was so cool. He came back to the Mansion again to film an episode of *Doggy Fizzle Televizzle* and brought with him these election stickers that said "Hef/Dogg 2004: A finer, hotter nation." It was hilarious.

Besides Snoop, my favorite person to see at Hef's birthday party was Jack Nicholson. He was standing in the corner of the dining room when I saw him. I think he was a bit overwhelmed by all of the attention and left fairly quickly.

Hef's party dress code was lingerie. Like with the other parties, anything goes really, but it was not as wild as Mardi Gras, not as whimsical as Midsummer Night's, and less formal than New Year's Eve. We usually wore something sexy and romantic—lots of lace and frills. One year, inspired by the Pussycat Dolls, I sported a faux-mohawk and dressed up my outfit with fishnets, stripes, stars, and bows. I think it was bit much for Hef, but the guests seemed to like it. On Hef's actual birthday, we would go out to dinner unless the party fell on that date. The toughest thing about Hef's birthday was getting him a birthday present. What do you get a man who has everything? Most of the time, we would get Hef photos of ourselves. In 2002, Emma, Lea, and I gave a him a photo of the three of us that he absolutely loved, and it became one of his favorites; he even put it in *Playboy*'s "Hanging with Hef" section. It was a photo of the three of us naked, but posing in such a way that nothing was revealed. I was in the center, and Lea and Emma were on either side of me. Our hair was long enough to cover our nipples and our bodies were posed sideways so that nothing at all showed. It was a sexy yet subtle and elegant photo. Hef hung it up in an alcove with a light above it, located at the top of the stairs of the second floor. I heard it has since been replaced and stored away. Some of the other things Hef would get were stuffed animals. It wasn't really worth getting him anything else because he is so set in his ways that introducing new things never worked. We usually did a group photo for his birthday, which was enlarged and displayed in the great hall so that Hef and the guests could see it upon arrival.

Midsummer Night's Dream Party

This is the party of the year, the most famous of Mansion parties. Every August, the Midsummer Night's Dream bash is the hottest ticket in Tinseltown. The theme of the party is fantasy, and the Mansion is transformed into a magical place. As the guests arrive, they see the Mansion sparkling in pink lights. As they enter, they see colorful flowers—the pool area is surrounded by plants, with flowers floating in the pool and beautiful mermaids lounging on the rocks surrounding the pool. The guests lounge on a veritable sea of colorful satin pillows, snacking on food from the sumptuous buffets. In 2003, the Mansion was turned into Mermaid Island for the annual bare-what-you-dare bash. A year later, it was a Greek bacchanal theme, where the lush grounds were decorated with giant statues of Greek goddesses and decorative flute-playing satyrs. This party seems to attract the most celebrities—not necessarily the most interesting ones, but the largest number. At 8 p.m., the gates were opened to a thousand friends—Playmates, Girlfriends, and celebrities, including Jenny McCarthy, Jimmy Kimmel, Sarah Silverman, Nikki Ziering, Tommy Lee, Michelle Rodriguez, Fred Durst, Marilyn Manson, J.C. Chasez, Leonardo DiCaprio, Tobey Maguire, Matthew Perry, Ali Landry, Jamie Foxx, Owen Wilson, Drew Carey, and Drew Barrymore. And to top off the star-power for the evening, Britney Spears arrived fashionably late. As testament to the party's desirability, Mansion security worked double duty with Bel-Air Police to corral all the crashers who tried in vain to scale the walls. After all, you have some of Hollywood's biggest names, rock stars, and hundreds of gorgeous women prancing about in the skimpiest of sleepwear.

It was to this party in 2002 that Stacy Burke wore the horse outfit with a gag in her mouth. Stacy is into fetish and bondage. I cannot help but laugh as I recall this; it was an ongoing joke among all of us. The girl was wearing a white lingerie outfit with a tail and hooves, and she had a gag in her mouth the whole night. It was over the top. We had never-ending fun with that, and soon after that, we voted her out of the group. So even though the Mansion is an open fantasy atmosphere, the fantasies do have their limits. It is not a free-for-all freak show.

Also at the same party, I met a couple who had paid $40,000 on eBay for an invitation. I went up to them and said, "I'm Hef's Girlfriend. Is there anything I can do to help make this experience worthwhile? You paid so much money to be here." They looked at each other and smiled. Then the wife said, "Yeah, you could go down on me!" I was speechless; I had been thinking more like an exclusive tour of the house. I laughed nervously and quickly walked away, mortified.

Then the busty British sexpot Jordan got totally wasted. She kept asking Hef if she could become a Girlfriend. Holly was getting jealous, and the whole thing was hilarious. But then Jordan began passing out on the table and we had to take her upstairs where she immediately crashed. We couldn't wake her up, and we were scared. She could have taken something; we didn't know. We called a doctor, but she turned out to be fine. I think she was just dealing with a lot of stress because her first baby had just been born blind. Jordan was really nice, and I wished she stayed longer. She flew back to the U.K. the next day with a bag full of Hello Kitty stuff for her bathroom.

Then there was a girl who tried out for Playmate and who played hard to get with Hef. When he lost interest, she tried anything to get into the group. I remember sitting at our table during the party talking to another

Girlfriend when she suddenly grabbed my arm. "Will you kiss me?" she said with a heavy Southern twang. All I could think was, "Eww, no," but I politely told her I could not. She ran off to the kitchen, crying to the butlers that she had been rejected. The freaks we had to put up with for Hef! There were some girls who really thought that most of the Girlfriends were into other girls, but that was simply not true. That party was a trip; it was one freak after another.

Halloween Party

The Halloween party at the Mansion is the most lavishly produced party, and it is amazing. It is my favorite party of the year! The usually tranquil Playboy Mansion is transformed into a wicked house of horrors. The decorations are incredible. In the front yard, we had personalized tombstones, and they are hilarious. Emma's said "Stoned to Death," Roxy, who is from the South, had one that said, "Too much Southern Comfort," while Susan's said, "From Neiman Marcus to Rigor Mortis." Mine was boring, it said, "Legally Blonde." Maybe it would have made more sense if it said, "Pronounced Legally Blonde"? The rooftop gargoyles glared from their perches, looking awesome flapping their wings. Monsters jumped out of the bushes, a gigantic, robotic, alien monster invaded the front lawn, and dismembered corpses oozed blood from guillotines along the driveway. The great hall is transformed into the "Hall of Heads," and the walls are ringed with fanged ghouls, blood-soaked monsters, and bug-eyed freaks.

One of the scariest, and most popular, diversions at the party was a horrifying haunted house constructed on the tennis court, which featured killer clowns, axe-wielding psychopaths, the Exorcist, and Freddy. I am not easily frightened, but Hef's haunted house is no joke—definitely not made by amateurs. Every year we began the party by walking through it and holding each others' hands tightly, while the camera crews from various news stations and entertainment shows like *Access Hollywood*, *Extra*, or *Entertainment Tonight* followed us and captured every scream and terrified look. Then they showed it on the late night news. It was a lot of fun.

Another great thing about the Halloween party is the costumes. All of the girls and all of the guests really go out of their way to dress up; no home-made stuff, this is the real deal. In 2001, I spent Halloween with Hef before I actually joined the group; I dressed up as a ballerina; it was actually a really cute one-of-a-kind costume. Unfortunately, that is the infamous party when I did my own makeup (before I learned the tricks of the trade). I got completely drunk, and all of the pictures from that party are horrible. The years after that I was a "Sexy Biker Chick" and the "Rite of Spring"—I just wore some flowers on my underwear and bra. Truthfully, we tended to choose costumes not based on the theme but on which ones we looked hot wearing. As for the guests, the Halloween party attracted the crème de la crème of Hollywood. At the 2002 party, I saw an actor I had always thought was good-looking. I caught him checking me out, so I walked up and introduced myself. He then introduced me to his beautiful wife; I didn't know he was married. We chatted, and I went on my way. Later on, they found me and gave me *their* number, just in case I wanted to "hang out" with the both of them. That was the first time I had been propositioned by a couple. (It was before the eBay couple.) They were both gorgeous and I was flattered in a way, but I was and still am way too chicken for things like that; I smile every time I see him on television.

Besides the five major parties, there are also a number of smaller gatherings such as Easter Day festivities, and the Fourth of July celebration. The Fourth of July celebration is a daytime party. It's a fun day with lots of celebrities stopping by, and a lot of Playmates show up; people are playing volleyball, swimming, or discovering the rest of the property. There are old-fashioned popcorn stands, ice cream stands, and all sorts of goodies you would find at a fair. In the evening, there is a buffet dinner, and around 9 p.m. when it got dark, we would have the fireworks. Hef is the only person in the city who has a private permit for a fireworks show, and it is always fantastic. The presentation starts off with a story about independence, followed by a salute to all of the branches of the military, and finally the fireworks start while beautiful patriotic songs are played in the background. It's all very touching; it makes you reflect on what this country stands for, and for someone who wasn't born here, like me, it fills me up with respect, admiration for America's beginnings, and a love for the American spirit. There are other firework displays that are bigger and brighter, but together with the songs and the atmosphere, so far the best Fourth of July I have been at has been at Hef's.

Easter at the Mansion is also a lot of fun because Hef has an annual egg hunt. The festivities start at noon, when all of the celebrities and Playmates arrive with their children. Hundreds of decorated empty eggshells are scattered around Mansion grounds, and prizes are awarded to the top gatherers. Hef announces the winners while the Girlfriends hand out the prizes. Everyone is dressed casually; we always wore pastel sun dresses. After the egg hunt, the children and adults would enjoy the petting zoo, ice cream and popcorn, and many other treats. Every child also left with an Easter basket full of sweets and toys. In the evening, there is a buffet dinner and a movie.

Also, not many people know that on many nights, the patio, pool, and backyard area (but not the grounds or the Grotto) are rented out for $10,000 per night for private parties. Hef agrees to come down and mingle with the guests and have his photo taken—like a prince or prime minister from one of those tiny European principalities who interrupts the affairs of state to greet the tour buses. It was all a little tacky, but I'm sure it went a long way toward defraying the costs of Hef's exorbitant lifestyle, which was a constant source of contention with the Playboy board of directors, particularly his daughter Christie. Hef argued that this was the best advertising money can buy—branding the company name and marketing directly to their demographic—anyone who secretly wanted to be Hef.

When security finally kicked everyone out, the attendees waited for the shuttle bus right under our windows. I remember how much it sucked to be drunk and exhausted, trying to fall asleep, people were screaming for hours right under our bedroom windows. And just when we fell asleep, the trucks arrived at 5 a.m. to take away all of the chairs and tables. They piled them up on the metal base of the truck as our nervous systems rattled. It was morning when we finally fell asleep. When we woke up, there was no sign that a party had gone on the night before, except that the grass was a little flat where the stage and the tent stood.

Besides the parties, the Mansion was also a much-sought-after location for movies, films, and TV, hosting everyone from *Politically Incorrect* to live ESPN boxing to episodes of shows like *Sex and the City*. The convent scene for *Charlie's Angels* was shot at the Mansion, and we got to meet George Clooney and Dick Clark when they were there to shoot a scene for *Confessions of a Dangerous Mind*. We were thrilled to have these exciting events take place at a place we called home.

16: Bunny 101

"She got her good looks from her father. He's a plastic surgeon."

—*Groucho Marx*

Bunnies are not born; bunnies are made. And they are made with the help of a whole army of people. How many times have you read or heard about celebrities preparing for a role or a photo shoot wherein they say, "I worked out with my trainer for five hours a day everyday and I had special meals delivered to me." And you thought to yourself, *Tough life. No wonder you look good. If I had that I would look even better!* And it's true: Celebrities have trainers and chefs and get regular massages, facials, treatments, and surgeries. They have their own makeup artists, hair stylists, clothing stylists, and personal shoppers. Who wouldn't look good with a support system like that? Although most Playmates and Hef's Girlfriends do not have this kind of an army of professionals, we do have access to and take advantage of many services to enhance our looks.

Many girls out there think that bunnies are like femme-bots, that not much is real. I can just hear women saying, "All those girls had so much surgery, and their hair is so bleached out, and they look so harsh." But every girl who became Hef's Girlfriend was pretty to begin with—Hef is not attracted to ugly girls. The face is the most important part. When people ask Hef what the first thing he looks for in a girl is he answers, "A beautiful face." And though I have seen him get completely sidetracked by a pair of huge breasts, it is the face that is the focal point. Bone structure and large eyes are the basics. The rest can be tweaked. And though we were all pretty, we all improved significantly with time. And it was not just the surgery. Yes, almost all of us had our noses altered to some degree, but that was the only facial surgery the girls had that had any significant impact. Bridget had laser eye resurfacing (erasing the wrinkles under the eyes), and Susan had an eyelid surgery, but other than that, no one else had anything done to her face that was permanent. We all tried Botox and lip-fillers such as collagen or Restylane, but those substances disappeared in time and did not change our looks dramatically.

What seemed to have made all the difference was actually what every woman can do for herself: makeup. Proper makeup technique, colors, and quality make a tremendous difference. For example, I did not know how to do the "smoky" eye shadow look at all; I put dark eye shadow on my lids and I looked like someone gave me two black eyes. I would look at the pictures afterward and wonder why I looked stoned. I also noticed that all of the girls were wearing fake eyelashes. I never had the need for them because I have naturally long lashes, but when you have so much eye makeup on, the extra lashes really enhance and frame your eyes. Most important, they look great in pictures. I remember the first Halloween party I spent as part of Hef's group, before I decided to move in; I did my own makeup and I looked horrible. Those pictures haunt me forever, and Emma never missed an opportunity to make fun of them when we walked by them in the Mansion gallery. When people see those pictures and then compare current ones, I look so different that they wonder what I "had done." The truth is often much simpler than we want to believe: makeup can do a lot of good—or a lot of damage in unskilled hands.

We all blossomed over time; there is not one girl that did not look significantly better after living at the Mansion for a while. I think it is because we learned from each other; how to do our makeup, how to wear our hair, what was flattering, and what was not. We asked each other and learned. There are no beauty secrets, just a lot of experimentation and coming to understand what works. But for those who want to "bunnify" themselves, I have come up with some essentials:

Bunny beauty basics:
1. Blonde hair
2. Tan
3. Perfectly white teeth
4. Fake nails
5. Fake eyelashes
6. Hair extensions
7. Full lips
8. Botox
9. Boobs
10. Photogenic nose

The most commonly altered feature is the nose. Six out of seven girls at the Mansion had their noses surgically altered. Nothing changes your look as much as nose surgery. Holly had her nose done twice. The first time was not enough of a change for her; she wanted a smaller, perky, button nose, so she went in the second time. She came out so bruised and swollen that she had to have tubes inserted to drain her nose. She looked scary at first, but she got the nose of her dreams. My procedure was very minor in comparison; I just had the tip of my nose shortened. Essentially, the doctor took off some extra cartilage from the tip. I had never had an issue with my nose, but after I moved into the Mansion and had to look at hundreds of pictures of myself each week, I began to scrutinize them and I realized my nose drooped when I smiled—the tip of my nose was close to my upper lip. Emma eagerly confirmed my realization. We were all quite critical of each other; other girls are very quick to point out imperfections, and of course when other people think there is a problem, you really begin to evaluate yourself. When I noticed that, I hated the way it looked when I smiled. And because all of the other girls had their noses done, I wasn't afraid to do it. When I woke up from the surgery, I came home and felt great; I was joking around with the staff and hanging out with the girls. I think what made a difference for me is that my nose didn't have to be broken like some of the other girls', so there was not much bruising or swelling. The worst part is that there is gauze stuffed up your nose and you can breathe only through your mouth. After the first night, your mouth is so dry that you get what I call the alligator tongue—all dry and rough. A couple of days later, I went in to have the stuffing removed and it was not painful at all, it was just surprising how much of it they put up there. About a week after the surgery, the protective cast came off. The nose looked swollen and weird, but in time I noticed that the tip did not drop down like it used to. When I went to Canada, no one noticed that I had my nose done; only when I told them and showed them pictures did they realize the difference. I was happy and relieved not to have the pinched, botched nose-job look that so many women sport in Los Angeles. In fact, when the girls ask for a nose job, Hef always warns them that accidents happen. But in the end, no one thinks that anything will go wrong in their case, and luckily, everyone's noses turned out great.

But I have to point out that no one was ever 100% satisfied with the results. There was always something: this side was different than the other, the bridge could have been flatter, the tip shorter, more refined, thinner, etc. And then the girls would say, well I did it once and it's better, so I'll do it again and it will be even better. I think that is when plastic surgery becomes addictive and dangerous; the never-ending quest for perfection can lead to the opposite effect. When Susan had her eyes done, she really did not need to—she looked great. After the surgery, the lids looked different and you could see the scars in the crease. It wasn't worth it; you should not do anything prematurely or it will have the reverse effect of making you look older. Bridget had laser resurfacing done underneath her eyes. I don't think it worked for her, because, to me, her eyes still looked tired and had lines underneath. This is what led us to think that she is older then she claims to be, because we did not know anyone who was having their eyes resurfaced in their twenties. What did make a difference for the eyes was the laser eye surgery. Many of the girls who moved into the Mansion wore contact lenses and glasses, and the first small surgery they had was the laser eye surgery. Holly used to wear these freaky blue contacts that looked cloudy or something, but she was almost blind and had no choice. That was the first treatment she had done when she moved in.

Besides the nose, the most popular procedure for girls living at the Playboy Mansion was breast implants. Some girls didn't have any before they moved in, and some girls wanted to upgrade. Everyone, except Bridget (at least when I lived there), had implants; we saw so many boobs on a weekly basis that we became breast connoisseurs. We could be happy with only the best. Boob jobs were as regular as a cavity fill. It was easy to get them; first of all, Hef did not need any convincing, he always agreed to pay the $8,000 or more it cost to have the procedure. We all went to the same surgeon, who always gave us preferential treatment and squeezed us in despite his busy schedule, so we could have them done whenever we wanted. We were driven in a limo to the doctor's office in Beverly Hills—five minutes down the street from the Mansion. We were picked up and escorted home, where our medication was waiting for us, as was a nurse if we needed one. We only had to press "0" to order anything to eat or drink. A breast enhancement surgery can be painful, particularly the bigger the implants and the smaller the breasts are naturally. It is also more painful to get them under the muscle. Usually it takes a week to get past the pain and discomfort. But for us, it was a piece of cake.

When a girl decides that she wants to get implants, there are many other decisions that must be made: Over the muscle or under the muscle? Saline or silicone? And of course the key decision of how many cc's to get, how big the implants will be. There was a degree of competition between the girls as far as the size and look of breasts; it seemed like everyone always wanted to have the biggest breasts. However, implants don't look the same on everyone; there are many factors that come into play in determining how they will look: the size of your natural breast, the shape, and of course your overall weight and height. It is an individual decision and must be discussed with your surgeon; and finding a good surgeon is the first step. Holly and I ended up getting the same amount. We had the largest breasts among the Girlfriends; no one had outrageously big breasts. Although Hef was fascinated when he saw really big breasts and slept with a couple of girls who had them, he thought they looked comical and did not want any of us looking that way.

Breast enhancement surgery is not always successful. It is a surgery, and there are always risks involved. The decision must not be made lightly. One of the girls at the Mansion had to have several surgeries to get them right. First she went too big and then switched to smaller implants. During the second surgery, the doctor (not our regular doctor) had injured one of her underarm muscles and she had a lot of discomfort there. She also developed a lot of scar tissue and her breasts did not look the same. When she moved into the Mansion, she went in for a third surgery so that the surgeon could remove all of that scar tissue. The surgery did not work, her implants looked tight, and she had to go in for a fourth surgery that finally made them better. Her recovery was not as easy; she had tubes in her breasts that were draining blood and liquids and needed a nurse the whole time. So although it is easy as pie for some girls, other girls have had complications. Also, breast surgery is not a one-time deal: those implants will have to be replaced in several years, and that means more risk, time off, and money.

Anything else the Girlfriends did was minor, such as lip enhancement. Everyone experimented with getting fuller lips at some point; collagen, Restylane, or Perlane. Emma had silicone put in her lips, and personally, I think it looked the best. The problem is that it is permanent, and if the doctor makes a mistake or you don't like the effect, you are out of luck. She had thin lips when she was younger, but you would never know; now she has fabulously luscious lips. And that is how it is in a house full of girls; one girl does something and she looks better, then everyone wants to look better too. I only tried Restylane because collagen required testing for an allergy and, having an intense dislike for needles, I wanted to avoid the extra poking. Restylane worked well initially, but it dissolved in about four months. After that we would go and have little touchups when special occasions like photo shoots or big parties came up.

To finish off the mouth area, a beautiful, healthy smile is also important. Bleaching is standard. You can get trays at the dentist office and buy special bleach and do it yourself, or do the one-hour bleaching at a specialist. I remember Susan remarking on how yellow Kendra's teeth were when she moved in. *Just give her time*, I thought. *She will go through the list and make the adjustments in time; we all did.* To fix teeth that are crooked, you obviously need braces. Braces are unsightly, and I don't think Hef would go for one of his girls having braces, but if the teeth were really messed up, the clear aligners are not so bad. Another possibility is veneers. A lot of girls had their teeth replaced with porcelain veneers. One of the girls had them put on because her teeth were badly damaged by drug usage as a teenager. Another girl had them to get bigger teeth. The con is that they are quite expensive, often costing $1,000 per tooth, and if not done properly, they can look too big and obviously fake.

Skin is key to the way you feel. We all tried to take care of our skin the best we could. We usually had a facial every two months. To treat minor facial lines, we all tried Botox. Even Holly at the age of twenty-four tried Botox, although she did not need it. But it was so easy to get sucked into doing what other girls were doing. I find that Botox doesn't last that long, maybe because they are diluting the solution so much. In any case, Botox won't change your look drastically, but it will take away or soften that one line you may have on your forehead or your frown lines. I tried it on my frown lines (the consequence of years spent studying and reading under dim lights), and it worked great but did not last long. For some girls, it became a regular treatment, while others did it when there was a need to look great for a special occasion.

We always sported a tan; it was hard not to when we live in a climate where your skin is always showing, not to mention the fact that we lived with a man who encouraged us to show as much of it as possible. With two tanning machines downstairs, it was easy to get and maintain a tan, and with the exception of Holly, who was smart not to tan, we all became dark after moving in. While I was mildly concerned about skin cancer and wrinkles, I thought I was still young and always planned to stop tanning when I was in my thirties. After I moved out of the Mansion, I noticed a weird spot on my upper back. It wasn't really a mole, just a round pink area that looked flaky and never seemed to heal. I had a bad feeling about it, but I was scared and put off going to the dermatologist for a while. When I finally went, I found out that I had skin cancer. *I'm only 29,* I thought. *How can I have skin cancer already?* I was devastated. I was also mad at myself for using those tanning beds at the Mansion. I had the cancer surgically removed, and hopefully it will not come back. But it can, and I have to get checked every six months for the rest of my life; I have that scar to remind me to be careful. Needless to say, I never tan anymore. I have grown used to my pale eastern European skin and when I need color, I go for the spray tan.

Now onto the hair: we all dyed our hair. We all came in with blonde hair but it always got blonder at the Mansion. The problem with constantly going blonder and then staying so blonde is that your hair gets very damaged and breaks, especially when you also style it frequently like we did. So besides using gentle shampoos and rich conditioners, I began alternating the intensity of the color; I would get bleach-free touchups to give the hair a break, and then every couple of months, I would get highlights or just lighten it all over. Being blonde is fun, but you do have to think long term unless you don't mind the so-called chemical haircut (when your hair is so fried by the bleach that it ends up looking like you cut your hair, when in fact it just all broke off). But Hef's Girlfriends are all blonde—that is the rule. He even went so far as to point out to the girls that their roots were growing out and that it was time to go to the salon. That must have been the one question brunettes asked him the most wherever we went: "Why all blondes, Hef?" As he so famously put it, "I'm presently dating seven girls, all baby-faced blondes. Picasso had his pink period and his blue period. I'm in my blonde period." For all you brunettes, it is worth mentioning that Hef's longest sweetheart, Barbi Benton, was a brunette, as was Carrie Leigh, a Canadian (who appeared with him in *Beverly Hills Cop*). Don't give up, ladies, Hef's brunette period may come yet.

If your hair did in fact break off and was short, or if it simply would not grow fast enough to a certain length, there was the miracle of extensions. Almost all of us, except Holly when she had short hair, had extensions (after we moved out, Holly finally got some individual extensions, and I think she looks the best that she has ever looked right now). The only difference was how long they were, and how many we each had put in. Although there are different types of extensions that I am aware of, we all preferred the individual extensions: pieces of hair with a protein-type glue at one end that is then attached to your own hair at the roots by a hot metal gun. Individual extensions sometime slide off on their own if they are attached loosely to your hair; otherwise, once they grow out and start showing, you can remove them by loosening the glue and sliding them off. Though they are fun to have, they do damage your hair. When you attach and remove them frequently, your hair gets ripped out. It looks thinner, and you begin to miss the extensions thereby falling into the vicious cycle of getting more in your hair and then losing more and more of your own hair as you remove them.

We were lucky enough to have a gym in the house with everything that a Bunny needs to stay in shape. During my two years at the Mansion, I used it about five times. Some of the girls work out like maniacs, some work out occasionally, and some never do.

Most girls try to eat healthy and stick to a diet. And yes, some do have eating disorders. I did not know anything about eating disorders until I noticed something strange about one of my law school roommates: she would bake cookies and cakes every day and order pizza all the time, and then disappear to the bathroom to brush her teeth for half an hour. After watching a talk show on eating disorders, I recognized the symptoms in my roommate. I wanted to help her and tried talking to her, but I did not want to embarrass her, so I did not push it. I really did not know how to deal with it. At the

Mansion, we all had our own rooms and did not usually share meals, so it was hard to see anyone's behavior—we only ate together at the Sunday buffet before the movie or when we went out to restaurants. But I know that when Holly first moved in, she went on a severe diet and security had to bring her home from clubs a couple of times because she was feeling weak. She told me she had been dieting and was not feeling well. Then there were times when we went out for dinner and some of the girls barely ate anything, like the time we went to Mastro's, a Beverly Hills steakhouse, and while Emma, Susan, and I indulged in filets with béarnaise sauce, potatoes au gratin, and creamed spinach, Holly ordered steamed broccoli. Hef came to us and wanted to know why we were laughing and giggling so much at dinner to make Holly lose her appetite, suggesting that we were laughing at her and Bridget. The truth was we had a couple of glasses of red wine and we were jovial and enjoying our delicious food. Somehow it seemed the other girls never missed any opportunity to blame things on us.

The fact that we had a twenty-four-hour food service at the Mansion was a plus and a minus. It was awesome to come home from a club and order nachos or cheeseburgers and fries, but it wasn't so awesome when the pounds started adding up. It was like gaining the "Freshman Fifteen" at college; this time it was the "Mansion Ten." I am blessed with eastern European metabolism, both of my parents are slim; in fact, not one person in my entire family is overweight. My weight has always fluctuated between 108 pounds to 115 pounds, no matter how many cheeseburgers I stuff my face with after my nights of drinking and partying.

In the end, I am happy with the two surgeries I had, and I have no regrets. If I didn't have them, I would still be a happy person. If I did not live in an environment that places so much emphasis on physical perfection, I probably would have never had any surgery. Although I would never encourage someone to have plastic surgery, I do advise my friends and support them if they truly believe that they need a procedure to be happy with themselves. I am also quick to discourage them when they are being overly critical of themselves. But sometimes a nose correction or a breast enhancement does wonders for a woman's self esteem and gives her confidence to go out into the world. I have a friend who had small breasts and always felt unfeminine and reserved sexually because she was embarrassed. Having her breasts enlarged changed her life. In a world full of hate and human suffering, there are more important things to worry about than a girl getting implants. But what I value the most is the fact that I improved my makeup skills.

Living at the Playboy Mansion is like living in an unrealistic bubble where everyone is beautiful. When I left the Mansion I could not help but notice how "normal" and ordinary most people looked. All of a sudden, not everyone had a perfect tan, blonde hair, and big breasts. Then I realized that it was the Girlfriends who looked like cartoon characters, too perfect and too exaggerated. I needed a reality check, and I needed to readjust to life outside of the Playboy bubble. I darkened my hair and took off the acrylic nails and am happy to be pale.

17: Playmates at Play ★

"Beauty is only skin deep, but it's a valuable asset if you're poor or haven't any sense."
—*Kin Hubbard*

The subject of being a "Playmate" was somewhat bitter for most of the Girlfriends because when you became a Girlfriend, you were not allowed to be a Playmate. It wasn't always that way; many Girlfriends such as Brande Roderick, Dalene Curtis, Stephanie Heinrich, and Tina Jordan were Girlfriends first and then Playmates. In fact, most girls became Hef's Girlfriends to become Playmates. However, as with many things, Hef learned his lessons from experience. When they achieved this goal, the women left. Being a Playmate would require a girl to travel and promote her issue, and with her Playmate status in hand, she would leave to pursue other opportunities and younger men. Brande left for *Baywatch Hawaii*; the other girls simply left. Hef knew that having a Girlfriend who was a Playmate was not compatible.

Holly, who really wanted to be a Playmate herself, would constantly tell all of the other Girlfriends that they would not become Playmates. I heard that Hef had told her that she wasn't photogenic enough, and she wasn't sure if she could be a Playmate, so she certainly would not allow anyone else to become one. She told all of us there was no chance Hef would make anyone a Playmate to discourage anyone from trying. She claimed it was because of the readers; in 2001, Hef had made several of his Girlfriends Playmates and the readers were sick of seeing the same type of woman. I understood that Hef had to please the readers, but after some time had passed, I thought they would be curious to see who Hef was dating. Although I did not care to pose myself, I know that it was a dream for some of the other girls. Emma had been a Page Three girl in England, and becoming a Playmate would legitimize her as a model in her niche of the modeling field. Susan also wanted to be a Playmate. I could understand everyone's desire to be a centerfold; after all, it provided occasional income forever and was a fun title to have. However, in my view, no one wanted it more than Bridget. I think she had an unhealthy obsession with becoming a Playmate. She demonstrated this on one of the first episodes of *The Girls Next Door*, when she encouraged the girls who were testing for centerfold to drink too much and then admitted on TV that she was glad that they were "not going to look their best tomorrow."

There was also the issue of equality; Hef felt if he made one Girlfriend a Playmate, the other girls would want the same thing, even though that was not necessarily true. In 2004, we found out by accident that Susan had done a Playmate test shoot. We flipped out. For me the issue was not that Hef let her test but that she didn't tell us about it; just a few days before we found out, she said she did not want to be a Playmate because it was cheesy, a career dead-end, and they were all hookers anyway. I was appalled that someone who was my friend would go to the trouble of saying all those things and creating this web of lies as if we wouldn't find out. Emma was upset, not only because Susan withheld the truth, but also I think her ego was a little hurt that Susan got to test and she did not. Even though she was denied earlier, she had hoped that as Hef's Girlfriend, she would be given another chance; plus, she looked better now than ever before, so why not try again? But I think no one was more dejected by the fact that Susan got to test than Bridget. We were also mad at Hef for being so deceptive and going behind everyone's back to do this, knowing what a sensitive issue it was for most of the girls. The kicker came at the end, when Hef told Susan her own friends ruined it for her. I didn't think it was very mature for a man of his stature to turn the girls against each other, and then tell the girl she wasn't getting it because of her own friends. Especially since everyone in the house heard that she was rejected for Playboy because apparently at 32, she was too old. I just couldn't believe Hef used us as an excuse instead.

There was also the drama of finding the right fiftieth anniversary Playmate. All year long, the girls kept coming to test and though some of them made Playmate, none was what Hef wanted for the fiftieth anniversary. They had such a hard time finding the right girl. Hef told the Girlfriends more than once that we were so much better looking than all of the other girls who had come through the door. "We know!" was the unanimous answer. But we knew he would not do anything about it. The funniest thing was when Bridget launched her campaign to become the fiftieth anniversary Playmate. She was telling us—Susan, Playmate Miriam Gonzales, and me—about her aspirations, and decided to go get the scrapbook she had prepared so that we could see it. I didn't have the heart to tell her I thought it was tacky and unprofessional; it was like a photo album with cut 'n' paste pictures of her and a letter written by her about why she should be chosen. Bridget sent the scrapbook to the *Playboy* offices in Chicago, New York, and the Santa Monica Studio. I wondered how many times a girl had to be rejected to move on. But she kept crying and whining about it and continued to do so when she saw that Hef felt bad for her. It seemed to me she learned how to work Hef with tears. I would not be surprised if he gave in and put her in the magazine out of pity.

For me personally, the matter of becoming a Playmate was inconsequential. That was not why I began dating Hef or moved into the Mansion. In fact, I was fairly certain that even if the opportunity presented itself, I would not do it. And I know people will think I am just saying that because I didn't become a Playmate or because I am bitter for some reason, but I am not. Hef told me several times that I was photogenic; I didn't make too much of that, and I never tested. I was the only one of the Girlfriends who did not test or become a Cybergirl, which all of us were "allowed" to become. The Cybergirl title was a concession in my eyes: you got a $1,000 for the same kind of pictures that Playmates got $25,000 for, except you were on the Internet and they were in a magazine. There are fifty-two Cybergirls each year, and there are only twelve Playmates. I am sure if Hef wanted to make all of the Girlfriends Playmates or wanted to feature us in the magazine, I would have gone along with the plan at the time. But it wasn't my dream or my goal like it was for Bridget, or Holly, who said on *The Girls Next Door* that "being a Playmate is all Bridget can achieve in body and mind."

I did not want to jeopardize my education and future to pose nude in a magazine. The money is good, but after taxes, all you were left with was about $13,000. I made a decision at the very beginning of my life at the Mansion that if I ever posed nude in *Playboy*, it would have to be for at least the amount of my school loans, never any less. It wasn't about being prudish. I am European and very comfortable with my body; I think being nude is natural, as natural as we can be. I remember being at nude beaches on the Black Sea Coast in Romania and Bulgaria when I was a little girl. I vividly recall seeing my first penis on one of those beaches. As perplexed as I was about its purpose, I giggled at the ridiculous sight of it, pointing up surrounded by a strawberry blond bush. I was five years old, and I refused to take off my bathing suit. It is comical to me now that I, the child, was the only modest one at a beach where people who should have stayed clothed were strutting their stuff. But after the initial shock of mass nudity, I relaxed and took off my bathing suit, perhaps aided by my discovery of how much fun it was to play with therapeutic mud. There were these fabulous mud baths and seaweed wraps for people to cover themselves with; I thought they worked well as a cover-up. Ever since then I have been comfortable with skin. I consider *Playboy* to be a classy magazine. I think the pictures are tasteful and artistic; my decision had nothing to do with nudity per se.

Being a Playmate is not a career in itself, at least for most Playmates. Yes, they get attention when their issue comes out. After that they move to

L.A. and try their luck in modeling and acting based on their Playmate status. What most Playmates want and hope the centerfold will get them, is a career in modeling or acting. Many went on to such work, though not at the high end. Anna Nicole Smith, Miss May 1992, modeled for Guess jeans, but others are more likely to end up in swimsuit or lingerie ads and, especially, in beer ads. In the meantime, they try to get Playboy promotional jobs through the company such as making appearances at Mansion parties and playing hostesses at charity or other events. They get about $500 for an evening and a couple hundred more if they wear their bunny costumes. I noticed that it was mostly the same group of Playmates who worked the events. I am sure there are the favorites who tend to get rehired because of their dependability and personality. I know some Playmates stopped getting hired because they had visible drug problems or hooked up with the guests; they did not reflect Playboy well. Because the cost of living in L.A. is so high and jobs are limited, a lot of the Playmates move back home. We had more than one stay at the Mansion when she ran out of money. There are a few who make it in the entertainment industry, but there are only so many jobs for the *Playboy* type. It seems like back in the days of Pamela Anderson and Jenny McCarthy, the look was more popular, but now the demand is not nearly that high.

Marriage, of course, was another thing the Playmates had in mind, and several of them landed rock musicians or professional athletes. Several Playmates' claim to fame is snagging a celebrity husband. Shanna Moakler got pregnant by Blink 182 drummer Travis Barker, and they got married soon after. Jaime Bergen married David Boreanaz, and Shauna Sand married and then recently divorced Lorenzo Lamas. And Shannon Tweed met Gene Simmons at a Mansion party. Playboy Mansion parties serve as the perfect opportunity for Playmates to hook up with rock stars or actors.

To say that all of the Playmates long to be Playmate of the Year (PMOY) is an understatement. First, there is the $100,000 prize to be won, along with a car and a motorcycle. Second, there is the title, and the title means jobs, promotions, appearances, and even more money. And of course there is the bonus sense of superiority in relation to all of the other Playmates of your year who thought they were going to get it. The PMOY is supposedly chosen by the people in a poll. However, the rumor is that it is really Hef, with his elite team, who chooses the PMOY.

It's funny, but you always know when it's that time of the year: the time before a PMOY gets chosen. All of a sudden the Playmates from that year start visiting the Mansion more, showing up at all of the parties. In 2002 a certain Playmate could be seen at the Mansion every single weekend playing Scrabble with fellow Playmate Julie McColough and even cards with Hef's secretary, Mary, and other older ladies. And then the PMOY title went to Dalene Curtis, and that other Playmate was seen only at Mansion parties, where she was always chatting up celebrities.

Some Playmates even visit Hef's bedroom in hopes of bettering their chances. Many girls think that sleeping with Hef will give them an edge over the competition. And there is good history to support that contention. After all, Brande Roderick and Dalene Curtis were his Girlfriends and then became PMOY. I would say that during the years I lived at the Mansion, half of the Playmates up for the title ended up in the bedroom. Though some only fooled around with the girls, many had sex with Hef. The reason I know it is connected to the PMOY title is that those girls never came up before the competition began, and they didn't come up after they lost the title.

Not only was the PMOY award good for Hef's sex life but we, the Girlfriends, also benefited. All of a sudden gifts were coming in the mail, and the girls were stopping by with little tokens for all of us. But we didn't have any influence on Hef, none of us, not even Holly, who is always in his ear. Yes, we told him who we thought was the prettiest and the nicest of the girls—not always one and the same. That is as far as it went. The Playmates always drilled us for information as to what Hef looks for and what they can do to better their chances. They were also more than willing to rat each other out; Playmates often gossiped about their competition and knew we would pass it on to Hef. I remember one year, a beautiful blonde whom I personally liked a lot was up for the title. All of a sudden this gossip about her drug use surfaced, followed by rumors of her sleeping with various men at the Playboy parties where she was supposed to be a hostess. Either way, Hef was uncomfortable with the image associated with her and she didn't get the title. The most beautiful girl does not always get the prize. Neither does the nicest, most wholesome girl next door. It's a combination of both qualities as well as star potential. If a girl goes on to land a movie role or a television job, it means added publicity for Playboy. Same with the guy she is dating; if she has a known beau, it raises publicity for her and Playboy.

There are other factors such as age, family, and political considerations. January 2004 Playmate Aliyah Wolf is beautiful, but she had two things going against becoming PMOY: Her married name is Hussein and she has a child. The same with Playmate Stephanie Glasson, she also has a child and is thirty years old. She is a great girl, and we became friends, but I told her before her issue even came out that she would not be PMOY. Is it fair? Of course not. Hef claims to be an equal opportunity employer, but if you are nearing thirty and if you have a child, despite how beautiful and educated you are, you have no chance. Sometimes the PMOY choice is downright confusing. In 2002 Christina Santiago, who was a contestant on the reality show *Playboy: Who Wants to be a Playboy Centerfold*, became the PMOY. People could not understand how she could win the title; although a beautiful woman, she didn't even win the show.

Then there was the quiet, well-hidden Playmate scandal. Hef kept getting e-mails and phone calls from madams in Los Angeles that a few Playmates, including some of his former Girlfriends, were showing up on their rosters of high-priced hookers. This finally became a household controversy when some of the main candidates for Playmate of the Year were implicated. Hef met with them to discuss the issue, but despite their claim of innocence and non-involvement, he could not take the chance. The PMOY went to a girl who was not implicated. Hef really had no choice, and while the girl was beautiful, she essentially got the job because others were disqualified.

Hef barely avoided it all going public, although there are a couple of articles on the Internet about it, and even Page Six of *The New York Post* recently reported that several models and Playboy Playmates are working as high-class escorts.

I learned it all from one of the girls in the house; she had been approached about working for a madam, but since she could not, she was telling some Playmates looking for the extra work to call that madam. Apparently another madam found out that this girl was sending Playmates to her competition and she threatened the Girlfriend. She was scared that Hef would find out about it all, and she confided in me; she also told me some of the names of the Playmates and former Girlfriends who were involved. The truth is that a lot of them did work as escorts, particularly in other cities and often in foreign places such as Turkey or the Middle East. We even knew some of Hef's ex-Girlfriends who bragged about how much money they were making. I stayed out of it all, not wanting to know too much. It was sad. For a lot of these girls the money is just too important to pass up; after they move out of the Mansion and cannot continue their standard of living on Playboy promotion jobs, they look for an easy way to make a buck. And apparently Playmates can charge a lot more than regular escorts because of their title. It isn't just Playmates who get involved in becoming high-class escorts though. I attended parties where I heard about celebrity women getting paid huge amounts of money to have dinner or attend a party with—and even spend a night with—some oil billionaire in the Middle East. This is not to say that most Playmates are gold-diggers and escorts. In fact, most of the girls I met are beautiful, really nice, friendly, and fun girls.

18 : Fiftieth Anniversary of *Playboy*

"To laugh often and much; to win the respect of intelligent people and the affection of children; to earn the appreciation of honest critics and to endure the betrayal of false friends; to appreciate beauty; to find the best in others; to leave the world a bit better whether by a healthy child, a garden patch or a redeemed social condition; to know even one life has breathed easier because you have lived. This is to have succeeded."

— *Ralph Waldo Emerson*

It was really special to be with Hef for the fiftieth anniversary of *Playboy* magazine. That is quite a milestone considering the humble beginnings of the magazine. He had been talking about the anniversary and all of the fun things we were going to do for months. The celebration started in August 2003, with a party at the Palms in Las Vegas. The drama began right away with the room assignments: Emma, Susan, and I had our own suite while Holly, Bridget, and Candy were to stay with Hef across the hall at the newly created "Hef suite," which is now open to all Palms guests. I didn't have a problem with the setup, but Emma and Susan felt it was unfair that he automatically assumed we didn't want to be with him. Why couldn't the other three have their own room? Of course the answer was Holly; Holly had to be with Hef and because Emma did not like Holly and vice versa, they could not be in the same room. It made perfect sense to me, but the inequity of the situation was really frustrating sometimes. I was excited to be out of the Mansion and did not want to focus on the silliness among the girls. We got dressed, took some pictures, and headed downstairs to an auction featuring Playboy memorabilia, including the famous Chicago round bed Hef used to hump on. We took some more photos and headed off to the street dedication ceremony for the "Honorary Hugh Hefner Drive." When we walked outside, there was a beautiful vintage Cadillac waiting for us (it once belonged to Marilyn Monroe and now belongs to Gavin's uncle, who kindly lent it out for the occasion). We drove in the car, like a procession, to the street corner a few feet away. It took a few minutes to go through the ceremony and unveil the street sign. Finally, we were off to Ghostbar for some drinks. Everybody, including dozens of Playmates, was already there, drinking and having fun. We realized we had not had dinner, so we went to the N9NE steakhouse at the Palms—my favorite restaurant in Vegas—for dinner. And we ended the night partying at the pool lounge Skin, where Paris Hilton joined us. She was very friendly with Hef; she sat on his lap for a photo and it made Holly so jealous. Holly actually told Hef that it bothered her when Paris came over to greet him and sat next to Hef in Holly's place. Paris was always so carefree that she never noticed. Who cares if she sits by Hef for a minute to say hi and take a picture? Next, Paris asked us if we wanted a "wet pussy." We looked at each other puzzled. It was a shot! Oh, okay, sure. So she went ahead and ordered "wet pussies" for everyone. We always run into Paris on the party circuit, and she is always friendly and sweet and likes to have fun.

The next day we lay poolside all day while Hef conducted countless interviews in our cabana, occasionally calling us over when he needed his blonde props. We were bored. Who wants to lay around in an area roped off from the public and guarded by security? It was not fun. Increasingly we felt like some sort of Playboy promoters who were not getting paid for any of the work. While everyone else was bedazzled by their exclusive invitation to the hottest party in town, for us it was similar to being in a car commercial. We had to appear charming, and gracious, and showcase the product—in this case, Hef himself. He made a lot of money off us and we sat there, lonely and isolated.

The second night we attended the premier of Zumanity, a Cirque du Soleil show that was absolutely fantastic. We sat right up front on the cozy little couches—Hef with Bridget and Holly on one, and Susan, Emma, and I on the other. Right before the closing act of the show, the emcee pulled Emma and I onto the stage to participate in the last act with them. It was a slow sensual dance. Our adrenaline skyrocketing, we began touching each other and moving our bodies erotically among the troupe, who welcomed us onto the stage. It was an amazingly liberating experience, and we got off the stage drunk with happiness. Holly rolled her eyes, but it didn't affect us anymore. We stole the spotlight.

We next went to dinner at the Voodoo Bar; we would have preferred to go somewhere else—Vegas has so many world-class restaurants—but we went there because Bridget, being a fan of horrors and all that is macabre, wanted to go there for the trademark drink, The Witches Brew. After the dinner, we were off to our big party at Rain Nightclub at the Palms. We were disappointed to discover that once again, we were isolated on our own balcony, our own little prison, far away from the celebrities and anyone that might actually be interesting to talk to. We could not just step over the rope and mingle—we would get in trouble with Hef. We weren't even allowed to go the bathroom on our own. And so we proceeded to drink and dance and tried to have fun despite our restrictions. The only person we got to talk to was Tony Curtis, who was very nice and friendly and invited us to come visit him in Las Vegas. The only reason Hef tolerated Tony's presence on his balcony was because Tony was with his sweet wife, Jill. Although when Hef noticed Tony talking to me a bit too much, he started getting irritated. It didn't matter though because we left the party soon after.

The fiftieth anniversary celebration continued with an official party at the Playboy Mansion in October. Although we had fun in Las Vegas and I knew we would have a great time on an upcoming trip to New York City, we were excited about having a people over at the Mansion. We were told that there would be musical performances, and it sounded like a lot of fun. In addition, the party at the Mansion was to be televised on A&E, which is a bonus for girls who enjoy attention.

My own personal level of enthusiasm was low. After years of suffering from chronic and severe back pain, my mother was going to have a risky back surgery: an artificial disc replacement. She was so hopeful that this surgery would solve her pain that I looked forward to it, but I was also nervous. After all, this was a serious, highly invasive surgery. It was scheduled for the day of her birthday, September 24, the day before my own birthday. I wanted to go home for at least two weeks after the surgery to take care of her, but the party fell on October 4. This meant I would be able to take care of her only for a few days. I resented not being able to be there for my mom, but I was keenly aware of my obligations. The night before I left, I went to say goodbye to Hef and asked him for my allowance early. All he had to say to me was, "You know, since you won't be here, you will not get your allowance next week when you get back." I was stunned. Here I was, so anxious and scared for my mom, and he just wanted to make sure I was aware of what I would lose out on? I was not going to Club Med for crying out loud, I was going home to be with my mom for her surgery and take care of her afterward. I paid for the plane ticket, I had to book some lousy motel to stay at right by the hospital, and I would be spending my mom's and my own birthday in a hospital waiting room, and here he was just making sure I knew that I was not going to get my allowance. I hated him at that moment. You would think that my boyfriend would offer to help somehow. He didn't even have the courtesy to say something hopeful, something encouraging or kind. He just tried to make me feel guilty about not being at the Mansion for a week and was making sure I knew the punishment would be no allowance. What kind of a "boyfriend" was that? What kind of a "family" was this? I knew then that if he ever tried to use those words again, I would throw up.

The week of my mom's surgery was one of the hardest in my life. To wait for five hours was torture. To see her so weak and in so much pain tore me up inside. My dad drove up to see her right after her surgery, but he had to go back to work while I stayed behind. I was not allowed to be with her all day, so I stayed alone in my motel most of the time. The morning of my birthday I had breakfast by myself at the motel diner; it was the saddest, loneliest birthday, or any day, of my life. I waited to see my mom and spend a few hours with her before returning to my motel room. After a few days I was able to take my mom home; that was a two-hour trip, but she made it through the drive. I got her special needs equipment, bought groceries, and cooked for her. My dad was unable to take time off to care for her. I did everything I could before I left. I hated to leave her but swore I would be back very soon.

My mom had waited so long to get the necessary treatment in Canada, only to undergo a horrendous surgery that did not help her condition. She was in pain immediately afterward and to this day does not know why her pain continues. It kills me to helplessly watch her suffer. Hef has access to the best medical care possible, but he never offered to help. I thought about writing Oprah a letter, like many people do on behalf of their mothers, so that she could help my mom figure out where the pain is coming from, and how to help her since the doctors in Canada are clueless and helpless to help her. So while my mom could not move out of bed, I was obliged to rush back to the Mansion so that there were enough blondes around to make Hef look good.

I got back to the Mansion the night before the party. Needless to say, I wasn't in a celebratory mood. I didn't even bother to buy a new dress or do anything special. I put on a white dress that was already in my closet and did my own hair and makeup. Now, looking back, the party was soothing. I had been so sad and scared the previous few days that it was nice to release that tension, even temporarily. The show was hosted by the funny, foul-mouthed Jenny McCarthy. There was a cool performances by Blu Cantrell, and Kelly Osbourne performed a song by Cindy Lauper. Sharon Osbourne had been so sweet to us (she came to interview us for her show a few months later), that Hef felt bad that Kelly's performance did not make it onto the air in the television special. I didn't understand it; I thought she was great. Some of the other celebrities in attendance included Pamela Anderson, Anna Nicole Smith, and Paris and Nicky Hilton. Barbi Benton, Hef's former longtime love, was also there. Hef stepped away for a while for a one-on-one conversation with Barbi. I thought it was charming that the two famous lovers were reunited, and I thought Barbi still looked cute. I ran into her and Gloria Allred as I was walking around the party and introduced myself. I told her that Hef speaks fondly of her. "See, I told you," remarked Gloria Allred. "Oh no, he doesn't," replied Barbi with a girlish coyness. I was so tempted to engage Miss Allred in a legal conversation, but I resisted. She gave me her card, and at times I have been tempted to contact her, but I don't know what to say. I wondered if she would be disappointed in me wasting my education or if she would understand that after years of schooling, I was trying something new.

Holly was not amused. She threw a jealous fit that Hef and Barbi had that intimate moment. She harped on it for a couple of days and made Hef feel bad about it. She couldn't believe he did that. She disappeared from the party for a while and then cried about it the next day. On one of the episodes of *The Girls Next Door* when Barbi comes to visit, Holly's dislike is clearly visible and she tries to belittle Barbi by dismissing her as too old for Hef. Although I felt that Barbi was a little condescending toward the girls, I think Holly's attitude toward her was unfriendly from the very beginning. I didn't understand it. I thought that Hef's connection with Barbi was very special, and that it was wonderful that she could be there to celebrate the fiftieth anniversary of *Playboy* with him. When I heard about Holly's reaction I thought it was ridiculous. She constantly made Hef feel guilty about his ex-Girlfriends; she would pout, cry, and then go sleep in the game house to punish him for her own feelings of inadequacy.

I thought she was also hostile to Kimberly Hefner. Whenever Kimberly came to greet Hef at parties or other events, Holly acted disrespectfully. I think she was jealous that the kids were an eternal connection between Hef and Kimberly. She constantly made negative remarks about the concept of marriage and family; I remember when we heard that one of Hef's ex-Girlfriends and a Playmate had a baby and got engaged, Holly thought it was lame. I thought it was comical that she found going out to clubs twice a week and having to share her boyfriend with many women so much more meaningful. That is why when I heard the rumor this year that Hef was considering having a baby with Holly, I was skeptical. Since she cannot marry him—as he is still married to Kimberly—I think she figures the only other way to guarantee getting her hands on the inheritance is a baby. Holly must know a child by Hef would provide her with money and power, and she would finally feel up to par with Kim. The sad thing is that Holly seemed to me barely able to take care of her dogs, with the assistance of several staff. I never saw Holly demonstrate any type of maternal instinct or love. I heard her speak with disdain about family; she never once went to visit her parents while I lived at the Mansion. She also announced that she had no friends to visit at home or anywhere else, and no one ever visited her. I think Holly will make a terrific trophy wife for someone, but I cannot imagine her as a mother.

Last but not least on the anniversary agenda was New York City. I love New York, and I was so excited to hear Playboy was throwing a big party there. Not only do I love the city, but it was also wonderful to get out of the house. It may be one of the most famous Mansions in the world, but when you live there day in and day out, it is still a house and you can feel cooped up in it. Sure, it was nice when we had a party and people came over, but that did not happen often enough. So off we went on our private plane. We stayed at The Pierre. As per usual, drama ensued with the room assignment. Emma and I snatched our own room, Holly slept with Hef, and Susan was stuck in a room with Bridget and Candy, who stayed in the other bedroom in Hef's suite. I stayed out of it as was my habit; no one was going to ruin my trip to one of my very favorite cities.

The first night we went to see *The Boy from Oz*, starring the talented Hugh Jackman, who was absolutely wonderful in it (the tight pants helped too!). We even got to meet him in his dressing room after the show, right out of the shower, and he was very friendly and handsome. At the end of the show, he was speaking about AIDS and the importance of contributing to the search for a cure, when he noticed Hef sitting in the audience and, right then and there, asked if Hef was willing to donate anything. Hef told him about the anniversary party, and agreed to donate a pair of tickets to be auctioned off with the proceeds going to the AIDS charity. After the show we went to Bungalow 8 for cocktails. We didn't stay out long since the big party was the next night.

By the time Emma, Susan, and I woke up the next day, everyone was gone. We found out that Hef went to ring the bell at the Stock Exchange; of course no one had mentioned it to us. When we asked why the three of us weren't informed, he said the other girls suggested we would not be interested. *Oh really?* I thought. *How convenient.* It was one thing after another, any opportunity to leave us out. We got our own limo and our own security guards—hot New York City police officers—and we hit the town. A little shopping at one of my fave stores, Henri Bendel (when we shopped for anything other than a dress for specific, formal events, we always spent our own money), followed by a visit to TRL, and last a stop at an authentic pizzeria. We came back to get ready for the main event, where we were met by a couple of makeup artists we had met at MAC the night before, who were fabulously talented and fun. Then off to the party!

The party took place at the New York State Armory, which is a huge venue. The décor was amazing. Some of the attendees included Donald Trump and his then girlfriend, and now wife, Melania Knauss, Dr. Ruth, Lara Flynn Boyle, our buddy Ja Rule, party girl Bai Ling, Jason Lewis and Evan Handler from *Sex and the City*, Dale Earnhardt Jr., and Gina Gershon. At the climax of the party, Ashanti came out of a big cake and began singing, serenading Hef from afar, and she was followed out of the cake by Pamela Anderson—the ultimate Playmate! She and the talented photographer David LaChapelle came to sit at our table for quite some time. Pamela was sitting next to me drinking champagne, hers and then mine. I asked her why she was wearing sunglasses when it was so damn dark in the place; turns out she had unsightly pink eye. She was flirting with Hef and telling him everything he wanted to hear—*ahh*, I thought, *so that is how she gets all the hot men!* That and the boobs, of course. She coyly asked Hef why they never see each other and why he never invites her over. He said she could come over anytime. She teased him that she is single now. She told me we were lucky; I told her she was the lucky one. She has dated some of the hottest men around, including one of my favorites, Kid Rock. "No, Hef is the ultimate rock star," she replied. I laughed, thinking, *Girrrl, you can have him, let's trade!* Then she borrowed my lip gloss and took off. I guess Hef wasn't as irresistible as she claimed after all.

And just like that, all of the anniversary parties came to an end. What were we going to do to make time go faster? We were bored with the Mansion routine, and having something, anything, to look forward to kept life exciting. We desperately wanted to go to the Cannes Film Festival. Just the opportunity to travel to Europe with Hef would be fantastic. But it was too expensive, and we didn't go. We were so tired, we kept asking Hef for a vacation. We were worn out from going out so much, from the constant drinking, staying out late and always wearing so much makeup. We asked Hef if he could take us to Hawaii. We told him he could play backgammon on the beach and we would just swim and relax. At night we could have dinner and hang out. He always seemed to brush it off. And whenever there was any problems with the girls, he would say, "See? How can we go on a vacation together when there is no harmony in the group." Well, maybe if we got a break, a chance to unwind and get away from the usual surroundings, everyone would be in a better mood. Maybe we could even bond while we were away. But it was futile, he wouldn't take us, he wouldn't let us go on our own. We were prisoners.

I know some people reading this ask why we, living a life of partying, with butlers and maids and all the luxuries, would need a vacation. The answer is complicated. We just felt trapped most of the time, the curfew was taking its toll, as was the life of constant tension among the girls, and always living life on someone else's terms. Yes, we chose this life, and at the beginning it was different. But it seems like life at the Mansion had gone through phases, especially for me: curiosity and intimidation, then fun and excitement, and finally boredom and fatigue.

When all the parties were over, Hef kept saying that the fun would continue with the fifty-city tour—fifty *Playboy* parties in fifty different cities in honor of the anniversary—and that we could go to some of those cities. He knew that we were getting restless; we had been there for almost two years. And he was lucky that we all stayed with him for the fiftieth anniversary instead of leaving him with only two girls. When the whole fiftieth anniversary year began, he said there would be so much publicity and girls would see how much fun we were having, that new girls would be knocking down the Mansion gates to join our party. "Shhh," we would say to each other all the time, "I think I just heard a girl knocking. . . ." We listened closely, but there was no one at the door.

19 ⁘ Bunny Trap

★

"A mind not to be chang'd by place or time.
The mind is its own place, and in itself
Can make a heaven of hell, a hell of heaven."

—Paradise Lost, Book I, Line 253

One day I woke up and had an epiphany: I was unhappy. I hadn't slept all night; they had rented out the pool to some alcohol company the night before and the rowdy guests did not leave until 2 a.m. For the next three hours, they cleaned up and threw the tables and chairs onto a truck. When I finally fell asleep at 6 a.m., the workers gathered under my window to chat. "Can you keep it down please?" I muttered, sticking my head out the window.

At 10 a.m., the office staff was in and the daily noise began. Holly apparently slept well because she came to Mary's office, her dog Harlow having barked all the way down the hall. I gave up. I woke up and ordered my usual breakfast, and by the time I got it, my over-greased English muffin was hard and as tasty as cardboard. The phone rang. "Dude, I am going to kick that stupid dog when I see it!" Emma said. Apparently Harlow woke up everyone who was sleeping. "Emma, don't even get me started. I need to have a pot of coffee before I can even begin to tell you how I feel right now." And that is when it came to me: What the hell was I doing? I visualized my apartment; it was no Mansion, but it was five times bigger than my room. It was cleaner, quieter, had nice furniture, and I could actually make my own breakfast. It was time to stop complaining like a spoiled brat and start living my own life once again. This setup was still perfect for people who were lazy and satisfied living off the fame of another, but that was not me, it never had been. I had a ton of fun and fantastic experiences, but that seemed to be over. It was time to move on and let someone new move in and enjoy the temporary bliss of the Playboy Mansion.

I felt exhausted. I was tired of the clubs, not just going out twice a week, but to the same places all the time being bound to our separated area. The late nights and drinking and stress made me feel like I aged twice as fast. I was also tired of living in a house with so many people around. No privacy ever, never just a chill day when you don't want to see anyone. I was also sick of getting sick. With so many different people handling your food before you got it, it was like a germ paradise, and my tired immune system was susceptible. I also wanted to do my own laundry. I was tired of getting things washed out, discolored or shrunk and stained—so many clothes ruined and missing. Every other day I got some other girl's laundry or random pairs of underwear, and that meant other people got mine. I was also sick of having a dead battery in my car every week from valets leaving something on, or worse, my car getting dents and scratches all the time by the workers. It was a big hassle to get the car fixed and have Playboy pay for it. I never thought I would get tired of living in a Mansion. More than anything, I got tired of the company I was keeping. The tension among the girls was ridiculous. We could not do anything without some drama ensuing.

I was at the Mansion by choice, and I was also free to leave whenever I chose. But like a captive who grows to care for the captor, I was not ready to leave all at once. The process would be gradual. Emma and I always talked about leaving the Mansion together, and although she and Susan complained daily and said they were leaving, I knew they had no intention of walking out on the best gig they ever had. I had to think of myself. I began saving money.

I decided that I would leave in May. I would sign up for the July Bar exam and hence force myself to leave so that I could study for it. In the meantime, because I knew I was leaving, my attitude changed. What was once tolerable became unbearable: the cattiness, the tensions, the dimwitted conversations.

We arrived at a point where the air itself was filled with animosity. It could not be ignored or wished away. I remember the time we had to do a photo shoot for the cover of YRB (*Yellow Rat Bastard*) magazine. It was tense from the beginning. The photographer told Bridget and Holly to sit on either side of Hef à la bookends because they were wearing the same color outfits (preplanning on their part); Emma then threw a fit about it—feeling she had no other choice. So she planted herself right smack in the middle on the floor in front of Hef. I could not have cared less about the whole issue, so I just sat back. The photographer then wanted to take individual photos of us outside. Hef went back to the office, and we went out onto the back lawn, tense as could be.

"Who is the leader of this clan?" the photographer asked.

"I am," Emma said testily.

"*Yeah*, right," was Holly's quick response.

Oh God, I thought to myself, *here we go*. I could not believe that Emma wanted to create a fight out of this simple event. The photographer and the crew instantly picked up on the vibe.

"So you all hate each other?" They could tell the group was divided.

"Yes, they are the nerd herd," was the mature response from Susan, Emma, and I.

"And what are you guys?"

Hmm. We hadn't thought about it.

"The cool group?" was our lame answer.

I couldn't believe things had deteriorated to this degree. We then had to undergo the torture of watching each other do individual photos. Holly and Bridget were great at keeping their hatred and fury inside. They did not say one word to each other or anyone else, they just did what they had to and left.

But I know as soon as they entered Holly's vanity area, in Hef's bedroom, they blew up. I knew Emma had gone too far. We already had so much tension; it really wasn't necessary to add to it. It was like two dogs trying to mark their territory. I knew Emma would lose.

In January 2004, Hef announced that we would be going to the Golden Globes as we did every year. We also found out that for the first time ever, there would be no clothing allowance. We were told that Holly complained to Hef that some girls—i.e. Emma—were not spending all their money on the dresses anyway. Apparently his secretary also urged him to give us less; she was always so nosy about what we wore, but I thought she was just curious. The other girls suggested that she was just checking to see if we had spent all of the money we were supposed to, and that is why she always asked where we got everything. I thought it was ridiculous—could Hef really be that gullible and easily manipulated by his secretaries and Holly? Apparently so. Once again, Emma and I went to reason with him; we could not wear things we already had because we had been photographed in everything, and it was embarrassing. This was a formal event, and we didn't have gowns lying around in our closets. But he would not budge. He said he would give us money for the Grammys that were coming up in a couple of weeks. We gave up. We knew something was different. In the meantime, I bought a dress for a couple hundred dollars, and some of the other girls bought dresses that they later returned. I guess desperate times call for desperate measures.

Then came the 2004 Grammy Awards. Hef usually gave us $2,000 because we had two events to go to—the MusiCares formal dinner gala and the actual Grammy Awards. That year, he gave us only $1,000 each. We couldn't believe it, especially since he didn't give us any money for the Golden Globes. A thousand dollars, truthfully, was not enough for us to dress the way he wanted us to dress for these two fancy events and for being photographed on the red carpet. Something was wrong. This was not Hef; this was the influence of other people. I wanted to go and tell Holly that the sooner we saved any leftover money for ourselves, the sooner we would go, so she was in fact working against herself by talking him out of giving us clothing money. We knew that this might be the last Grammys we would attend—none of us had any musical talent, so the only way we would be going again in the future was on the arm of some rock star—so we decided to make the most of it.

We wanted to wear something fun and cool, very representative of the Grammys. Susan wanted us all to wear the same thing since Hef likes the whole idea of twins or triplets, and if it appealed to him, then Holly and Bridget would be upset—icing on the cake. It was up to me to create the outfits, and I found this dress—actually it was a top—in three different colors. I envisioned them with over-the-knee glitter boots for the extra bling. Emma wore a yellow dress with gold boots, Susan wore a red dress with red boots, and I wore a pink dress with pink boots. It worked. On the red carpet, everyone was focused on us and our outfits.

"Who are you girls wearing? You look hot!" asked the amused reporters.

"Izabella Creations," Emma kept answering, as the eager reporters scribbled it down.

I laughed. Pictures of us showed up at stores around L.A. with knock-offs of the dress/top we wore. When photographers took photos, it was of the three of us and Hef; when they asked the names of the girls they didn't go any further than inquiring about our names. We knew the other girls were mad, and we loved it. You wanna play games? We can play! The show that year was really good; Beyonce was amazing, and I loved the White Stripes. After the show, as we were walking out toward our limo, I noticed Scott Stapp standing there. I had to say something. "Hey Scott, my name is Izabella, I live at the Playboy Mansion. . . . I am the one you talked to for six hours that time. Did you ever end up making it to the party?" I asked, even though I knew he did.

"Oh yeah, I did but it was really late. Can I get your number?"

I wanted to give it to him again, but I had to run; Hef was way ahead of me.

"I'm sorry, I gotta go."

"Fine, whatever," was his cool response.

Two minutes after we got into the limo and started driving, someone rear-ended us. It wasn't a hard hit, but it jolted us and the pause made us lose our party streak. We ended up only going to one of the after-parties—despite having planned on attending three—for about fifteen minutes, and then going home. It was so pathetic, but we knew we were not going to have fun with Hef anyways, so why bother going to all those places? It was the great irony of the situation for us; we were invited to all these fabulous parties and events, but we could not go, and even if we could, we could not enjoy ourselves. This routine was getting really old.

And like always, as soon as we were in the limo heading home, Hef would reflect on what a great night it was, and Holly and Bridget would obligingly "ooh" and "ahh" while the rest of us grieved for the fun that was not to be had. His tone wasn't genuine. It was like he was asking for praise and thanks for taking us there, and at the same time trying to convince himself that he was living the life of a real Hollywood player. Of course we were grateful, but at the same time our attitude was, "Why lead the horse to water if you aren't going to let him drink?" But that was not Hef's plan; he just wanted to be seen bringing the prettiest horses and then taking them right back to the stable, while at the same receiving their gratitude for allowing them to see the water. And if we weren't grateful enough, he would be sure to tell us how he did it only for us and how much money he spent to get us there.

I remember I was driving somewhere with Emma and Susan when they began talking about leaving the Mansion and finding another sugar daddy. Susan kept harping on the fact that Donald Trump gave her a compliment at the *Playboy* fiftieth anniversary party, and now she and Emma wanted to take full advantage of it. Emma got the phone number for his office and wanted Susan to call him. I was in awe. They called and left a message with his secretary. Their grand plan was that since he gave Susan a compliment, he must have been interested, so when he called back Susan would get together with him, but would be with him only if he would take care of Emma as well. I could not believe what I was hearing!

"He has a girlfriend, Melania Knauss, who he has been with for years, just in case you girls did not notice!" I pointed out.

"So?" they chimed in.

I could not believe how silly they were. More than anything I longed to be independent and try to build my own life. I could not believe they were desperate to go into the arms of another man who would take care of them *again*, versus taking care of themselves. I remember telling them, at that moment, that I never met such characters, and one day I would have to write about them. Then they began talking about other men who were like Hef, men who were wealthy and wanted to copy his lifestyle. Despite what Hef would like to believe, he is not the only playboy around. Hef wannabes who had as much if not more money than him had emerged, and offered more benefits to the girls, more money and more freedom. The only thing they did not have was their own magazine and a legend.

Although we had always reassured Holly that no one wanted her position as number one Girlfriend, I slowly realized that perhaps Emma and Susan thought otherwise. Although Emma didn't want to do any of the work involved in having that position, she would have loved for Susan to take Holly's place, and Susan would surely go along with it. I couldn't believe they were even thinking in those terms. Maybe Holly knew that, and that was why there was so much animosity between her and Emma? All I knew was that I just wanted to stay out of it and make the last few months as pleasant, or as painless, as could be.

Susan was worried about leaving the Mansion because she did not have enough money saved up at the time, and Hef never asked if you had any money when he kicked you out or you were leaving by choice. He did not ask a girl if she had enough money to make a deposit on an apartment, if she was going to be okay, or if she needed money to get started. Even the maids got severance pay when they got laid off. Hef's Girlfriends get nothing. When you told him you were leaving or if he told you that you should leave, you were out of his sight and out of his concern.

I was disappointed that Emma and Susan were looking for another sugar daddy instead of looking to themselves to build their own lives. But they always reminded me that they had no qualifications and no education; Susan worked at a department store, and what was Emma going to do? A sugar daddy was actually much better than some of the other options they discussed. I understood them, but it made me sad to recognize that we had nothing in common past our shared experience of life at the Mansion. I realized that the end of my stay at the Mansion would most likely equal the end of my friendship with the girls.

20 ⁚ Fear and Loathing in Holmby Hills

"Our discontent begins by finding false villains whom we can accuse of deceiving us. Next we find false heroes whom we expect to liberate us. The hardest, most discomforting discovery is that each of us must emancipate himself."
—*Daniel J. Boorstin*

It is amazing how you can come to despise the things you once thought so luxurious and glamorous. When I first moved into the Mansion, I felt like a princess; after two years, I felt like the princess that was locked up in the tower and yearned to escape. I recall that when I first moved in, I thought Tammy was crazy for staying at the Mansion for *two* years, how could she not want her own life? Now I found myself approaching the two-year anniversary. I had to leave, for so many reasons. What toll did this silly hedonistic life ultimately have on the participants? I don't know about long-term damage, but in the short run it made me very tired. At the most basic level, I grew tired of my surroundings. My room was small and claustrophobic. The furniture in it was old and damaged. I love antiques, but there was nothing to love about this setup. And it wasn't just my room—the glamorous veneer of the Playboy Mansion started to peel off and I saw a house that was old and grimy. The dirty hallway carpet and the curtains that smelled like dog-piss. I felt stifled in that house. Yes, the grounds are stunning, but there is only so much time you can spend outside.

The tension and the antipathy among the girls became insufferable. At the end of December 2004, Candy departed, leaving the group sharply divided—Holly and Bridget on one side, and Emma, Susan, and me on the other. There was no buffer. There was no one else to pick on, talk about, or mutually dislike. The battle lines had been drawn, and it was just a matter of time before something big occurred. At the beginning of the year I gave myself until the two-year mark, May 2004, to leave the Mansion. The last few months were just a matter of getting by, so I stayed neutral. While the hatred between Holly and Emma grew, I stayed out of it. I maintained a good relationship with Holly and stayed friends with Emma and Susan. I avoided Bridget because we had nothing to talk about. And then a new girl entered the group. Her name was Kendra, and she was one of the naked painted girls at Hef's birthday party in April 2004. Her job was to hand out Jell-O shots to all the guests, but Kendra stood firmly in front of our table all night to be sure that Hef saw her. He did. He invited her out with us, and strangely enough, Holly and Bridget took her under their wing. We understood what they were up to, but we were too disinterested to do anything about it. We knew Kendra was really just like us; I saw her doing her booty dance at the clubs, looking around for boys, and flirting with the security guys. I knew she wanted to be a Girlfriend and it was in her interest to befriend Holly and Bridget, but I realized the limits of that friendship. I knew as soon as we were gone, they would turn against her because she was younger, more attractive, and had an outgoing personality. I couldn't figure out why Kendra, at eighteen, would want to live at the Mansion. I was twenty-six years old when I moved in, I had several boyfriends, and I had accomplished all of my educational goals before that. And all of the other girls, except Holly, were older than me. But the butlers told us that Kendra was a stripper from San Diego, and thought that moving into the Mansion was the best thing she could do in her life to that point. I was also a little disappointed in Hef; I thought dating an eighteen-year-old was a bit much, even for him.

The situation was getting progressively worse. We would hear rumors, from the butlers, from Playmates and other Mansion guests, about all of these plans Holly and Bridget were concocting. For example, to make us look bad in Hef's eyes, they decided to suggest going to movies that they knew we would not be interested in going to. So when Hef planned the movie night, we would decline, and they would have a chance to point out to him that we did not want to spend time with him. At this point, not one of the three of us was having sex with Hef. It was pointed out to him that he didn't really need us to have a good time because we were not contributing anything. Other random rumors began appearing, such as the one that I had a boyfriend and he was in a band. I almost fell over with laughter when I heard that one. I had worked with Henry two years before at Playboy, maybe for two months total. I had not spoken to the guy in months. Now for some reason, two years later, there was another outbreak of rumors that I had this rocker boyfriend. They also planned on following me and catching me in the act. The act of what, I don't know, but I welcomed them to try. They were only helping me keep the real identity of the closest thing I had to a boyfriend—Justin—hidden. I wasn't afraid of getting caught, nor did I feel attacked. I just could not continue living in the same house as these unbearable people whose main goal in life was to plot against me and my friends. It made me question who I was and why I was allowing myself to be surrounded by such mean-spirited people.

The most important and powerful reason to leave was personal. After all those years in school, I could not help but wonder if I wasted my youth with my nose in the books, while people were having the time of their lives. My moving into the Mansion was totally out of character for me, but I wanted to make up for lost time, to drink life up. Living at the Mansion allowed me to catch up and even exceed everyone else. You could say I was "drunk with life." In a total reversal, I was now wondering whether I was wasting my late twenties living a superficial life without any meaning. I could not help but feel that I was a character in Hef's Bunnyland. We were all riding his coattails. I had too much pride to continue doing that.

I began focusing on my life and spent my free time preparing to leave the Mansion. I saved any money leftover from my allowance and looked into buying a condo. I found a place in my beloved Malibu and made an offer on a condo. I was so excited, the future looked bright, and I could not wait to live my life. At the same time, Emma had found a condo in Hollywood and purchased it. She spent her time decorating it and planned for Susan to move in with her, which was mutually beneficial since Susan would have a place to go and Emma had someone to help her pay the mortgage. Holly and Bridget had no idea that we were ready and able to leave the Mansion. We had great places to live and lives waiting for us; all of their plans and schemes were nothing but entertainment to us at that point.

Life at the Playboy Mansion wasn't all parties, money, and clothes. When the fog of drinking and partying cleared, the overwhelming tension among the girls became excruciating. Like I said before, it was comparable to the reality show *Survivor*; the main Girlfriend and her sidekick were always plotting to have us voted off. We knew it, and we went on having as much fun as we could and throwing it in their faces. On *Survivor* the contestants swallow their pride, bear the pain, and fight through the day, knowing that they can win a million dollars and it will change their life. What was I playing for? I got the car, I got the fake breasts, but there wasn't a million dollars at the end of the struggle, so why continue to struggle? I decided it was time to vote myself off. The last few months at the Mansion were just going through the motions. In retrospect I wish I would have enjoyed it more, but I didn't. I was in a rush, in a rush to save money and live freely. It was a waiting game—waiting to leave, waiting for an excuse to make a graceful exit. An opportunity presented itself sooner than I expected.

In light of the fact that I was going to leave soon, and that Emma and Susan had to prepare for this possibility as well, we decided to get some last-minute benefits. Susan asked for eye surgery for her birthday—well before her birthday. Emma and I went to talk to Hef about possibly getting new cars. Emma's car constantly had problems, so she was hoping to trade it in. I did not want a new car; I thought I could ask him for a couple thousand dollars to pay on the car to lessen my monthly payments. We asked him to think about it. A few days later, Emma and I spoke about it in the morning and wondered if he made a decision. She decided to call him in his bedroom to find out. A minute later, she called me back; I knew it was her, but she was silent at first. Then she said, "He asked me to leave." I was incredulous. My mind raced—he has no reason to kick her out, she didn't do anything. "He said, 'I can't believe you are asking me for a car, I think it's time for you to leave.'" I was shocked. I immediately realized that this had been brewing for quite some time. I'm certain it was the result of systematic bad-mouthing of Emma to Hef by others.

I grabbed my purse and left. I really did not want to run into Hef; I needed time to think. I did not know what to expect. Was he going to let me go as well? Was this the right time to tell him that I was going to move out? When I got home a few hours later, Hef came into my room to talk. He informed me that he had asked Emma to leave, and he wanted me to think about what I wanted to do and was hoping we could work things out. I didn't hesitate. I took the opportunity to tell him that I thought it was time for me to go as well. He was shocked; I think he was hoping that I would stay and give it a shot considering Susan was still there. I told him I wanted to take the Bar exam in the summer and that I really couldn't study while I was still living there. He said, "But you don't have a place to live. Where are you going to go?" I told him I had just gotten a place, which was true. He wasn't expecting me to be prepared. I told him I was not in a hurry, but I thought it was time for me to move on. I admired Hef for living out his fantasies, and the fantasies of others. He is an example of not accepting the life you are handed, but holding onto the dreams of your childhood and pursuing them.

I told him I had dreams of my own that I wanted to pursue, and I reminded him that when he was my age, he began *Playboy* magazine. I needed to go figure out who I was and my calling in life. I told him I would talk to Susan and that we would both wait and see how it went, but I knew this was the end for us; it was time to move on. Hef did not realize that letting Emma go that morning would start a domino effect and cost him two more Girlfriends. In recent interviews, Hef said he chose to downsize his group of Girlfriends. But that was not the case entirely; I had made my own decision to leave.

It was all happening so fast. And it could not have happened at a worse time. On Monday, he asked Emma to leave. Tuesday was awkward in the house, so I spent all day running errands. Wednesday was a club night, and I knew it might be the last time I ever went out with Hef. Thursday I had to pack because Friday morning I was flying out to Toronto for one of my best friends' weddings. I did not know what would happen when I returned.

I was actually looking forward to going out that Wednesday night. I wanted to show Hef that even though I was going to leave soon, I still cared about him. Inside I knew that this might be the last time, or one of the last few, so I wanted us to have a great time. I was also hoping that now that Holly and Bridget knew I would be leaving, we could all just let our guards down and have some fun. There wouldn't be any more struggle. I couldn't have been more wrong.

We all met downstairs as per usual. Emma was told she was not invited to come out, although she was still at the Mansion packing her stuff. When we got into the limo, Susan told me to sit beside Hef one last time, and I thought I would do it for old times' sake. It was nice to sit beside him and chat with him, knowing that it would most likely never happen again. My reasons for sitting next to him were innocent. I didn't even think about it; for me, all of that petty stuff was over. When we got to the club, we ordered our drinks and some of the girls got up to dance. Bridget sat there alone, looking miserable, and began crying. I asked another girl what was wrong with Bridget, and she told me that Bridget was crying because I sat beside Hef in the limo. Apparently Bridget claimed I did it on purpose to hurt her feelings. I was furious. I could not believe that this girl was taking something that I did for sentimental reasons and turning it around to make something ugly out of it. I felt sorry for her. I was *leaving*, I was no longer a threat to her, and she was still so insecure that she had to take that last opportunity to create problems. Normally I would have ignored her. However, I had nothing to lose at this point and could not resist the opportunity to be myself. I went up to her.

"Are you really crying because I sat next to Hef in the limo?" I asked. "That is really pathetic. I'm leaving. You can sit next to him for the rest of your sorry life. This isn't about you. You really need to take your medication." I suddenly remembered that she used to take meds.

All she could say in reply was, "I don't take any medication."

"That's the problem. You should start taking your meds again, you psycho bitch."

I walked away and saw her immediately run to Hef to complain. I saw his face fill with anger and his eyes found me across the dance floor.

He came over to Susan and me, and grabbed our arms and started shaking us.

"I have had enough of this shit!"

I couldn't control my emotions. There was too much built up. I started crying. "You always choose their side!"

"Oh yeah, I am so unfair," he yelled.

"You *are* unfair! I am glad you realize it!" It felt so good to call him on it.

"You are both going home right now," he said sternly and motioned for the security.

"*You* can go Hef, we are staying!" I yelled. There was no stopping me now.

I realized what a scene that made. People were staring, but I couldn't have cared less. I ran off to the bathroom to compose myself. I came out to find Susan sitting at the table, bawling, her face buried in her hands and Hef down on his knees trying to talk to her. I grabbed her and we walked off. She said that he told her she doesn't have to be involved in this fight, that it was my fault for fighting with Bridget. I couldn't believe he was trying to turn us against each other again. He had realized he lost me and I think he was trying to save Susan. I hated him at that moment. I hated him for being so easily blinded and manipulated. I hated him for being weak. I looked over and saw Bridget, who was so devastated and crying two minutes ago, now all smiles, dancing—or flopping her body around, as I called it. At that point I realized the bitch did it on purpose. I did not think she was upset; she just wanted to make sure that I kept my word and left the Mansion by making the situation irreparable. *How could Hef not see the manipulation, the set-up?* I wondered.

Susan and I weren't standing there for one minute before guys approached us offering us drinks. We accepted, determined to get drunk and have fun. Five minutes after we had walked away from him, Hef and the other girls left. Susan and I stayed at the club for another hour, flirting and drinking. As we walked out of the club, *Celebrities Uncensored* and other paparazzi cameras were in our face. Drunk and free, Susan and I didn't hold back. "We got in trouble with Hef. We broke up! We're free! Now we have to take a cab home to the Mansion." Then we jumped into the first available cab and told the cabdriver to take us to the Playboy Mansion. We called Emma on the way to fill her in. We screamed and ranted, laughing about how much fun they must be having in the bedroom right now and how we'd bet Hef couldn't get it up. The cabdriver must have had a blast. As soon as we pulled up the driveway and got out, Mark, Hef's main security man, was there to pay for it, which was great because we had no money with us. We ran to Emma's room to vent. I think she was happy that all this happened because now she didn't have to leave on her own. I knew it would have hurt her a lot to walk out of there and to have her two best friends stay behind. Now we were all going to leave together like we always talked about.

I was high on adrenaline, so I went back to my room and started to pack. It was three o'clock in the morning, but I kept at it. Box after box went into my truck. I meant to fill it up, drive to my apartment, unload, and come back to do it all over again until every single item was out of there. I was not going to stay in this disgusting house of hypocrisy and lies. Finally at 8 a.m.,

I collapsed from exhaustion. I woke up two hours later to find the office workers already aware of what happened and the house buzzing with people. It was the annual PMOY luncheon, the formal brunch where the new PMOY is announced and receives her prizes.

I continued packing until late in the evening. All that was left in my Mansion bedroom were some random things in the closet. I would have moved those, but it was already night time and I still had to pack for the wedding. I finally got to bed at four in the morning only to wake up three hours later and get on the plane. That was a disastrous weekend. I was beyond exhausted at Niki and Angelo's wedding—I actually had to walk away from the altar during the ceremony because I almost fainted. I was physically and emotionally beat up and I couldn't even enjoy her wedding properly.

Three days later, I was back in L.A. When I drove to the Mansion to pick up the rest of my things, I found them already packed for me. The butlers told me that they had been asked to pack all of my stuff. I ran into Hef in the hallway as I was leaving.

"I am sorry it all happened like this. You are still welcome to come to all the parties and everything," was all he said. I was glad he said that, but I don't know if I would even want to come to the parties. He hurt my feelings, and I was disappointed in him. Would I want to run into Bridget? Plus, if you have been to a couple of parties at the Mansion, you have been to them all. We exchanged niceties, and I left. As I struggled to find a spot for a fish bowl (with the water and fish in it) in my truck, I saw Hef watching me out a window. I smiled, and he smiled back. I know he is a sentimental person, and I know he was feeling a sense of loss and sadness at that moment. I was too; after all, we had been a part of each other's lives for two and a half years. I waved to him, and he walked away as I drove off.

That was the last time I really saw Hef.

21: Post-Bunnydom

"I'm not afraid of storms, for I'm learning to sail my ship."

— *Louisa May Alcott*

The first year after I moved out of the Mansion was like living in the twilight zone. The world seemed a strange place, and I was even stranger to myself. I felt like I needed to be deprogrammed. There's a little bit of the Stockholm syndrome in being isolated from everyone and everything in your life, and then you start to identify with your captor. Pretty soon, you become the Bunny.

It was weird not to have a curfew. I remember driving my car after 9 p.m. for the first time in years. The world looked different. I kept having a feeling like I was going to get in trouble from someone. It was strange to be able to do whatever I wanted and go wherever I wanted again. But I had become so unaccustomed to having my own social life, particularly at night, that I really didn't know what to do. Emma's apartment was right in the middle of Hollywood, and she and Susan did not waste anytime getting into the Hollywood party scene. On one of their nights out, they ran into a guy who had dated Holly; he told them Holly had been after Hef for a long time. She had researched everything about him to appeal to him once she was able to get close enough to him and then set out to become one of the Girlfriends. It made a lot of sense, since she claimed to have studied psychology just like he did, and claimed that her favorite food and movies were the same as his, and all of this other stuff that we thought was more than a coincidence.

I partied with Emma and Susan for a couple of months. Every time I did, I came home at six in the morning. Although I had a lot of fun, I could not keep up with that lifestyle. I really needed a break. I changed my phone number, settled into my place by the beach, and began getting used to life once again. I had this strong urge to nest. I spent my time decorating my apartment to perfection. I cleaned it every day—every room had to be spotless. I knew something was seriously wrong with me when I learned how to cook and actually liked it. It was so bizarre not to be able to order room service anymore. Every morning when I woke up, I had the urge to dial "0" and order my usual. But the last few months, I had missed doing things for myself and this was my opportunity. I became a total domestic. I didn't know what was happening to me. I guess for two years I felt like I didn't really have a home, a place of my own, and so when I finally did, I wanted to enjoy it, to savor every minute. I also wanted to prove to myself that I did not need to live in a Mansion with a staff of seventy to have a good life and be happy.

But nothing works in the extreme, and my newfound domesticity was soon not enough. I have learned that a balance is necessary; sometimes it's nice to stay in and cook dinner, watch a movie, and go to bed early; other times it's great to get dressed and go dancing, come home late, and drink too much coffee the next day. Being a true Libra, I am constantly seeking the perfect balance in my life. When the scales tip to one side too much, the equilibrium is lost, and I make impulsive decisions. Life in the spotlight—while fun, exciting, and exhilarating, proved very empty and lonely. For me, fame and fortune only mean something if you can share them and enjoy them with the people you love. Without my family close by, and without being able to spend time with my friends, it was a very empty lifestyle.

Although I felt like a fish out of water after I left the Mansion, I didn't miss it. I was sorry that things had ended the way they had because I always planned on leaving on good terms with everyone, particularly Hef. I was curious to see what kind of a relationship, if any, I would continue to have with Hef. I decided to test the waters.

I had inherited a goldfish named Bob. It had been given to Marston, Hef's teenage son, as a birthday present, but because his mom Kimberly has so many cats, it was not a good idea for Bob to stay at their house. Marston brought him over to the Mansion to find someone willing to take him. I have a soft spot for animals, so I took Bob in. The pugs didn't mind; in fact, Balbina used to lie on the bed and watch Bob swim. I bought him a new small tank and all of the necessary supplies. But Bob had grown fast, and by the time I moved out of the Mansion, he was way too big for the tank and I needed a new one. About two weeks after I moved out, I e-mailed Hef's assistant and explained that Bob needed a new tank, but since I needed my savings to start my new life, I could not afford to spend the money on a new fish tank. Could Hef help me out, since I adopted the fish as a favor to Marston. I knew it sounded hokey, but I wanted to see what Hef would do. I got a reply that Hef would not pay for the fish tank. Okay, so I knew where things stood between Hef and I; I e-mailed back saying I was disappointed that Hef has chosen to be on unfriendly terms with us. It wasn't about the fish tank. I had already bought one, before I received the reply e-mail. I bought Bob a huge mansion of a tank with all the luxuries he could require and charged it to my credit card. A week later a letter came from HMH (Hugh Marston Hefner):

"Dear Izabella,
Here is the check for the new fish bowl.
I don't have "unfriendly" feelings about you, Emma or Susan. The only concern I have in that regard is related to Holly and Bridget. I care about all of you, but I don't want to have to deal with any more of the negativity that prompted the break up. That isn't the way any of us should have to live.

Love, Hef."

I knew it. Of course it all had to do with Holly and Bridget. Now that we were gone, God only knew what they were saying about us. Hef wasn't allowed to be nice to us or invite us to the Mansion or the parties until they got over it; he wasn't going to jeopardize his sex life when he was only left with two Girlfriends. But he did send money for the fish tank; that meant he still cared at some hidden level.

After that, it was time for the Midsummer Night's Dream party. I did not receive an invitation, and neither did the other girls, despite the fact that the last thing Hef said to me was that I was still welcome at all of the parties. The first invitation to a party arrived for New Year's Eve. I spent Christmas in Canada and was unable to attend the party. And why would I go without a date? Since I was Hef's ex-Girlfriend, I thought it was time that I be allowed to bring a date, Justin, with me; I thought I had earned that right. I spoke to Emma, and she told me she had not been invited to any of the parties. She also told me that when her son went to play with Hef's kids (they had become friends during the time Emma lived at the Mansion), some of the girls there objected to having him hang out at the Mansion. Despite Emma's letters to Hef asking to be invited to parties, he refused to allow her to come to the Mansion. I thought it was really sad how Hef let those girls influence him. After all, we did live at that house for more than two years. We didn't do anything to Hef; there was no reason for him to act this way. It never ceases to amaze me what little backbone he has and how he can be such a successful businessman but cannot be a man when it comes to his own relationships.

In July 2005, I received an invitation for the MSND party. At that point it had been more than a year since I moved out. I had not been to the Mansion at all. I decided to go. I wanted to see what it would feel like to return. Everyone, the Mansion staff and Hef's friends as well as many Playmates, were very nice and happy to see me. I realized that I cared about a lot of those people and had missed seeing them around. All of the butlers said that it is so boring at the Mansion without Emma, Susan, and I, and that Hef and the three current Girlfriends hardly ever go out because Holly doesn't want to. *So that Hef doesn't meet new girls*, I thought. Hef's close friends told me that Hef does what he does to keep the harmony in the group and to keep the girls who remained with him happy. Holly was friendly to me, but Bridget was cold, which was expected. And then there was Hef. I said "hi" to him and he looked at me like he barely recognized me. I felt uncomfortable and awkward. It made me sad to think that that was all that was left of the time we spent together.

In an ironic twist, I ran into my friend Vivian, who had started this whole Playboy experience with me, at the party. Seeing her there reminded me of those first parties we came to, and seeing Hef and his then-Girlfriends, wondering what the hell that was all about. And here I was once again, having lived that life, looking at him like a stranger again, wondering the same thing. I didn't stay long. I realized that when you have been to all those parties so many times, they lose their luster. But I was glad that I went. It reminded me of all of the good times I had and all the people I still cared about and missed. But I also remembered the things that were not so great, so I was able to close that chapter of my life. In an ideal world, Hef and I would be friends; I could come to the Mansion for movie night or parties with my significant other and have a nice respectful relationship with Hef. I would hate for the two and a half years I spent living at the Mansion with him, and all the memories we share, to be ruined by jealousy and pettiness.

And then there was Justin. My moving into the Mansion turned out to be a good thing for our relationship; it allowed us to become friends. Without the pressures and expectations of a relationship, we had more fun together, and despite our independence we found that we really needed each other for comfort and support. We became best friends, and Justin always knew everything about my life at the Mansion as it was happening. He listened and advised me, and without him, I really don't think I would have lasted as long as I did in that lifestyle. He kept me grounded, and whenever I got out of control, he was my reality check.

We grew closer when I was at the Mansion than we ever had been before even though we were not in a relationship. I know a lot of people gave him a hard time about the fact that I lived at the Mansion. "Your chick left you for an old dude," they would tease. And he swallowed his pride and stood by me like the loyal friend that he is. Only a strong man could do that, a man who knows who he is and does not have to prove anything to anyone. Justin is a good man. He does things for the right reasons, not because he wants to impress people. He is honest, caring, and loyal.

A common lawyer joke alludes to the fact that there are no honest lawyers, but Justin is an honest and ethical lawyer. He gets it from his father, a hardworking, salty yet loving man who raised three boys alone after he and his wife separated. It wasn't easy; he sacrificed his own needs and pleasure for the well-being of his children. Despite the obstacles, he devoted himself to God and hard work, and managed to instill great values in his sons. I realized what a good man Justin was and how lucky I was to find such a man, especially in Los Angeles. Plus, Justin lets the pugs sleep on the bed and snore all night; if that is not love, then I don't know what is! He is not perfect by any means, but he is one of the best people I have ever met. I don't know what the future holds; there are no guarantees. Only time will tell if he is the love of my life.

Justin was right when he told me a couple of years before that I would fall off the law track. I was not the same person when I left the Mansion. I tried to take the Bar exam, but my heart and mind were not in it. The beautiful thing about an education is that no one can take it away from you and it never expires. And though right now my dream is to be an attorney on one of David Kelley's brilliant legal shows (can we resurrect my favorite show, *Ally McBeal?*) rather than a real-life attorney, it does not mean that one day I will not use those skills and knowledge. Despite my bunny-fication over the years, I am still a nerd deep down inside, one who loves to read and learn and have political discussions. In the meantime, the events of the previous two years kept circling in my head, begging to be organized. I began having this repeating dream about moving back into the Mansion, just to wake up sweating and confused. I didn't know what to do with my memories, with my thoughts or feelings. And so I began writing.

When I found out that Hef and his current three Girlfriends were doing a reality show called *The Girls Next Door*, I thought it was ironic. Emma and I were the ones always telling him that with all the drama going on at the house we should do a reality show. I even spoke to my boss at Playboy Entertainment about it a couple of years ago, trying to make the idea a reality. Hef was always hesitant because he thought it was going to be an inconvenience in his life, an intrusion upon his work, but I told him it should be about the lives of the Girlfriends, since we create all of the interesting turmoil anyway. I imagined the show to be something like the Playboy version of *The Real World:* people from various walks of life together under one roof, sharing a common boyfriend. You don't have to imagine all the jealousy, trash-talking, back-stabbing, and catty girl behavior going on. It would have been great. In fact, when I started writing my story, the subtitle was "The Greatest Reality Show Ever," and even though that was written at least a year before this show was born, I am going to change it, as I shall likely be accused of copying the idea.

I had a chance to watch a few of the shows' episodes and I think it is cute and fuzzy. I am sure it is interesting for people to take a look into the life of Hugh Hefner and the girls he dates, but though it is a "reality show," I don't think it is very real. I find that every episode is scripted and a version of the truth is portrayed, the version they want people to believe. Almost every episode centers around an event or a party that I believe is happening only because the cameras are rolling. All of the butlers and Mansion regulars have told me that nothing much happens at the Mansion anymore, other than the annual parties, and that they have to come up with themes and stories for the episodes. And it seems to me that everyone on the show is on their best behavior, and their most likeable.

Had Emma, Susan, and I still been there, it would have been a totally different show: real and sassy. What I think would be even more exciting is glamorous fiction. Perhaps I can pitch a *Dynasty*-style saga to one of the networks: an aging but handsome magazine tycoon with multiple girlfriends, but he is still in love with the ex-wife who lives next door, two gorgeous sons wanting to take over the business (imagine if Hef's sons were much older) from the older sister who refuses to relinquish her control, the girlfriends lusting after the sons (they would be the same age) and having affairs with the butlers out of boredom. Drama, love, lust, intrigue . . . Mr. Spelling, give me a call if you want to collaborate.

★ Epilogue

"Miserable creatures, thrown for a moment on the surface of this little pile of mud, is it decreed that one half of the flock should be the persecutor of the other? Is it for you, mankind, to pronounce on what is good and what is evil?"

—*Marquis De Sade*

I feel naked. I have exposed my innermost thoughts, feelings, and experiences for the world to judge. I have told the truth, and that gives me satisfaction. If I told the story well, the reader will understand where I come from, why I chose to live at the Mansion, and why the experience was incredible, liberating, and rewarding, while being difficult, tormenting, frustrating, and lonely. If I didn't tell my story well, I anticipate words like bimbo or gold-digger to be tossed in my direction; however, those words can only hurt me superficially because this experience has taught me what is important in my life. What hurts is never knowing my grandfather because he was in Auschwitz and died before I was born, or not knowing my grandmother because she died early after the horrors of World War II. What hurts is vividly remembering leaving my native country because of the oppression of communism, the memory of the hopeful look in my first dog's eyes, a look begging me to take her with us while I knew I could not even cry about it because it would raise suspicion. The fact that I have lost almost every token of my childhood, the trauma of moving across the world and learning two languages within a year. What really hurts is remembering my proud parents taking any job they could to fulfill the dream of giving their only child a better life, ultimately sacrificing their health and themselves to make it come true: sending me off to McGill University and Pepperdine University School of Law. What hurts is losing one of my best friends in a plane crash well before his time, and not being able to be at my grandfather's or grandmother's funerals in Poland. And what hurts the most is seeing my mother suffering from pain today and being unable to help her, to take that pain away after her whole life has been devoted to helping me and others. Those are the things that penetrate my heart and make me feel pain with my entire being. Not words spoken by people who look at me and can't get past the outside appearance. Those are merely scratches upon the surface.

From the day I met Hef to today, it has been a long and emotional journey. When I moved into the Mansion, I was looking for a break. It was not about the money because I could have made more as a first-year legal associate, nor was it about becoming "famous" by association to Hef; it was about living a carefree, fun lifestyle, one that was drastically different than my own was at the time. And at first, living at the Mansion was just that; it was like an extended spring break. My mistake was staying longer than the few months I initially intended to stay. I got caught up in the drama and tension between the Girlfriends and what was once enjoyable, turned into a miserable waiting game. If I could go back, I would do it all over again; the only difference would be that I would have left after a few months.

Living with Hef was a one-of-a-kind experience. I learned that you must follow your dream and believe in yourself and that you do not have to conform to everyone's expectations. But I also learned that a life of pure hedonism is only briefly satisfying; it leaves you lonely and empty in the end. Having lived a life of learning and discipline and then one of fun and pleasure, I learned that neither is satisfying in itself, and that you have to find a balance in life to be truly happy and fulfilled. I imagined that I would learn some sort of a formula for greatness from Hugh Hefner; what I learned is that Hef is just a human being, like all the rest of us, with faults, vulnerabilities and insecurities. I learned that being wealthy brings with it a lot of responsibilities, even more stress, and attracts many fake, insincere people. In the end, money doesn't bring you happiness unless you have loved ones to share it with, and you use it to help those less fortunate than you. I also learned that I would not dumb myself down myself for anyone. I would never again be a woman who belittles herself to make someone else—a man—look bigger. I was never just having fun, and I certainly never meant to contribute to the trend of stupid blonde girls. It is quite possible to be blonde, be comfortable with your sexuality, and be intelligent; it may be an exception to the rule, but it is possible.

The greatest legacy that life at the Playboy Mansion with the iconic Hugh Hefner has left me with is the enjoyment of the simple things in life; it used to be a cliché to me, but now I truly understand the meaning of that phrase. Nothing makes me happier than to hear my mom say that her back hurts a little bit less today than it did yesterday, or waking up with Balbina's little pug head lovingly tucked into my neck, the kisses Bogart bestows upon me as soon as I open my eyes, or the times Justin surprises me with a latte and a blueberry scone in the morning. I treasure the daily ritual of making my own coffee and reading the newspaper, going for a walk with the dogs and making dinner with Justin. I realize that I used to take these small things for granted, and I am happy that I learned not to. If I had not lived at the Mansion, it might have taken me a lot longer to learn many valuable lessons about gratitude, true friendship, and love. The burden of my memories has lifted. Maybe the tormenting, vivid dreams about living at the Mansion again will finally stop. I don't know what the future holds, but I have finally made sense of my past. At thirty, I feel like I have lived many lifetimes. I look forward to the future and the new unexpected adventures it will bring.

And that movie star I mentioned in the prologue? He got over my past, and called a few days later to apologize. But that's a whole other story.

THANK YOU

Thank you Hugh Marston Hefner for making me a part of your fascinating life; for your kindness and generosity. I care about you very much and hope we can build a friendship. To the girls—thanks for the memories. I have learned something from each and every one of you. To my partner in crime, you know who you are—you made me laugh, you made me cry, and then laugh again. This special experience would not have been the same without you. The staff at the Playboy Mansion, thanks for making a mansion feel more like a home. To all the butlers, the chefs and kitchen staff, thanks for the best French toast, fajitas, cheeseburgers, and skinny fries. Thank you to the ladies who cleaned my room, David in the video department, Mickey for just being you. Thank you Mary, Norma, Elizabeth, Joyce, Bob, and Jenny. To the yard workers who always cleaned up after my dogs. Elaine, I didn't mind cameras in my face as long as you were behind the lens. To all of the Security, especially the unparalleled Mark, and Freddy and Eddy, the best limo drivers around. I want you all to know that everything you ever did for me was always appreciated. The employees of PEGI who took me in, and were patient and understanding while I made my guest appearances at work every week.

Laurent, Gary, Holly, and Edgar thanks for all your great work and the good times we had at the salon. Also thanks to Janet and Edon. I would like to thank my vet, Dr. Werber for always being there for me and the pugs, beyond the call of his duties. My acting coach D.W. Brown for many words of wisdom and countless moments of inspiration. Mark Ebner for our brief yet enjoyable collaboration; I hope one day to be as compelling a writer as you are. Thank you to Chris Nassif and Zach Solov at Diverse Talent. Gavin Maloof, thank you for so many things. You are truly one of the kindest, most generous people I have ever met. You are amazing; may God continue to bless you and your family.

A special thanks to my agent Frank Weimann, for your immediate confidence in me and my story. I realize how lucky I am that you took me on. At Running Press: Greg Jones for your belief in the story and for your enthusiasm. Lisa Clancy, my editor, thank you for your hard work and patience. Janet Saines, thank you for your clarity and for being the only one who always answered my e-mails. Joshua McDonnell, thanks for a fabulous time in Philadelphia and all your talented, creative work. Craig Herman, it is a pleasure working with you. Diane Mancher, you crack me up, thanks for your work on behalf of the book. And thank you to everybody else at Running Press who made this book happen. Thank you to James Creighton and Pier Nicola D'Amico for the beautiful photography.

Thank you to my friends, those who were there for me during this turbulent time. Pamela, thank you for the frequent phone calls, your kind words, and your belief in me. Laura, thanks for the sound advice, and for being there for me when I really needed you. Denise, thank you for the encouragement, it has always meant a lot to me. Niki, you were one of the first people who originally encouraged me to tell me story. Gena, thanks for reminiscing. Sean, thanks for being there for me during some of the hardest times in my life, you are a great friend. I would like to thank Justin's family and friends for their understanding and respect. Papa Leonard, thank you for always buying Canada Dry ginger ale for me, you know I love you. Debbie, thank you for your positive encouragement. My precious pugs, Balbina and Bogart, for your unconditional love, endless kisses, and entertainment. Although I could do without the snoring at night, I would have not made it through it all without you.

Justin, I could not have done this without you. It was you who selflessly encouraged me to write this book, and who pushed me along when I didn't think I could go on. You were my rock when I lived at the Mansion, you were my best friend when I left, and you were patient and supportive when I was writing. And you kept the wine bar fully stocked when it was desperately needed. I am lucky to have an intelligent, honest, kind man like you in my life.

Most importantly, I want to thank my wonderful parents. I love you.

Thank you for your hard work, your sacrifices, and your unconditional love. Everything I am and I have is because of you. I can only wish to be as hard-working as my father, as loving as my mother. Dad, you are my courage and strength. Mom, you are my best friend, my inspiration, and everything that is good in me. Thank you for being my angel on earth.

I thank God for all the blessings bestowed upon me.